Operating Environment

BLACKWELL
Business

Leeds Metropolitan University

17 0167644 2

THE
OPEN
LEARNING
FOUNDATION

Operating Environment

by:

Tom Burden

Leslie Hamilton

Philip Webster

Copyright © Open Learning Foundation Enterprises Ltd 1995

First published 1995

Blackwell Publishers Ltd
108 Cowley Road
Oxford OX4 1JF, UK

238 Main Street
Cambridge, Massachusetts 02142, USA

British Library Cataloguing-in-Publication Data
A CIP catalogue record for this book is available from the British Library

Library of Congress Cataloging-in-Publication Data
A catalogue record for this book is available from the Library of Congress

ISBN 0-631-19673-0

Printed in Great Britain by Alden Press

This book is printed on acid-free paper

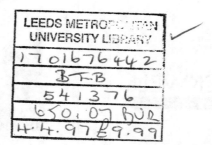

Contents

Foreword

BTEC is committed to helping people of any age to acquire and maintain the up-to-date and relevant knowledge, understanding and skills they need for success in current or future employment.

These aims are greatly enhanced by this series of open learning books for the new BTEC HND and HNC in Business Studies.

These books will provide more students with the opportunity to successfully achieve a widely recognised national qualification in business by allowing flexible study patterns combined with an innovative approach to learning.

Our active involvement in a partnership with the Open Learning Foundation and Blackwell Publishers ensures that each book comprehensively covers the specific learning outcomes needed for a module in this Higher National programme.

Acknowledgements

Authors

Tom Burden (Leeds Metropolitan University)

Leslie Hamilton (Leeds Metropolitan University)

Philip Webster (Leeds Metropolitan University)

Open Learning Editor: Maurice Bennington

For the Open Learning Foundation:

Director of Programmes: Leslie Mapp

Design and Production: Stephen Moulds

Text Editor: Paul Stirner

Academic Co-ordinator: Glyn Roberts (Bradford & Ilkley
                                                    Community College)

Academic Reviewer: Martin Gibson

The Open Learning Foundation wishes to acknowledge the support of Bradford & Ilkley Community College during the preparation of this workbook.

For BTEC

Dianne Billam: Director of Products and Quality Division

John Edgar: Consultant

Françoise Seacroft: Manager of Futures Department

Mike Taylor: Deputy Head of Department of Service Sector
                         Management, University of Brighton

For Blackwell Publishers

Editorial Director: Philip Carpenter

Senior Commissioning Editor: Tim Goodfellow

Production Manager: Pam Park

Development Editors: Richard Jackman and Catriona King

Pre-production Manager: Paul Stringer

Reviewers: Steve Ellis (Herts Regional College)

            Alan Prest (West Herts College)

            Pete Robinson (Highbury College)

Introduction

Welcome to this workbook for the BTEC module Operating Environment.

This is a book specifically designed for use by students studying on BTEC Higher National programmes in Business, Business and Finance, Business and Marketing and Business and Personnel. However, it can be also used by people who wish to learn about this aspect of business.

How to use the workbook

Please feel free to:

- write notes in the margins

- underline and highlight important words or phrases.

As you work through this module, you will find activities have been built in. These are designed to make you stop to think and answer questions.

There are four types of activities.

Memory and recall These are straightforward tests of how much text you are able to remember.

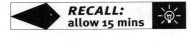

Self-assessed tasks (SATs) These are used to test your understanding of the text you are studying or to apply the principles and practices learnt to a related problem.

Exercises These are open-ended questions that can be used as a basis for classroom or group debate. If you do not belong to a study group, use the exercises to think through issues raised by the text.

Assignments These are tasks set for students studying at a BTEC centre which would normally require a written answer to be looked at by your tutor. If you are not following a course at college, the assignments are still a useful way of developing and testing your understanding of the module.

There are answer boxes provided below each activity in this module. Use these boxes to summarise your answers and findings. If you need more space, use the margins of the book or separate sheets of paper to make notes and write a full answer.

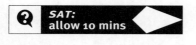

SAT:
allow 10 mins

Managing tasks and solving problems ✔

EXAMPLE ACTIVITY

As an 'icebreaker' try this exercise.

Interest rates charged by banks have gone up by 1 per cent. How could this affect business?

Commentary...

In general, interest rate rises are seen negatively by business because they put up the price of borrowing money for firms. However, interest rate rises can be used to stabilise an economy which is 'overheating'; this occurs when demand is rising too rapidly. They can also be used to try to bring down inflation.

The emphasis of the workbook is to provide you with tasks that relate to the general operating environment of business. The work that you do on these tasks enables you to develop your BTEC common skills and a skills chart is provided on page 7 for you to note your practice of each skill. One sheet is probably not enough, so cut this sheet out and photocopy it when you require new sheets.

Aims of the workbook

This workbook is concerned with increasing your awareness and understanding of the environment in which organisations operate. It provides a framework in which to review the economic, political and social contexts of business activity.

The book has three sections which are designed to cover the learning outcomes (as shown in bold in the boxes below) for this core module. These, with the suggested content, are as given in the BTEC publication (code 02–104–4) on the Higher National programmes in Business Studies. Where appropriate, the suggested content may be reordered within sections of the book.

SECTION ONE: THE NATIONAL ECONOMIC CONTEXT

On completion of this section, you should be able to:

> ▶ **recognise the structure of the national economy and assess the significance for business of the operation of mixed economic systems**

> ▶ **analyse the role of government in economic management and its impact through participation in, and regulation of, the business environment**

> ▶ **identify the key components of the UK financial system and its role and functions within the business environment**

> ▶ **assess the significance of international economic relations on UK business.**

Suggested content

Economic systems: the mixed economy and the role of government economic policy; fiscal and monetary policy and industrial policy

Role of government: the role of government in the provision of goods and services, as a regulator and as manager of the financial framework

UK financial system: the banking system and international trade; internationalisation of business in a global environment

SECTION TWO: ENVIRONMENTAL FACTORS AFFECTING BUSINESS ACTIVITIES

On completion of this section, you should be able to:

> ▶ **assess the impact of technology and technological change on business**

> ▶ **assess the role of social and community processes in business activity, including social protection and social safety nets**

> ▶ **examine the significance of the environment and its protection, for business decisions**

> ▶ **evaluate the impact of political pluralism and democracy on business relations.**

Suggested content

Technology: high technology, developing technology, work patterns and changes in production or operations

Social and community processes: the social welfare system, impact on employment, health, housing

Environment: environmental damage and social responsibilities

The political process: political parties and groups, lobbying, contrasting political processes

Section three: Business firms in markets

On completion of this section, you should be able to:

> ▶ analyse the competitive environment in which business firms operate and identify competitive strategies likely to generate successful results

> ▶ examine the role of businesses in factor markets

> ▶ investigate and interpret the main regulatory controls on the operation of organisations

> ▶ identify the main regulatory bodies within both the UK and the EU and investigate how they influence the operation and activities of business organisations.

Suggested content

Competitive environment: competition and competitive strategies in product and factor markets, monopoly and restrictive practices

Regulatory controls: regulatory controls and the law relating to business, employment, sale of goods, safety and the environment

Regulatory bodies: regulatory agencies – UK and EU

Market factors: labour market, capital market

In working through the BTEC Higher National programme in Business Studies, you will practise the following BTEC common skills:

Managing and Developing Self	✔
Working with and Relating to others	✔
Communicating	✔
Managing Tasks and Solving Problems	✔
Applying Numeracy	✔
Applying Technology	✔
Applying Design and Creativity	✔

You will practise most of these skills in working through this Module.

Recommended reading

Section One

Cuthbertson, K. and Gripaios, P. (eds), 1993, *The Macroeconomy: A Guide For Business*, 2nd edn, Routledge.

> This provides you with more general analysis on the British economy.

Bishop, M., Kay, J. and Mayer, C. (eds), 1994, *Privatisation and Economic Performance*, Oxford University Press.

> This book enables you to study in more detail the impact of privatisation on the economy.

Section Two

Abercrombie, N. and Warde, A., 1994, *Contemporary British Society*, 2nd edn, Polity Press [Section 2.4, Chapters 3–9, Section 11.3 and Chapter 12.

> This book enables you to study in more detail the social structure of modern Britain.

Section Three

Cole, B., Shears, P. and Tiley, J., 1993, *Law in a Business Context*, Chapman & Hall [Chapters 1, 4, 5, and 6].

> This is a general text on the impact of law on business.

Grant, R.M., 1995, *Contemporary Strategy Analysis*, 2nd edn, Blackwell Publishers.

> This book examines competitive strategies.

Weir, S. and Hall, W. (eds), 1994, *Extra-governmental organisations in the UK and their accountability*, Democratic Audit.

> This enables you to take a closer look at regulatory agencies.

Name

Module

BTEC Skill	Activity No./Date	Activity No./Date	Activity No./Date	Activity No./Date	Activity No./Date	Activity No./Date
Managing and developing self						
Working with and relating to others						
Communicating						
Managing tasks and solving problems						
Applying numeracy						
Applying technology						
Applying design and creativity						

The National Economic Context

The UK labour force

Objectives

After participating in this session, you should able to:

▶ describe the main demographic trends

▶ identify the major changes in the structure of the
labour force

▶ explain the reasons why labour tends to move from the
primary sector to the other sectors

▶ understand what is meant by the 'flexible workforce'.

In working through this session, you will practise the following
BTEC common skills:

Managing and Developing Self	✔
Working with and Relating to others	✔
Communicating	✔
Managing Tasks and Solving Problems	✔
Applying Numeracy	✔
Applying Technology	
Applying Design and Creativity	

The population of the UK

The basic function of business is to produce goods and services that people want. In this process, organisations act as a transformation unit turning resources into goods or services. Although the goods and services of one firm may become the inputs of another (e.g. the production of machinery or management information systems) the ultimate consumers will be the people of a country. These people will also provide the labour force.

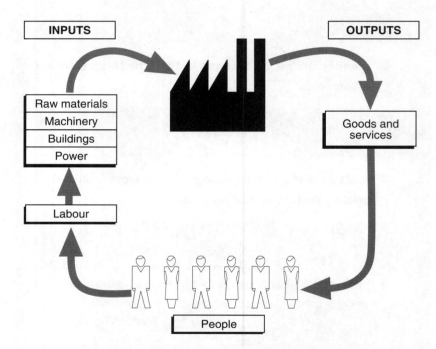

FIGURE 1.1: *The firm turns resources into goods or services.*

People are important both as consumers and producers. The population of a country does not consist of people all of the same age and sex, but of a mixture. This mixture is referred to as the structure of the population and it varies over time in several ways:

- in the proportion of males to females

- in the proportion of the population in different age groups

- in the proportion of people of working age.

This last group is also made up of a mixture of people which can be analysed according to:

- the proportion of males to females

- the proportion in different age groups

- the proportion of employed to unemployed

- the type of jobs people do

- the different type of employment patterns (e.g. full-time, part-time, temporary)

SAT:
allow 10 mins

Managing tasks and solving problems ✔

ACTIVITY 1

It is vitally important for business to be aware of the changes taking place in both the structure of the population and the working population. Can you think why this is so? Think of the population both as consumers and producers.

Commentary...

You should have remembered that people are the final consumers of the goods and services that are produced. Businesses must take this into account when planning what it is they are going to produce. If more babies are being born, this increases the demand for baby products. If people are living longer then there is a greater need for products associated with older people, e.g. old people's homes, health care services and walking sticks.

People also make up the labour force and changes in the structure of the population affect the structure of the labour force. A reduction in the birth rate means that in 16 years' time, there may be a shortage of young people entering the labour market. If the population is ageing then the labour force may also be ageing. These two factors taken together may mean a change in recruitment policies for firms. If more married women are seeking work, firms may have to provide childcare facilities or provide more generous maternity breaks than the minimum legal requirement in order to retain valuable workers.

These are just a few examples and you may have thought of many more.

This session looks at changes in both the overall population and the working population of the UK. It analyses the type of jobs people do and in which industries they do them; this tells us something of the changing structure of the economy.

The UK population was 56.5 million in 1991 compared with 38.2 million in 1901 and less than 12 million in 1801. The population more than trebled between 1801 and 1901 but grew by less than half between 1901 and 1991.

Changes in total population are largely determined by changes in the birth rate, the death rate and the net migration rate. The very rapid increase in total population in the nineteenth century was the result of dramatic reductions in the death rate while the birth rate remained relatively high. The birth rate only began to fall in the late nineteenth century and into this century (see table 1.1).

The total population grew steadily between 1951 and 1971, an average annual increase of around 300,000. Growth slowed in the 1970s averaging only 42,000 per year, picked up in the 1980s and 1990s and is expected to fall back in the twenty-first century (see figure 1.2).

Within these long-term trends, there are important short-term fluctuations in the birth rate which are of considerable importance to business. In this period, total live births peaked in 1964 at over one million but fell to a low of 657,000 live births in 1977. This has important consequences for business not only in the considerable reduction in demand for goods and services associated with children but also in the effects on the supply of new labour some 16 years later. This is, however, one of the more easily forecast variables in the operating environment and one of which organisations should be well aware. Live births were rising again by the mid-1980s but more

	Pop. at start of period	Annual average change				
		live births	deaths	net natural change	other (a)	overall annual change
1801	10,000(b)					
1851	22,300					
1901–11	38,200	1091	624	467	−82	385
1911–21	42,000	975	689	286	−92	194
1921–31	44,000	824	555	268	−67	201
1931–51	46,000	785	598	188	25	213
1951–61	50,200	839	593	246	6	252
1961–71	52,700	963	639	324	−12	312
1971–81	55,500	736	666	69	−27	42
1981–91	55,800	757	655	103	42	145
1991–2001	56,500	786	633	154	53	207
2001–11	59,700	721	626	95	44	139
2011–21	61,100	725	644	81	6	87
2021–31	61,900	710	698	12	0	12

(a) net migration plus others
(b) excluding Northern Ireland   *Source: Annual Abstract of Statistics, 1994.*

TABLE 1.1: *The population of the UK: past and projected patterns ('000s)*

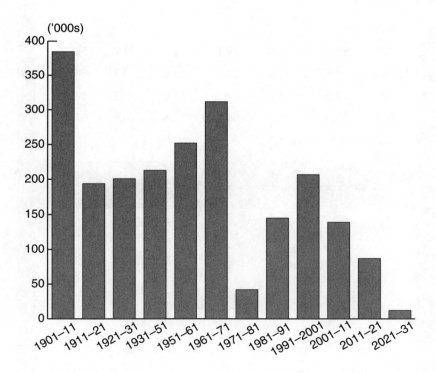

FIGURE 1.2: *Annual average change in UK population by decade 1901–2031.*

slowly than the 1950s and 1960s. They are expected to rise further in the 1990s but fall again in the next century.

THE AGE STRUCTURE OF THE POPULATION

ACTIVITY 2

Answer the following questions using table 1.2.

1. What is happening to the age structure of the population?

2. What is the balance between males and females in the population?

	Under 16 %	16–39 %	40–64 %	65–79 %	80+ %	Total (millions)
			All ages (=100%)			
1961	24.9	31.4	32.0	9.8	1.9	52.8
1971	25.5	31.3	29.9	10.9	2.3	55.9
1981	22.3	34.9	27.8	12.2	2.8	56.4
1991	20.3	35.3	28.6	12.0	3.7	57.3
Male	21.4	36.7	29.0	10.6	2.3	28.2
Female	19.3	34.0	28.2	13.3	5.2	29.6
Projections						
2001	21.0	32.8	30.5	11.4	4.2	59.7
2011	19.5	30.3	33.7	11.9	4.7	61.1
2021	18.5	30.0	32.3	14.0	5.2	62.0
2031	18.4	28.7	30.3	15.6	6.9	62.1

Source: Social Trends, 1994.

TABLE 1.2: *Age and sex structure of the population of the UK*

Commentary...

The UK has an ageing population (see table 1.2). In 1961, only about 1 in 8 of the population was aged 65 years or over. The proportion had increased to 1 in 6 by 1991 and is projected be 1 in 5 by 2031. The age group which has shown most significant changes are the over-80s, increasing from 1.9 million in 1961 to 3.7 million in 1991. Put simply, people are on average living longer. This allied to a low birth rate, results in an ageing population. Besides the effects on the pattern of consumption, the most serious consequence is the increased dependence of retired people on a working population which is growing very slowly and which may eventually shrink in numbers.

In 1991, there were more females than males. This was not true of all age groups. For some reason more boys are born than girls but male death rates are higher in almost all age groups. Consequently males dominate in all age groups up to the age of 50 (OPCS – 1989 figures). Thereafter females dominate, particularly so in the older age groups as a result of their greater longevity.

The working population

The working population consists of the employed labour force (both those in employment and the self-employed), the armed services, the unemployed and those on work-related government training. In Great Britain, in March 1994, the working population totalled 27.2 million of which 20.8 million were employees in employment, 3.2 million were self-employed and 2.7 million were unemployed (*Employment Gazette*, July 1994). This figure is about 49 per cent of the total population although the proportion in work is only about 43 per cent.

Changes in the labour force

1986–1991	Working population increases by 2 million
1991–1993	Working population falls by 0.4 million
1993–2006	Projected increase of 1.5 million to 28.5 million

Source: Employment Gazette, British labour force projections, April 1994.

The employed labour force can be classified in a number of ways – by sex, age, occupation/industry, type of employment (i.e. part-time, full-time, temporary), and sector.

	1993	1994	1997	2001	2006
Men					
All ages 16 and over	15.6	15.6	15.7	15.8	15.9
Working age	15.4	15.3	15.4	15.5	15.7
Women					
All ages 16 and over	12.2	12.3	12.6	13.1	13.5
Working age	11.7	11.8	12.1	12.5	12.9
All					
All ages 16 and over	27.9	28.0	28.3	28.8	29.4
Working age	27.1	27.1	27.5	28.0	28.5
Women as a percentage of all					
All ages 16 and over	43.9	44.1	44.6	45.3	45.8
Working age	43.2	43.4	44.0	44.6	45.0

Source: Social Trends, 1994.

TABLE 1.3: *Estimates and projections of the civilian labour force in Great Britain (millions)*

AGE STRUCTURE

The UK not only has an ageing population but also has an ageing workforce. In 1986, almost 1 in 4 of the workforce was under 25. By 2001, this ratio is expected to be 1 in 6. It is expected that, by the year 2006, there will be 2.4 million more people aged 35–54 and 0.7 million aged 55 and over compared with a fall of 1.6 million people aged under 35 in the labour force (*Employment Gazette*, British labour force projections, April 1994).

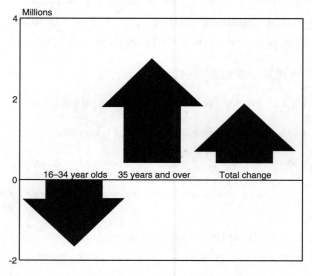

FIGURE 1.3: *Changes in the average age of the workforce 1993–2006.*

SEX STRUCTURE

Women's employment rose much faster than men's during the 1980s reflecting both the increase in traditional female employment areas (e.g. clerical and secretarial work) and the increased willingness/ requirement for women to work. The proportion of the population above 16 who are in the civilian labour force is referred to as the economic activity rate. From table 1.4 it can be seen that the economic activity rate for women has increased from 48.8 per cent in 1984 to 52.6 per cent in 1993 and is projected to rise to 56.5 per cent by the year 2006. However, in December 1993, 47 per cent of all female workers were part-time compared with 6.5 per cent of male workers.

				Projections			
	1984	1987	1990	1993	1997	2001	2006
Males	74.5	73.7	74.3	71.9	70.9	70.1	69.0
Females	48.8	50.2	52.8	52.6	54.0	55.2	56.5

Source: *Regional Trends*, 1993; *Employment Gazette*, April 1994.

TABLE 1.4: *Economic activity rates (percentages)*

Industrial structure

There are two main methods of classifying different occupations each of which has its particular uses:

- Occupational grouping – according to the job

- Industrial grouping – according to the industry

An analysis of jobs by occupational structure tells us about the types of jobs undertaken and an analysis by industry tells us about types of business in which these jobs are located.

A useful way of describing the general changes in the structure of industry is to classify economic activity into one of three sectors: primary, secondary or tertiary.

- The **primary sector** refers to the first part of the productive process, e.g. extracting minerals, growing crops, rearing animals, fishing.

- The **secondary sector** refers to the subsequent stage in the cycle of production and includes firms which either process materials or manufacture products or both. The main element is manufacturing but this sector also includes construction and the utility industries of gas, water and electricity.

- The **tertiary sector** refers to firms involved in the final stages of the cycle of production. This sector is often known as the services sector and includes firms who are directly involved in production (e.g. retailers, wholesalers, transport firms, insurers) and those less directly involved who provide a service to clients (e.g. education, health, police and fire services).

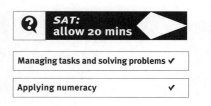

Managing tasks and solving problems ✓

Applying numeracy ✓

ACTIVITY 3

1. **Classify the following activities into the appropriate sector — primary (P), secondary (S), tertiary (T).**

bricklayer ☐

shop assistant ☐

meat packer ☐

chartered accountant ☐

swimming instructor ☐

coal miner ☐

police officer ☐

secretary in an engineering firm ☐

insurance broker ☐

	TOTAL Employees & Self-emp.	Agriculture Fishing A–B	Energy and Water C,E	Manufacturing D	Construction F
All persons					
Spring 1984	23,072	526	568	5,347	1,874
Winter 1993/4	24,329	438	331	4,725	1,741

	Distribution Hotels Restrnts G–H	Transport and Comms I	Banking, Finance and Insurance J–K	Public Admin, Education and Health L–N	Other Services O–Q
All persons					
Spring 1984	4,718	1,402	2,415	4,824	1,312
Winter 1993/4	4,918	1,521	3,306	5,894	1,386

Source: Employment Gazette, July 1994.

TABLE 1.5: *Industry sector (employees and self-employed) coded to SIC(92)*

2. **Using the information from table 1.5 complete the table below. The first column contains the figures for the total employees and self-employed.**

Employees by sector (per cent)

	A–B	C,E	D	F	G–H	I	J–K	L–N	O–Q
Spring 1984									
Winter 1993/94									

Commentary...

1.

bricklayer	S
shop assistant	T
meat packer	S
chartered accountant	T
swimming instructor	T
coal miner	P
policeman	T
secretary in an engineering firm	S
insurance broker	T

2. Employees by sector (per cent)

	A–B	C,E	D	F	G–H	I	J–K	L–N	O–Q
Spring 1984	2.3	2.5	23.2	8.1	20.4	6.0	10.5	20.9	5.7
Winter 1993/94	1.8	1.4	19.4	7.2	20.2	6.3	13.6	24.2	5.7

C,E includes primary activities like mining and quarrying as well as industries in the secondary sector, therefore it is not possible to calculate percentages for the primary and secondary sectors.

ECONOMIC DEVELOPMENT AND STRUCTURAL CHANGE

Economic development involves structural change as some sectors grow more rapidly than others while some decline. From figure 1.4 it can be seen that the UK has witnessed a considerable movement of workers from the agricultural sector, from around 36 per cent of workers in 1801 to just over 1 per cent in 1991. What is not clear is whether these workers were displaced into the secondary sector and subsequently the tertiary sector or into both sectors at the same time.

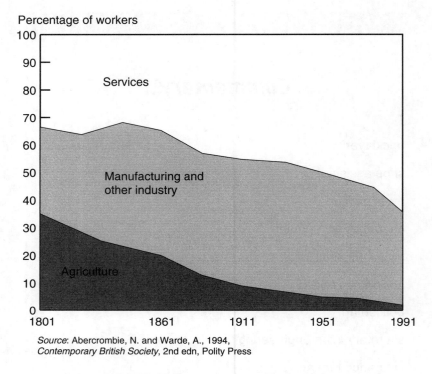

Source: Abercrombie, N. and Warde, A., 1994,
Contemporary British Society, 2nd edn, Polity Press

FIGURE 1.4: *Changing size of the sectors of the economy.*

The Fisher/Clark thesis According to the Fisher/Clark thesis, as economies develop, labour moves gradually from the primary sector to the secondary sector and then to the tertiary sector. To be able to explain why this should happen you need to understand two concepts – **income elasticity of demand** and **labour productivity**.

> **\!?/ Income elasticity of demand** refers to the relationship between changes in demand and changes in income.

If people have more money then usually they want to spend most of it. So an increase in income generally leads to an increase in demand for goods, but to varying degrees. Look at the following list of goods and consider whether your family would buy more of them if your family income increased by 50 per cent:

videos, potatoes, computer games, holidays, bread, ballpoint pens, motor cars, light bulbs, magazines, soap, pensions, health.

You probably decided that your family would spend more money on videos, computer games, holidays, motor cars, pensions and health. The income elasticity of demand for these goods is positive. As income rises, buyers tend to buy more of these types of goods. Economists refer to these as **normal goods**; most products fall into this category.

Your family would probably not buy any more ballpoint pens, light bulbs or soap. The demand for these does not change as income increases as you are already in a position of being able to buy as many as you require. The income elasticity of demand is zero.

This may also be the case with bread and potatoes, although you may actually consume less, preferring to buy more expensive food. Your family may also substitute more expensive brands of soap. Rising incomes can cause the demand for some products to fall. The income elasticity of demand for these products is negative. Economists refer to these as **inferior goods**.

The goods which fall into each category depend very much on the current standard of living. The demand for bread has been declining in western Europe for many years but this is not the case in many poorer countries.

> **‼️ Labour productivity** refers to the amount of goods and services each worker is able to produce.

It is usually measured as the output per employee hour. Improvements in labour productivity can come about in a number of ways:

- better food and living conditions

- better working conditions

- improved organisation of work

- education

- greater use of machinery.

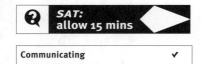

Communicating ✔

ACTIVITY 4

Now that you understand what is meant by income elasticity of demand and labour productivity, use these concepts to explain why labour moved from agriculture to industries in the secondary and tertiary sectors in the nineteenth century.

Write up to 100 words.

Summarise your findings in the box below.

Commentary...

In the nineteenth century, greater farm mechanisation, improved transportation, the application of fertilisers and better farm management techniques allowed for substantial productivity improvements, freeing surplus labour for the expanding secondary sector.

At this time, most people were concerned with earning enough money to survive. As productivity increased so did incomes, allowing expenditure on things other than basic foodstuffs, and creating a demand for manufactured goods. The transition from an agricultural society to an industrial society further increased the incomes of workers leading to even greater spending on manufactured goods and services. A diminishing proportion of their income was spent on basic foodstuffs.

THE GROWTH OF THE SERVICE SECTOR

This logic can be equally applied at a later stage in the development of an economy to the growth of the service sector. The income elasticity of demand for services is very high at high levels of income. If you think back to the exercise above about income elasticity of demand you can see that much of our increased income is spent on services, especially leisure, health and financial services.

There is an increasing demand for services. There is also an available supply of labour as many factories today have automated their production lines and are able to operate with very few workers. In other words, labour productivity has increased considerably.

Taking this thinking a step further you might like to consider how many and what type of jobs will be available in the future. Most people now work in the services sector but substantial productivity improvements are now taking place in this sector, most notably in the financial services sector but also in health and education. Will we all end up in leisure services?

ALTERNATIVE VIEWS ON THE SHIFT OF EMPLOYMENT

Other writers have agreed that this view of the shift of employment from one sector to another is too simplistic. Instead, they claim that the shift was from the primary sector to both of the other sectors simultaneously. A look at the graph in figure 1.4 shows that there was already a significant services sector in 1801 which grew throughout the nineteenth century. Many services are an essential part of the production process (e.g. distribution and financing) so clearly a substantial part of the services sector would have to grow with the secondary sector.

THE POST-INDUSTRIAL SOCIETY

Although there may be disagreement about the pattern of development, there is no doubt that the UK is an economy in which most people are employed in the services sector. Some writers (notably Daniel Bell, in *The Coming of Post-Industrial Society*, Basic Books, 1973) refer to this as the post-industrial society.

The post-industrial view of society recognises three stages of development of an economy:

- the pre-industrial economy

- the industrial economy

- the post-industrial economy.

In a pre-industrial economy or agrarian society, the major service activity will be domestic service. In the industrial phase, the major services will be those which support industrial development, banking, insurance, transport, retailing. The post-industrial phase is recognised by the growth of personal service industries such as health, welfare, education and leisure.

Certainly over the last 30 years increases in jobs in the services sector have dominated employment growth. Between 1983 and 1993 the total number of workers in the service industries expanded by about 2.4 million so that about 70 per cent of all workers are now in service industries. Total employment in the economy grew by only 1.9 million due to the decline of the production and construction sectors.

According to the Institute of Employment Research (IER), these trends are set to continue. Manufacturing, primary and utility industries will continue to decline up to the year 2000 but these job losses will be more than offset by growth in the services sector.

THE SWITCH FROM MANUFACTURING TO SERVICES

Within these broad sectoral changes lies another change which has been of much concern, i.e. the decline of manufacturing relative to other sectors. The share of manufacturing in total employment in the UK has fallen from 34 per cent (8.2 million jobs) in 1971 to 26 per cent in 1981 and 19.4 per cent (4.7 million jobs) in 1991. The IER projects a further fall by the year 2000 to 17 per cent of all employment or 4.4 million jobs.

This loss of the manufacturing base is referred to as **de-industrialisation.**

There is little agreement as to the exact meaning of the term de-industrialisation. It has been variously defined as:

- the decline of the manufacturing sector's share of output or employment (i.e. the relative decline of manufacturing)

- the absolute decline in manufacturing employment

- the inability of UK manufacturing to compete successfully in both domestic and overseas markets.

By the first definition, de-industrialisation started in the mid-1950s when manufacturing's share of total employment started to decline. The second, and most popular, definition would date the start of de-industrialisation as 1966 which saw the peak of manufacturing employment. The focus in this session is on jobs but mention should be made of **manufacturing output** which continued to grow until 1973 but then fell until, by 1981, output levels were comparable to those in the mid-1960s. From 1981 manufacturing output rose but did not achieve 1973 levels until 1988.

The third definition points to the particular problems of the UK economy and its relationship with the rest of the world. All advanced economies suffer de-industrialisation to some extent but the decline in the UK seems to be greater than that experienced by our competitors, indicated by the loss of domestic and export markets.

Traditionally the UK was an exporter of manufactured goods and an importer of food and raw materials. In 1899, the UK accounted for a third of the world manufacturing exports. Although the UK share declined from this date, this was hardly surprising in that other countries were developing their manufacturing capacity. By 1950, the share had declined to 25.5 per cent but subsequently the deterioration accelerated so that, by 1979, the share was only 9.7 per cent. In the same period, West Germany's share increased from 7.3 per cent to 29.8 per cent and Japan's from 3.4 per cent to 13.6 per cent. In 1983, for the first time, the UK imported more manufactured goods than it exported.

Although it was only in the 1960s that the extent of the relative decline became apparent as the UK slipped down the international league table of living standards, the decline is long-term. Many writers (e.g. Gamble, A., 1990, *Britain in Decline*, 3rd edn, Macmillan and Hobsbawm, E., 1968, *Industry and Empire: An Economic History of Britain Since 1750*, Weidenfield and Nicholson) trace the origins of decline to the late nineteenth century. It was at this time that the USA and Germany became major industrial powers and the UK share of world manufacturing output and exports started its long decline.

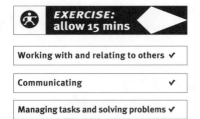

EXERCISE:
allow 15 mins

Working with and relating to others	✔
Communicating	✔
Managing tasks and solving problems	✔

ACTIVITY 5

Form into groups of four and complete the following task.

Explain why there has been a shift from the primary and secondary sectors to the services sector.

Summarise your findings in the box below.

Commentary...

Your answer should make reference to the two concepts of income elasticity of demand and labour productivity.

The first concept can be used to explain different spending patterns as the economy develops. In pre-industrial economies people do not generally have much money to spend and therefore all their spending tends to be on basic foodstuffs. As the economy develops into an industrial economy and people become better off, more money is spent on manufactured goods. Ultimately in very rich economies, such as the UK, many people are able to satisfy much of their material wants and switch their spending to services such as health, education and leisure.

This establishes the demand for the goods and services produced by each sector but it is increases in the efficiency of people which releases labour to move from the primary sector. Improved food and living conditions initially make people more productive but greater use of machinery and ultimately automation releases many people from the primary and secondary sectors. In the long term, education is also an important factor in increasing people's productivity.

Changes in the occupational structure

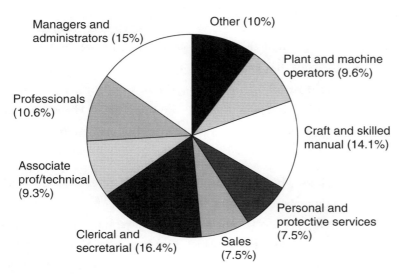

Source: Labour Market and Skills Trends

FIGURE 1.5: *What the jobs are today – total employment by occupation*, 1993.

The dominant feature revealed by figure 1.5 and table 1.6 is the shift from manual to non-manual occupations. This trend is not new. In 1911, manual occupations accounted for almost 75 per cent of all employment but, by 1951, this had fallen to 62 per cent. Many people worked on construction sites and in factories, tending machines or standing at conveyor belts doing simple repetitive tasks which needed

	1951	1961	1971	1981
Employers and own account	6.7	6.4	6.5	6.4
Managers and administrators	5.4	5.3	8.0	10.1
Professionals and technicians	6.6	9.0	11.1	14.7
Clerical and sales	16.3	18.6	19.5	19.3
Supervisors and foremen	2.6	2.9	3.9	4.2
Skilled manual	23.8	24.1	20.2	16.0
Semi-skilled manual	26.6	25.1	19.3	19.0
Unskilled manual	11.9	8.5	11.6	10.4
Total ('000s)	22,514	23,639	25,021	25,406

Source: Hamnett, C., McDowell, L. and Saarre, P., 1989, *The Changing Social Structure*, Sage and Open University, Table 3.3.

TABLE 1.6: *Distribution of economically active population by occupational category, Great Britain 1951–81*

a minimum of training. But many more were going into clerical work or supervisory jobs. Others took jobs in the growing public sector as doctors, nurses, teachers, social workers or civil servants.

This shift from manual to non-manual work continued throughout the post-war period but the rate of change accelerated from the late 1960s with manual occupations (according to the IER) now accounting for only 35 per cent of all occupations. Absolute numbers of manual workers have been decreasing since the late 1960s. These workers are still heavily concentrated in the construction and manufacturing industries.

There has obviously been a corresponding increase in the proportion of non-manual workers who now form 65 per cent of all employment. Workers with higher level occupations (managers, professionals and technicians) now account for almost 35 per cent of all employment while the largest single occupational group is clerical and secretarial covering 16 per cent of all employment. These workers tend to be concentrated in the business and miscellaneous services and distribution sectors but are also well represented in public services.

The IER expects these trends to continue with 1.7 million (45 per cent of all employment) jobs being created in higher level occupations by the year 2000, of which over 1 million will be occupied by women. The number of manual jobs will continue to fall probably by more than 1.3 million in the same period.

CHANGING SKILLS

Another important feature of the occupational structure is the changing job content in terms of the skills required to carry out jobs. We have seen that there is a general growth in higher level occupations but there are also increasing skill demands within many occupations. Another changing feature of the labour market is the wider range of skills needed by many employees.

A 1993 study by the Centre for Research in Employment and Technology (CREATE) analysed future job needs in terms of numbers and skills. Figure 1.6 summarises their findings.

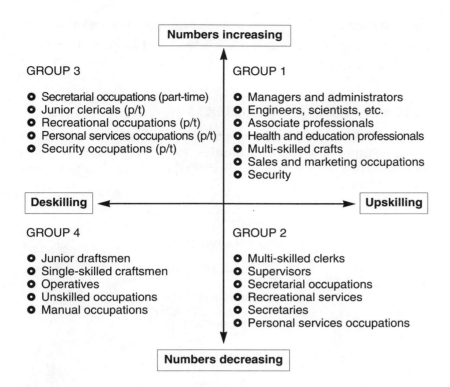

FIGURE 1.6: *Jobs affected by changes in numbers and skill levels.*

The groups on the right of the diagram are those occupations where the level of skill requirements will rise whereas those on the left will see their jobs simplified (de-skilled) as a consequence of improved technology. Technology will also have the effect of reducing the demand for some occupations, e.g. groups 4 and 2.

Group 1 occupations will be those where demand and the skills content will be increasing – mainly knowledge-based occupations. Group 4 occupations will be facing a reduction in demand in both numbers and skills.

These changes pose a challenge to the training and educational worlds to fill the 'skills gap'. An increasing supply of 'knowledge-based' workers with high-level education and training qualifications will be needed; organisations will require problem solvers and decision makers with the ability to take responsibility.

TYPE OF EMPLOYMENT — THE FLEXIBLE WORKFORCE

Some 9.7 million people (38 per cent of all UK workers) were either part-time, temporary, self-employed, on a government training scheme or unpaid family workers in Spring 1993 — an increase of 1.25 million since 1986.

Source: Watson G., The flexible workforce and
patterns of working hours in the UK, *Employment Gazette*, July 1994.

One of the aims of the government over the last 15 years has been to promote a 'flexible' labour market believing it to be an important contributor to economic growth.

CORE AND PERIPHERAL WORKFORCES

Atkinson (*Flexibility, incertainty and Manpower Management*, report no.89, Institute of Manpower Studies, 1984) put forward a model (figure 1.7) of a flexible firm which divided its workforce into a 'core' and a 'peripheral' workforce.

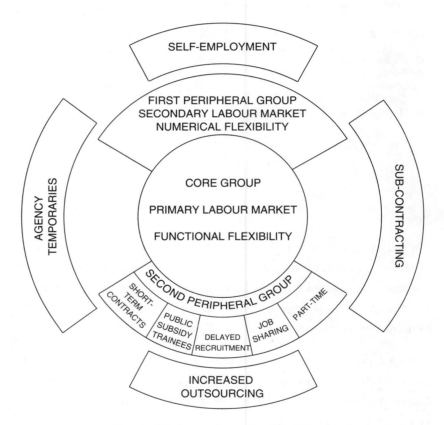

FIGURE 1.7: *Core and peripheral workforces.*

Each of these groups of workers provided the firm with different kinds of flexibility.

The core workers provide 'functional flexibility'. This group of workers would be full-time staff. They would be permanent staff. They would be expected to adopt working practices which cut across traditional demarcation lines, i.e. have greater task flexibility. They would enjoy job security and a high level of investment in their training. Typical groups would be managerial and professional staff and multi-skilled workers. These skills would not be easily available in the labour market and therefore the firm would be keen to keep this group.

The peripheral group provide numerical flexibility. They enable firms to adjust the number of workers or the number of hours worked as demand for goods and services changes. A number of different groups of workers would fall into this category. Some would be full-time workers but unlike the core workers, this group would have much less job security. They would be in lower skilled jobs of a fairly routine nature. Labour turnover would be high so that a reduction in demand for a firm's goods and services would cause a reduction in recruitment activity. Other 'peripheral' groups would be part-time, temporary, contract workers or those on government training schemes. All of these groups of workers could be adjusted relatively easily as the level of production fluctuated. Other sources of numerical flexibility could be achieved by subcontracting, outsourcing and self-employment, especially for specialist services such as printing or routine tasks such as security.

The evidence for businesses employing this as a strategy is fairly thin and it has been suggested that the model is an 'ideal-type' rather than a picture of reality. It has been said that the growth in the peripheral workforce simply reflects the broad structural changes taking place in the economy. The increase in service sector employment leads to an increase in part-time and temporary work and the reduction in manufacturing produces a reduction in full-time work because these are the traditional working patterns in these sectors.

Another criticism points to the fact that employers have always sought labour market flexibility and it is only the economic and political climate of the 1980s and 1990s and the consequent shift in power towards employers that has allowed the greater use of flexible types of employment.

Nevertheless the growth of peripheral type employment is undeniable (table 1.7) and Atkinson's model is still useful in highlighting two features of the present day economy:

- the ways in which firms may achieve greater flexibility in their operations

- the possibility of a polarised workforce into a highly paid secure group of 'core' workers and a low paid, insecure group of 'peripheral' workers.

**CHANGES IN THE
OCCUPATIONAL STRUCTURE**

	1983		1993	
	Men	Women	Men	Women
Traditional workforce				
Full-time permanent employees	83	53	73	48
Flexible workforce				
Part-time permanent employees	1	34	3.7	36.7
Full-time temporary employees	2	2	2.8	2.3
Full-time self-employed	13	3	15.6	3.7
Part-time self-employed	0.4	3	1.4	3.4
Government training workers			1.7	1.1
Family workers			0.3	1.0

Source: Watson, G., The flexible workforce and patterns of working hours in the UK, *Employment Gazette*, July 1994; Hakim, B., *Employment Gazette*, November 1987.

TABLE 1.7: *The traditional workforce and types of flexible worker (percentages) 1983–93 (men and women)*

**SAT:
allow 5 mins**

Managing tasks and solving problems ✓

ACTIVITY 6

Which of the following characteristics apply to core workers (C) and which to peripheral (P)?

a high level of company specific training ☐

numerically stable ☐

a general level of skill ☐

low job security ☐

multi-skilled ☐

relatively good career prospects ☐

part-time work ☐

flexible between functions and activities ☐

temporary contract ☐

jobshare ☐

relatively few career prospects ☐

permanent contract ☐

government training scheme ☐

Commentary...

a high level of company specific training (C)

numerically stable (C)

a general level of skill (P)

low job security (P)

multi-skilled (C)

relatively good career prospects (C)

part-time work (P)

flexible between functions and activities (C)

temporary contract (P)

jobshare (P)

relatively few career prospects (P)

permanent contract (C)

government training scheme (P)

PUBLIC AND PRIVATE SECTOR EMPLOYMENT

The workforce can also be classified between those employed in the public sector (public corporations, central government and local authorities) and those employed in the private sector (generally private profit and non-profit making organisations).

Peak employment in the public sector occurred in 1979 at 7.5 million. This total fell to 5.8 million by mid-1992 (*Economic Trends*, January 1993), a fall of nearly 23 per cent. Most of this decline took place in the public corporations as a result of the government's privatisation programme. Central government employment peaked at 2.4 million in 1981, fell gradually to 2.3 million in 1990 but has since lost about 300,000 jobs.

	1961	1971	1981	1991
Total workforce in employment	24,457	24,533	24,345	26,028
Private sector	18,598	17,906	17,160	19,799
Work-related gov't training	0	0	423	353
Public sector	5,859	6,627	7,185	5,876

Source: *Economic Trends*, No.471, January 1993

TABLE 1.8: *Analysis of workforce in employment by sector ('000s)*

CHANGES IN THE
OCCUPATIONAL STRUCTURE

SAT:
allow 10 mins

Applying numeracy	✓

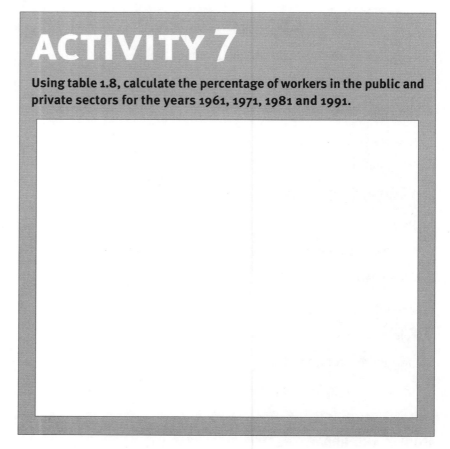

ACTIVITY 7

Using table 1.8, calculate the percentage of workers in the public and private sectors for the years 1961, 1971, 1981 and 1991.

Commentary...

You should have calculated the following figures:

Percentage of workers in each sector				
	1961	1971	1981	1991
Private	76	73	72	76
Public	24	27	28	24

ACTIVITY 8

From your own experience and reading and through discussion with your colleagues suggest some reasons for the decline of the manufacturing sector in the UK.

Use a separate sheet of paper to record your answer. Summarise your findings in the box below.

Write about 250 words.

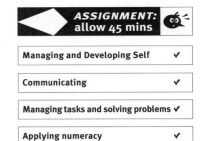

ASSIGNMENT:
allow 45 mins

Managing and Developing Self	✔
Communicating	✔
Managing tasks and solving problems	✔
Applying numeracy	✔

summary

This session has described the UK economy by analysing changes in the structure of the UK labour force. The main characteristics are:

> ▶ an ageing population

> ▶ an ageing workforce

> ▶ an increasing proportion of females in the workforces

> ▶ a declining share of employment in primary and secondary sectors and an increasng share in the tertiary sector

> ▶ a declining manufacturing sector (de-industrialisation)

> ▶ a shift from manual to non-manual occupations

> ▶ a greater skill content in many jobs but de-skilling in others

> ▶ a shift to a more flexible workforce

> ▶ a mix of public and private sector workers with the latter increasing in size.

The UK economic system

Objectives

After participating in this session, you should be able to:

- explain the basic economic problem

- list the strengths and weaknesses of central planning

- analyse the economic process in a market system

- assess the effect of government intervention into the market process.

In working through this session, you will practise the following BTEC common skills:

Managing and Developing Self	✔
Working with and Relating to others	
Communicating	✔
Managing Tasks and Solving Problems	✔
Applying Numeracy	✔
Applying Technology	
Applying Design and Creativity	

The economic problem

We live and work in an extremely complicated economic system in which, daily, we depend on many thousands of workers for our survival. If you take a moment to consider your daily routine and the goods and services you consume in one day, from the house in which you live, the way you travel to work or college, the food you eat and the electronic gadgets you use, it does not take long to realise how dependent we are on the co-operation of the rest of society.

LEVELS OF DEMAND

Most people would like to be able to increase their standard of living by laying claim to more of the goods and services that are produced. Unfortunately, there is not enough production to satisfy everybody's wants even though the volume of production is continually increasing. Many of the goods we now think of as essential – automatic washing machines, videos and freezers – were thought of not so long ago as luxuries. How long will it be before the non-essentials of today, such as cellular phones, automatic dish-washers and camcorders become the essentials of tomorrow? Perhaps some of you already think they are. These rising expectations form part of what economists refer to as the 'economic problem'.

LIMITS TO SUPPLY

The other side of that problem is the limited resources available to produce goods and services. Resources in this sense refer to land, raw materials, machinery, tools and labour available for production.

These resources are not scarce in themselves but only in relation to the demands put upon them. In other words, the demand for goods and services constantly outstrips the resources available to satisfy them.

It follows from this that choices have to be made. Society has to have some way of deciding which goods and services are produced and which are not. Should we produce more cars or more video recorders, or build more hospitals? Resources used for one cannot be used for another. Economists refer to this concept of alternatives foregone as 'opportunity cost' and point to this as the 'real cost' of production. From an individual point of view, choosing to go on holiday may mean giving up the opportunity to buy a new CD-player. Hence the real cost to you of the holiday is the CD-player you cannot buy.

The first problem facing society is: 'What goods and services should be produced?'

The second problem facing society is how best scarce resources can be used to maximise production. The level of production depends not only on the volume of resources at a country's disposal but also on the way in which those resources are used. Should we produce goods using lots of machinery rather than labour (capital intensive methods) or more labour than machinery (labour intensive methods)?

The third and final problem concerns the distribution of the goods and services once they are produced. How should they be divided?

These problems exist in all societies at all times no matter what stage of development that society has reached. Imagine yourself cast away on an island with a group of 40 people and ask yourself what you would need to survive. You might decide that food and shelter are high on your list of priorities but how are you going to produce them? Does anybody have any relevant skills? Should you make a net to catch fish? Can you and will you have time? What will you eat while you are making the net? The crunch question of course is who gets what? How do you divide ten small fish between 40 people?

PLANNED AND MARKET ECONOMIES

The problems may be the same for all societies but the ways of solving these problems, i.e. the systems created, will vary from one society to another. At one extreme is 'a market system', a completely decentralised system. An analysis of the market system forms the major part of this section. At the other extreme is the 'centrally planned economy' in which the three problems are solved by a centralised bureaucracy. These are theoretical extremes and in reality all economic systems are a mixture of the two. Perhaps the USA and Hong Kong could be said to be closer than most to a market economy. Central planning was most widely attempted on a country-wide basis in the former Soviet Union and Eastern Bloc countries. Those attempts have now been abandoned as they did not produce the same material wealth as the western market-based economies. Central planning is usually associated with communist countries, but it can take place under right-wing dictatorships.

The essential differences between the systems are the degree to which the means of production (land, factories and machinery) are either publicly or privately owned and the method of decision making and of control.

RECALL:
allow 2 mins

What three basic economic problems face all societies?

1.

2.

3.

Central planning

In a centrally planned economy such as the former Soviet Union, the means of production were publicly owned by the state. Decisions were made by a hierarchy of planning bodies from factory managers through regional councils to Soviet planning bodies to the central state authorities.

The state planners would decide the level of resources to be devoted to each particular sector and then set production targets. They would also decide where that production would go and set the prices for each particular industry. These plans would be implemented by the Soviet and regional planning bodies within their area of jurisdiction ending with instructions to each plant manager who would be informed of the relevant targets, destination of output and prices to be charged. The success or otherwise of the individual plant was to be judged by whether the targets were met.

THE MERITS OF CENTRAL PLANNING

According to those who favour it, central planning has a number of advantages:

- Theoretically, production is carried out to maximise common welfare therefore there should be no great extremes of income or wealth and no poverty.

- Workers work for each other and not for a capitalist employer whose main interest is maximisation of his/her own income by exploiting those who are employed.

- Private monopolies in which powerful owners exploit both workers and consumers do not exist.

- State administration should mean that unemployment, inflation and the variations in economic activity that occur in western economies do not exist.

- The state, by determining output targets can ensure that social priorities (e.g. education and health) are available to all.

- Planning can reduce the uncertainties and stresses associated with life in a competitive market economy.

Some of these merits look very attractive, particularly in an economy which has a large part of its workforce unemployed and in which income differentials are widening rather than narrowing. Unfortunately, there are drawbacks.

Drawbacks of central planning

Opponents of central planning cite a number of weaknesses:

- The planning apparatus requires a huge amount of resources.

- Country-wide planning entails a high degree of co-operation and communication between the different elements in the economy. Experience shows that these plans often go wrong.

- Individual freedom and decision making is greatly curtailed.

- State direction reduces individual initiative and effort.

- The range and quality of consumer goods on offer is determined by the sate rather than consumers.

- Firms tend to be inefficient by western standards as the emphasis is on meeting targets rather than achieving efficiency.

What this meant for people who lived in these regimes was a much lower material standard of living than that enjoyed in the West. Shops were often faced with long queues of consumers as planners' objectives were not necessarily the same as consumers'. The Soviet economy became associated with shortages of consumer goods (which were of inferior quality) while at the same time the Soviets were able to produce an arsenal of nuclear weapons, send astronauts into space and win a haul of Olympic gold medals.

However, the transformation from a centrally planned economy to a market or mixed economy has not meant greater prosperity for everybody. Workers are now for the first time having to come to terms with unemployment, inflation and a rationing system based on price rather than queues.

Central planning has now been largely discredited as a way of solving the basic problems (what, how and for whom) facing society. There now seems to be widespread agreement that the market system of allocation is necessary for an efficient economy.

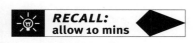

RECALL:
allow 10 mins

List the advantages and disadvantages of a central planning system, as practised in the former Soviet Union.

The free market economy

At the other extreme from the centrally planned economy is the totally de-centralised market economy, sometimes referred to as capitalism, free enterprise or *laissez-faire*. You need to understand the operation of the free market to understand the many economic policy changes made in the UK in the last 15 years. Government ministers talk about the 'discipline of the market' or 'leaving the market to get on with the job'. Indeed an article in the Treasury's *Economic Progress Report*, No. 145, May 1982 started with this sentence: 'A major aim of the government since coming into office in May 1979 has been the restoration of market forces throughout the economy.'

In this type of economic system, the means of production are in private hands with complete freedom over their use. The decisions about what, how and for whom are left to individuals operating through markets. There is no single agency directing resources. The system is also typified by competition between individuals. Everyone tries to achieve what is in their best interests. The role of the government in this system is limited to creating a framework within which markets can operate.

> **\!?/   Market** A market is defined as any situation in which buyers and sellers are brought together to determine a price.

This is most easily observed at an auction when buyers and sellers gather together to fix a price for the goods on offer. Goods we consume daily are usually sold in shops where prices are generally fixed by the shopkeeper, but buyers will still have some influence. If prices are too high, shoppers will go elsewhere; if prices are too low, stocks will soon disappear. Other markets, such as foreign currency markets, stock exchanges, gold, oil and cotton, are conducted over the telephone, often worldwide.

BASIC FEATURES OF A MARKET ECONOMY

There are a number of basic features which need further explanation before we look at the operation of the market economy.

Private property In a market economy, all resources are owned by individuals or groups of individuals who may have joined together for some purpose, e.g. to run a business. Property rights (rights over land, buildings, machinery and other natural and man-made resources) are enshrined in law (part of the minimal function of the state). Owners are free to do what they want with their property as long as their actions do not infringe upon the property rights of others.

Following the investigation by the Monopolies and Mergers Commission into the brewing industry (1989), the government ordered the brewers to dispose of many of their public houses. One of the arguments used by MPs to defend the brewers was that this struck at the heart of these basic property rights.

Freedom of choice Individuals are free to set up in business to produce anything they choose; these individuals are known as entrepreneurs. They are equally free to close the business. Workers are free to choose which occupation they will follow and consumers are free to spend their money as they see fit.

Self-interest The assumption is that individuals attempt to do what is best for themselves. Entrepreneurs attempt to make as much profit as possible by selling their goods and services at the highest possible price while producing at the lowest possible cost. At the same time, consumers try to buy goods at the lowest possible price and workers move to jobs in which they can maximise their earnings.

Competition Individuals, in attempting to achieve what is in their best interests whether as producers, consumers or workers, are in competition with others. The producer is trying to capture the market by reducing prices while at the same time staying in business. Consumers compete with other consumers in searching out goods at the lowest price and workers compete with each other for the best paid jobs.

For competition to take place, there must be a relatively large number of buyers and sellers. This is so that no one individual, by monopolising the market as a seller or buyer, can have more influence than any other buyer or seller. Further, there must be freedom of movement in and out of markets. It is the pressure of competition which acts as a check on the pursuit of self-interest. Without it some may achieve a position where they are able to exploit others.

Limited government The role of government in this model is to provide a framework within which individuals are free to act. This includes national defence and a system of law in which property rights are protected, contracts enforced and so on.

THE ECONOMIC PROCESS

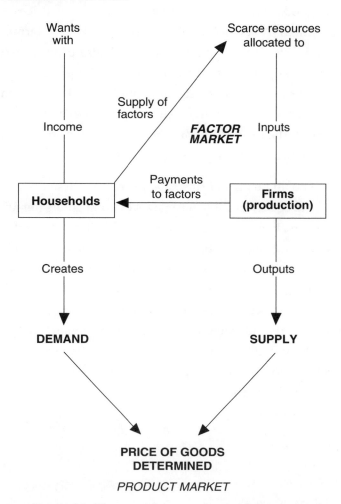

FIGURE 2.1: *The economic process in a market economy.*

Figure 2.1 is a simplification of the operation of a free market economy in which there is no government sector or overseas trade. The decisions in this system are made by individuals acting as producers and consumers. In the diagram, households are the buyers of goods and services and sellers of resources, mainly labour. Firms produce the goods and services and buy resources. There are two markets in operation in this model: the market for goods and services (the product market) and the market for resources (the factor market).

THE PRICE SYSTEM

The key element in this model is the operation of the price system. It is movements in price which communicate the decisions of buyers and sellers. Price is determined by the interaction of the forces of supply and demand.

In the product market, consumers distribute their spending on the alternative goods and services on offer. They want low prices; sellers want high prices. A balance is reached and a price is determined. If consumers decide they want more of a particular product, demand will rise while supply stays constant causing the price to rise. The movement in price will act as a signal to producers. They will employ more resources to produce these extra goods. They may also move resources from the production of other goods whose price is falling relative to the products whose price is rising.

In order to stay in business firms have to react to these changes. The alternative is to be driven out of the market by competitors pursuing the same customers. In order to be competitive producers adopt the least-cost combination of factors obtained in the factor market. That is, they use a combination of resources which enables them to produce each unit of output at the lowest possible cost. They buy these resources in the factor market. Prices in this market, just as in the product market are determined by the interaction of supply and demand with prices generally reflecting the relative scarcity of particular factors. If wages are low relative to capital, then producers will tend to adopt labour-intensive methods of production and vice versa.

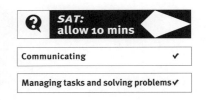

SAT:
allow 10 mins

| Communicating | ✔ |
| Managing tasks and solving problems | ✔ |

ACTIVITY 1

Explain how each of the basic problems facing society is solved by a free market economic system.

What is to be produced

How is it to be produced

For whom is it to be produced

Commentary...

It is consumers who determine 'what' is produced. They cast their votes by spending money in the market for goods and services. Suppliers take note of what consumers wish to buy through changes in price.

'How' these goods are produced is determined by competition between suppliers. They must use the most efficient (least-cost) methods of production in order to stay in business.

'For whom' is it produced is determined by the distribution of income. In other words, the more money somebody has, the greater the claim to the limited supply of goods and services.

So, these problems of what, how and for whom are solved not by a single agency as in a centrally planned economy but by millions of individuals making their own decisions, acting on their own initiative but co-ordinated by the price mechanism.

THE MERITS OF THE MARKET

Many economists argue that the free market system is a much more efficient system than a centrally planned economy. Producers aim to reduce their costs and charge as high a price as possible so as to make as much profit as possible. In other words, producers will always seek out the cheapest methods of production and eliminate waste and duplication.

When firms make large profits they will expand production to make even larger profits. These large profits also tempt other producers to enter the market. The result is an increase in supply. This increase in supply will drive prices down towards the cost of production. The end result is:

- low cost, efficient production

- low prices.

Furthermore, the goods and services which are produced are determined by the spending decisions of consumers and not by producers. In this, consumers are said to be sovereign, i.e. 'they rule'. If the distribution of income in an economy is acceptable then it follows that the types of goods and services produced are socially acceptable.

Besides these advantages of a market economy, there are other features which can stimulate economic growth. The increased availability of consumer goods can act as a strong incentive to individuals to increase their earning capacity by working harder or acquiring new skills. Access to markets provides opportunities for inventors to profit from the exploitation of new goods and technical innovations. There is also a big incentive to capital accumulation of all kinds as such capital earns extra income.

In summary, it is argued that a properly functioning market economy stimulates both economic efficiency and economic growth. This takes place automatically requiring no great bureaucratic administration, no central decision making process and very little policing.

WEAKNESSES OF THE MARKET ECONOMY

Having read the description of the operation of a free market you may be wondering why more economies, and in particular the UK economy, do not operate more like the model described. The first point to make is that successive governments since 1979 have been opening more of the economy to market forces yet the economy is still very much a mixed economy.

\?/ A mixed economy This is an economy which has a mix of public and private ownership of resources and in which decisions concerning the allocation of resources are made by individuals and the state.

Market forces may well produce a greater volume of goods and services but they do not necessarily work to everybody's advantage. There are several major deficiencies which have prompted governments to intervene.

Monopolies and market concentration Part of the dynamic process of competition means that there will be winners and losers. In the goods market, the losers go out of business. According to the model, they are replaced by others (freedom of entry) but there are powerful forces which may work against this happening. One of the factors which enables some to 'win' is that they are able to reduce costs and therefore final prices. As some producers leave the market, the winners are able to gain more customers, increasing the scale of their operations and allowing further cost reductions (economies of scale). They also gain cost reductions from what is known as the 'experience curve', i.e. as a company gains experience of producing a product it can make further efficiency savings. This can act as a quite substantial barrier to the entry of new firms; they find it difficult to compete on price with established companies (See Section 3, Session 1).

The end result of this process is evident in many product markets which are dominated by a few producers (economists refer to this as concentration). Indeed most business people tell you that they are rather keen on less competition, not more, and that the well-known strategy of merger and acquisition is designed to produce exactly that. Once a market is dominated by a few producers (what economists refer to as **oligopoly**), there is the possibility of producers abusing their dominant position and charging higher prices than they would be able to do in a truly competitive situation. It also allows the possibility of inefficiency in production if price competition is restricted.

This is not to say that competition does not take place, but once a market is dominated by a few producers, it allows forms of competition other than the price competition assumed in the model. Advertising is a major competitive weapon used by many firms in this situation. A good example is the detergent market dominated by two firms, Proctor and Gamble and Unilever, each with massive advertising budgets.

A situation in which a single firm produces the whole output of an industry is known as monopoly. A firm in this situation faces no competition and is able to set prices at any level. However, the monopolist cannot make consumers buy at any price. It must therefore set a price at which it is able to generate sufficient income to cover costs and make a profit.

Pure monopolies are rare. British Gas may be the only producer of piped gas to households but it faces competition from other sources of power, e.g. electricity. Even so, it is still in a powerful position. If prices rise, people do not immediately start replacing their gas heating systems. Now that British Gas is in the private sector, the government has established a watchdog body called OFGAS which tries to ensure that it does not abuse its monopoly position.

Consumer sovereignty A key feature of the model in both economic and political terms is the freedom and power of the consumer to 'pull the strings'. In other words, it is the consumers who cast their votes (i.e. spend their money) in this economic democracy. They determine how the resources of the economy will be used.

This makes two assumptions. The first is that there is 'a balance of power' between producers and consumers. The second is that consumers are 'rational' and pursue what is in their best interests. To do this, they would need to be fully aware of all the alternative products on offer, their various attributes and their prices. Ask yourself how this accords with your own experience. Have you ever bought a car or a CD-player? If so, were you able to compare the various technical merits of the products on offer? Were you aware of all the products on offer? Were you really able to compare prices after special offers, discounts, trade-ins, interest free periods, low interest loans, etc.? Were you able to relate the price to the different technical specifications?

Income differentials Closely related to this last point is the influence that each member of society has on the system. Unlike our political system in which those of voting age each have one vote, power in the economic voting system is determined by the amount of money each person has available to spend. The more money you have, the greater the influence you have on what is produced. Businesses are only interested in the actual demand for goods. If you look back at the model you can see that wants (let alone needs) only become demands when backed by the ability to pay. It follows from this that there may be many people whose needs are not being met by the economic system.

The pure free market produces an unequal distribution of income and wealth regardless of whether people start from a position of equality. Distribution depends on a number of factors, including abilities, skills, wealth, luck and on how others judge what each other has to sell.

Externalities In producing goods and services, firms are concerned to maximise revenue and minimise costs. These costs and revenues appear in the profit and loss accounts of the firms but they are not the only costs and benefits that might arise in the production process. Some costs and benefits are external to the market process and hence are known as 'externalities'.

What might be good for a firm's profit and loss account is not necessarily good for society because a company's 'private' actions may impose social costs (pollution, unemployment). For example, a transport firm which economises on maintenance may run dirty and dangerous vehicles which are a hazard to the public. There may also be benefits. Some firms (so-called 'free riders') may benefit from the training efforts of another.

These externalities can arise from consumption as well as production. Motoring, for example, causes pollution of the atmosphere, increases congestion and thereby increases transport costs for firms.

The type of goods and services produced Some goods and services are such that a pure market system may either not produce them at all or not produce them in suffcent quantities.

These goods are known respectively as **public goods** and **merit goods**.

Pure public goods are goods which would not be produced at all in a free market economy. This is because they are non-rival in consumption (this means that when one person consumes a product it does not reduce the consumption of any other person). They are also non-excludable (consumption cannot be restricted to those who pay).

National defence is a good example of a pure public good which meets both these conditions. Street lighting and roads are others which are treated as public goods although in principle they could be provided by the market. The government in seeking market solutions to some of our transport problems, is considering introducing tolls on motorways and systems to charge car owners when they bring their cars into a city, thereby restricting traffic on some roads to those who can pay.

A merit good is one whose consumption is seen as intrinsically desirable and which confers a benefit to society as a whole. The obvious examples are health and education. The market could and does provide both services up to a point. Some economists think that if people are left to decide what they spend on health and education there may well be under-consumption. The case for public investment could be made by a paternalistic state deciding that people are not always the best judge of what is good for them or by the state recognising the considerable external benefits arising from a healthy and educated labour force. One of the reasons often put forward for the relatively poor performance of the UK economy is that, compared to our major competitors, we fail to educate and train people to a sufficiently high level.

Instability Another criticism of the market economy is its tendency towards instability. The level of economic activity tends to follow a cycle in which periods of economic growth, coupled with rising employment, inflation and balance of payments problems are followed by a period of falling growth, rising unemployment, lower

THE FREE MARKET ECONOMY

levels of price inflation and a more satisfactory balance of payments. This is the typical pattern of a market economy although, in the UK the 1970s saw a period of rising unemployment and inflation. The 1980s and 1990s have seen persistently high levels of unemployment irrespective of the rate of economic growth or inflation.

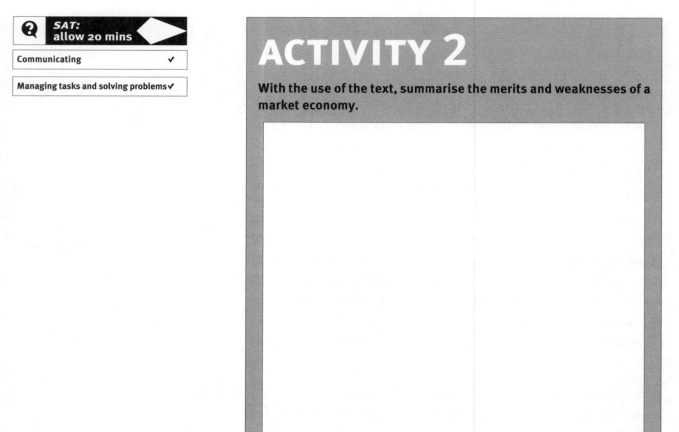

SAT:
allow 20 mins

Communicating	✔
Managing tasks and solving problems	✔

ACTIVITY 2

With the use of the text, summarise the merits and weaknesses of a market economy.

Commentary...

The merits of a market economy:

- efficiency
- maximum production
- high volume of consumer goods
- large range of choice
- good quality
- flexibility
- responsiveness to consumers

- strong incentives

- freedom of individual in decision making

- encourages innovation

- no bureaucracy.

The weaknesses of a market economy:

- economic power concentrated in a few hands

- intensification of economic inequality

- instability – unemployment/inflation

- some goods may not be produced – public goods

- insufficient merit goods produced

- ignores externalities

- system based on greed rather than need

- crime/corruption.

THE MIXED ECONOMY

The weaknesses of the market economy provide a reason for forms of government intervention into the free market process. This may mean replacing the market system entirely, particularly in the case of public and merit goods. It may mean helping the market to work better by making markets more competitive (e.g. controlling mergers and acquisitions), or by helping the movement of resources (e.g. labour to jobs or vice versa). It may mean manipulating the market by adjusting prices, e.g. by imposing lower taxes on unleaded fuel, or by providing subsidies for public transport or by more direct controls such as land planning regulations.

The government also takes responsibility for the direction of the whole economy. Through a mixture of monetary policy, fiscal policy and more direct controls, it is able to influence the level of unemployment, economic growth, inflation and the balance of payments (see Session 3 for an explanation of these terms).

The relationship between government and business is investigated in much more detail in the third and fourth sessions of this section. The final part of this session looks at the attempts, since 1979, by the Conservative government to 'roll back the frontiers of the state'.

Rolling back the frontiers of the state

Since 1979, a belief in the virtues of the free market by successive Conservative governments has underpinned a set of policy initiatives broadly labelled 'privatisation'. One of the main targets of the privatisation programme was the return to the private sector of many of the nationalised industries.

NATIONALISATION

Nationalised industries are, broadly speaking, those parts of the public sector which supply goods and services in the market economy. This excludes defence, health, education, social services and organisations like the BBC which for the main part operate outside the market economy. Most nationalisation has taken place since the Second World War and is, therefore, relatively recent historically.

THE REASONS FOR NATIONALISATION

There have been both economic and political reasons for nationalisation. Economic reasons include the following:

- **Natural monopolies** Utilities such as gas, electricity, telephone and water are likely to be monopolies whatever the form of ownership. Competition would lead to an unnecessary waste of resources as the supply of pipes, mains and cables and so on would be duplicated. Nationalisation was a way to control these monopolies and ensure that they were run in the public interest.

- **Capital investment** Investment in many industries had been neglected, especially during the war. Nationalisation was seen as a way of injecting large amounts of capital to restructure and modernise key industries.

- **Management of the economy** In the period after the Second World War, the government took much more responsibility than previously for managing the economy. Nationalisation gave the government a powerful tool for economic management.

- **Social benefits** In some industries, the revenues that could be obtained from their operation may not cover operating costs but the social benefits outweigh social costs. For example, an efficient transport system which delivers goods and people on time confers a benefit to more than the user.

- **Equity** Some argue that people are entitled to the same standard of essential service at the same cost wherever they live, e.g. postal services.

- **'Lame ducks'** Some firms, e.g. Rolls Royce, were saved from bankruptcy by being taken into state control.

- **Planning** In the areas of transport policy and energy policy, it was felt that a long-term view was needed. This was made much easier if these industries were under public control.

Political reasons advanced for nationalisation include the following:

- **Improving government planning** Ownership of the major industries of the economy would aid planning of the economy.

- **Promoting social equality** This would be delivered by redistributing wealth and income more equitably. (Abolition of high profits would lead to higher real wages for workers and lower prices for consumers.)

- **Improving industrial relations** By giving workers more democratic control in the workplace, conflict between employer and employee would be reduced.

The arguments against nationalisation include the following:

- **Lack of competition** As most nationalised industries are monopolies this may lead to inefficiencies, a lack of innovation and little consumer choice.

- **No profit motive** Therefore there is no incentive to improve performance.

- **No threat of bankruptcy** The guarantee that losses will be paid by the taxpayer may lead to complacency.

- **Problems of size** Nationalised industries are generally big. They may therefore suffer from too much bureaucracy, poor communications and inflexibility.

- **Political interference** Although politicians were not supposed to interfere in the day-to-day management of the nationalised industries, they frequently did. Decisions were imposed on the nationalised industries which served the interests of government rather than those of the industries themselves. For example, prices might have been held down to combat inflation when they should have been raised.

For many years after the Second World War, the major UK political parties had agreed about the benefits of a mixed economy. It was generally felt that the production and distribution of consumer goods and services was best left to the private sector. It was also agreed that the 'natural monopolies' ought to be nationalised and that services such as education and health should be provided by the state and financed by taxation.

From the late 1960s, some began to blame the mixed economy for the relatively poor performance of the UK economy. It was argued that the public sector was wealth consuming, reliant on wealth created in the private sector. At the same time, it was using resources which would have been better utilised in the private sector. Industries in the public sector did not face the same constraints as those in the private sector. They were therefore less efficient and some were loss making, relying on state subsidies for their existence.

Since 1979, successive Conservative governments have sought to change radically the 'mix' of the economy through 'privatisation' policies.

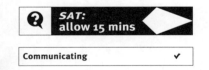

ACTIVITY 3

In your own words, summarise why nationalisation took place.

Commentary...

You should have summarised the points made above, but the major points you could have made are:

- natural monopolies

- control of the economy

- rescuing inefficient industries

- social welfare

- ideological commitment.

PRIVATISATION

The term 'privatisation' has come to include all of the following:

- The sale of public sector assets to the private sector, most notably the denationalisation of many public enterprises, e.g. British Gas, British Telecom, water companies and regional electricity boards. (Other sales have included local authority council houses and land owned by various bodies such as the Forestry Commission and the Land Settlement Association.)

- The reduction of state controls (de-regulation) over both public and private sectors, e.g. building societies being able to offer banking services.

- The contracting out of publicly financed services, e.g. school meals, refuse collection, hospital laundry, cleaning and catering.

THE REASONS FOR PRIVATISATION

A number of reasons have been put forward to support privatisation:

Reducing government intervention in industry The main purpose of privatisation has been to open up more of the economy to market forces in a belief that this would increase productive efficiency and consumer choice. The government believed that activities in the public sector were cushioned from the realities of commercial life in the private sector. Public sector enterprises did not need to respond to customer wishes as did the private sector, nor did they need to ensure that revenues covered costs as they could simply turn to the Treasury to make good any loss. There was no threat of bankruptcy.

Improving efficiency in privatised industries If management and workers are free to pursue commercial objectives (e.g. profit maximisation) rather than government objectives then this would lead to greater efficiency. Privatised companies would have greater freedom to organise to reduce costs, improve productivity and encourage innovation. The introduction of incentive schemes such as performance related pay and/or employee share ownership would improve performance.

Widening share ownership Privatisation not only offered the opportunity of share ownership to employees but also to the general public. This policy allied to the sale of council homes and general encouragement to home buyers was intended to create a 'property-owning democracy' in which the fortunes of individuals were closely related to the performance of the economy.

Increasing government revenue Sale of public sector assets boosted the income of the government at a time when it was trying to reduce taxation.

Political It was also part of the process of changing the culture of the British people, i.e. from a 'welfare dependency' culture to an 'enterprise' culture.

This philosophy has also been extended to those sectors of the public sector not so easily privatised. The civil service has been reformed to provide incentives to individual civil servants which mirror the type of incentives available in the private sector. Many other areas of the public sector are now subject to performance related pay in the belief that this will increase individual effort.

RECALL:
allow 10 mins

List the main arguments put forward in favour of privatisation.

THE CRITICISMS OF PRIVATISATION

Performance and consumer choice Whether or not the performance of the privatised companies has improved is difficult if not impossible to measure. What yardstick should we use? Would profit be a good indicator?

One of the reasons for privatisation was to open up the nationalised industries to increased competition but many of the privatisations have simply transferred public sector monopolies to the private sector with no increase in consumer choice. It was the government's belief that efficiency came from competition. If this were the case, then these industries should have been broken up into smaller competing units before privatisation. Ironically, privatised industries (water, gas, electricity, telecommunications) have been subject to the discipline of government appointed regulators (OFWAT, OFGAS, OFFER, OFTEL), rather than the discipline of the market. Their profits have increased but is this because they have improved their performance or because they have taken advantage of their monopoly position?

We could use productivity as a measure of performance but this also leads to confusing conclusions. There have been substantial productivity improvements, largely as a result of redundancy programmes, but not so great as the productivity improvements in British Coal (only recently privatised) and British Rail, which is still in the public sector.

Any measure of efficiency must also take into consideration external costs and benefits. British Telecom is obliged to provide telephone lines to isolated communities but charge consumers standard national rates; these social considerations must be taken into account when assessing efficiency. Large-scale redundancies may reduce costs for companies but unless there are other employment opportunities, the cost is transferred to the wider community. If the measure of success is profit and shareholder satisfaction then many of the privatised companies may be judged as successful but this success may be at the expense of consumers and employees.

Revenue The government has raised much needed revenue but has also been condemned for selling valuable public assets too cheaply. Many of these industries now have market values which are far greater than the sale value. This would seem to be a major loss to the public purse.

Shareholders There are now more shareholders. But many purchasers of privatisation share issues sold their shares soon after purchase making a quick profit as share prices rose. The government claimed a 66 per cent average retention rate but according to Bishop and Kay (table 2.1) this average is much lower and has since slipped to around 40 per cent. Additionally, some 70 per cent of shareholders have shareholdings of less than £3,000 and most in only one company. Financial institutions own something in the order of 76 per cent of all equities. This would seem a long way from the vision of a 'property-owning democracy' (Clarke, T., 1993, The political economy of the UK privatisation programme: a blueprint for other countries? In *The Political Economy of Privatisation*, ed. by Clarke, T. and Pitelis, C., Routledge).

Company	Successful applicants	Number of shareholders: end 1st year	latest	Percentage of original number
Amersham Int'	165,000	8,601	6,048	9.3
British Telecom	2,300,000	1,692,979	1,311,139	57.0
BAA	2,187,500	1,064,815	1,064,815	48.7
British Gas	4,407,100	3,111,872	2,903,416	65.9
British Airways	1,100,000	420,526	347,897	31.6
Jaguar	125,000	54,104	42,790	34.2
Britoil	35,000	39,558	*	*
Assoc Brit. Ports	45,000	15,500	n/a	n/a
Enterprise Oil	13,700	14,146	10,714	78.2
Rolls-Royce	2,000,000	924,970	924,970	46.2

Note: * Acquired by BP.
Source: Bishop, M. and Kay, J., 1988, *Does Privatisation Work – Lessons from the UK*, London Business School.

TABLE 2.1: *Size of privatised company share registers in the UK*

It is difficult not to conclude that privatisation has been driven more by ideology than by an objective analysis of the merits of public or private ownership. Nationalisation was seen to have failed and the assumption was that it was due to the form of ownership rather than any other cause. The solution then was simple, change the form of ownership. But privatisation was also part of a programme of reducing the size of the government sector in general and the creation of an 'enterprise culture'.

THE SIZE OF THE GOVERNMENT SECTOR

We have already established (in Session 1) that the public sector share of employment has fallen from a peak of 30 per cent in 1981 to 24 per cent in 1992. We are now going to measure the public sector in terms of its contribution to gross domestic product (GDP).

> **⟍?⟋ Gross domestic product (GDP)** is the total money value of
> all final goods and services produced in an economy over a one-
> year period.

In spite of the government's declared intent to reduce the size of the
public sector (as a percentage of GDP) this has proved difficult to
achieve. At its lowest in 1988–89 (39 per cent), it was only similar to
levels in the late 1960s and the recession of the late 1980s has pushed
this ratio back up to about 45 per cent, similar to levels in the late
1970s.

The government is still committed to reducing the ratio of public
spending to GDP and, in November 1993, announced budget plans to
reduce the real growth in public expenditure for 1994–95 by 1.3 per
cent. There will be a small increase in real terms in the two years
following. The ratio of general government expenditure to GDP is
forecast to fall to 41 per cent by 1998–99.

> **⟍?⟋ Real terms** This refers to the measurement of a figure
> adjusted for the effect of prices over time. For example, GDP may
> rise in money value by 5 per cent from one year to the next. Some
> of this increase will be because the prices of the goods and
> services which make up GDP will have risen. If prices have gone
> up by 2 per cent then the real increase in GDP will be about 3 per
> cent.

**ROLLING BACK THE FRONTIERS OF
THE STATE**

Managing and Developing Self	✔
Managing tasks and solving problems	✔
Applying numeracy	✔

ACTIVITY 4

Convert the figures in table 2.2 to percentages. Study the figures and note down your main conclusions about changes in government spending over the period. Write about 300 words.

	£ billion		
United Kingdom	78/79	84/85	92/93
Defence	21.1	27.1	23.6
Public order and safety	7.1	9.9	14.2
Education	25.4	25.6	32.2
Health	21.8	26.0	34.7
Social security	47.3	62.3	79.7
Housing	12.5	6.9	6.2
Transport	8.3	8.8	10.7
Overseas services	3.0	2.7	3.5
Agriculture,fisheries, food and forestry	2.9	3.8	3.2
Trade and industry, energy and employment	11.3	12.5	8.6
Environmental services	7.4	6.8	9.0
National Heritage	2.0	2.2	2.6
Personal social services	3.8	4.5	6.4
Miscellaneous expenditure(*)	7.7	6.1	7.2
Total expenditure	181.6	205.2	241.8
% of GDP	44.0	46.75	44.75

(*) includes contributions to the EC and activities required for the general maintenance of government, such as tax collection and the registration of the population
Source: Statistical Supplement to the Financial Statement and Budget Report, 1994– 95.

TABLE 2.2: *Government expenditure by function in real terms 1978–79 to 1992–93*

Use a separate sheet of paper to record your answer. Summarise your findings in the box below.

summary

▶ All societies face the same basic economic problem of what to produce, how to produce and for whom to produce.

▶ Economic systems developed to solve these problems vary from centrally planned systems to decentralised market systems.

▶ In centrally planned economies, the state solves the basic problems. These systems require huge bureaucracies, are inflexible and have proved to be inefficient.

▶ In market systems, freely operating individuals make the decisions concerning the basic economic problem. The decisions are co-ordinated by the price system.

▶ The market has proved more successful at producing a large quantity and variety of consumer goods. It does have its weaknesses and this has resulted today in what is known as the mixed economy.

▶ In the mixed economy, the government intervenes in the market process in order to correct market deficiencies.

▶ Recent Conservative governments have tried to reduce the size of the public sector, believing it to be partly responsible for the poor performance of the UK economy.

The financial sector

Objectives

After participating in this session, you should be able to:

▶ describe the structure of the financial system

▶ describe the functions of financial institutions

▶ explain how the financial sector has developed since 1945 and give reasons for this development

▶ explain why the financial sector is important in the UK economy

▶ describe the role, and extent of control, of the regulatory bodies and assess their effectiveness.

In working through this session, you will practise the following BTEC common skills:

Managing and Developing Self	
Working with and Relating to others	
Communicating	✔
Managing Tasks and Solving Problems	✔
Applying Numeracy	✔
Applying Technology	
Applying Design and Creativity	

For this session you need a copy of the *Financial Times* and a calculator.

Functions of the financial sector

All the activities concerned with making, selling and buying goods and services is called the economy. When we think about the economy, it is often convenient to speak of it as though there were different sections or sectors, each concerned with different aspects of the production, sale and purchase of goods and services. For example, we talk of the agricultural sector, the industrial sector and the financial sector as though they were separate entities. In fact, they are closely linked. In this session, we study the financial sector – the part of the economy concerned with money, loans, interest rates, credit cards, shares, etc. We see how important this sector is, in that it affects the way every other sector of the economy works.

The functioning of a modern economy and the activities of the organisations and individuals within it – local and national government, businesses and consumers – is lubricated by a variety of financial institutions. Banks, building societies, insurance companies, pension funds, investment trusts, unit trusts, the stock exchange, all act as intermediaries between those:

- who wish to borrow money and those who wish to lend it, or

- who wish to save money and invest it, or

- who want to trade in financial assets such as company shares.

There are four main areas of activity within the financial sector:

- borrowing and lending money

- insurance

- trading in stocks and shares

- pensions.

BORROWING AND LENDING MONEY

Businesses require money to finance their production of goods and services. Governments need money to provide national services such as education and health, defence, and the social security system. Businesses get their money partly from retained profits and governments get it mainly from taxes. But often these sources of finance are not enough, and both businesses and governments must borrow money.

Sometimes governments, businesses and individuals have surplus money that they are willing to lend (at a price) to people wanting to borrow, but the problem is that the would-be lenders may not know who wants to borrow. An individual living in Scotland say, who has money to lend, is unlikely to know that a small company in the Midlands needs money. Even if the would-be lenders knew this, it might be that the amount of money the company requires is much greater than he or she can lend. One function of the financial sector is to bring together the needs of borrowers and the wealth of lenders. Banks and other financial institutions act as go-betweens. They collect funds from many lenders which they can then make available to borrowers.

When a business wants to borrow money, it looks for a lender (such as a bank) who can meet its needs. When a bank wants to lend, it will try to find a suitable borrower. So what do lenders and borrowers look for?

Lenders look for:

- low risk borrowers (people and businesses who will not default on their loans)

- high returns

- liquidity (the ease with which the loan can be converted into money at the convenience of the lender)

- confidence that the value of the asset representing the loan such as a share certificate will be maintained.

Borrowers require:

- funds at a particular point in time

- funds for a given period of time

- the lowest borrowing costs and charges.

It is possible for an individual borrower to find an individual lender – as when you borrow money from a friend for a drink. But instead of borrowing directly from individuals, businesses and governments usually borrow from organisations – called financial institutions – which have got their money from individual lenders.

**FUNCTIONS OF THE FINANCIAL
SECTOR**

SAT:
allow 5 mins

Managing tasks and solving problems ✓

ACTIVITY 1

There are a number of benefits for individuals, businesses and government – which we have not yet described in the text – for having financial institutions acting as go-betweens between borrowers and lenders. Before reading on, see if you can list some of these benefits.

Commentary...

That may have been quite a difficult activity, but we hope you could list one or more benefits. The benefits include:

- ○ creating a large pool of savings for borrowers to access

- ○ spreading risk – so that if any one borrower defaults on the loan there is very little risk of lenders losing all their funds

- ○ buying and selling financial assets so as to transform short-term lending into long-term lending or vice versa.

It costs businesses time and money to find suitable lenders. Businesses can avoid these costs by using financial institutions which bring together lenders and borrowers. Financial institutions can also take advantage of economies of scale, some of which are passed on to customers. These advantages arise from their ability to:

- ○ collect and interpret financial information easily and cheaply

- spread fixed overhead costs over a large output

- employ specialist personnel who are expert in assessing the creditworthiness of borrowers and the profitability of different investments

- advertise and thus reduce search costs for lenders and borrowers.

INSURANCE

Insurance enables businesses and individuals who suffer a loss or accident to be paid financial compensation. For example, a chemical company can avoid being financially crippled by a costly fire at one of its plants by insuring against that risk. Insurance companies take money (called premiums) from individuals and businesses who wish to protect themselves against events that might happen like theft, flood, fire and accident; this is called **insurance**. They also offer cover against events which will definitely occur such as death; this is called **assurance**. When these events take place the insurance company pays compensation to the policy holder. In simple terms, policy holders not putting in claims, compensate those who do claim. In this way, insurance firms spread the cost of an individual loss or accident over all the policy holders.

TRADING IN STOCKS AND SHARES

Businesses and governments raise money by issuing stocks and shares. These are bought by financial institutions, other businesses and individuals. Once issued, stocks and shares are traded on the stock market. Investors look for stocks and shares paying high dividends and those whose prices are likely to rise.

Traded stocks and shares are like second-hand cars. Just as the original producer of the car receives no money when the car is subsequently resold, so the business issuing the shares gets no money when the shares are traded on the stock market.

PENSIONS

A pension is a regular payment received by someone who has retired. People pay for pensions through personal pension plans or through pension schemes provided by their employer. Payments are made during their working lives in order to provide a regular pension on retirement. The contributions are invested by organisations called pension funds in a wide range of shares, property, and works of art and antiques. Sometimes big businesses run their own pension funds.

Structure of the financial sector

> **\?!** The 'structure' of the financial sector simply means the different types of institutions that belong in the sector and the relationships between them.

In this text, we look mainly at the different kinds of institution, and we pay less attention to their inter-relationships.

We listed four main areas of activity of financial institutions:

- borrowing and lending money
- insurance
- trading in stocks and shares
- pensions.

Institutions have tended to specialise in one or other of these activities. Banks borrowed and lent money, but did not sell insurance or trade in shares. Building societies made long-term loans on the security of private houses but did not provide banking services such as **current accounts**. Recently this has changed and there is more competition between the various institutions as they increasingly sell similar services and products.

> **\?!** **Current account:** sometimes called a cheque account because customers can write cheques up to the amount of money in the account, or beyond that to an overdraft limit agreed with the bank. These accounts are designed for businesses and individuals who wish to draw out money regularly. Most banks charge customers for current accounts.

The current areas of activity of each type of financial institution are detailed in figure 3.1. Remember that the activities of the institution are constantly changing.

	Retail banks	Building societies	Insurance companies	Wholesale banks	Pension funds	Unit trusts
Current accounts	✔	✔	✔	✘	✘	✘
Deposit accounts	✔	✔	✘	✔	✘	✘
Loans and overdrafts	✔	✔	✘	✔	✘	✘
Money transfer services	✔	✔	✘	✘	✘	✘
Mortgages	✔	✔	✘	✘	✘	✘
Buying and selling shares	✔	✔	✘	✘	✘	✔
Insurance policies	✔	✔	✔	✘	✘	✘
Life assurance policies	✔	✘	✔	✘	✘	✘
Pensions policies	✔	✘	✔	✘	✔	✘
Foreign currency	✔	✔	✘	✘	✘	✘
Financial advice	✔	✔	✔	✔	✘	✘
Payroll Services	✔	✘	✘	✘	✘	✘
Export finance	✔	✘	✘	✘	✘	✘

FIGURE 3.1: *Activities of financial institutions.*

Some institutions such as the banks and building societies rely very heavily on deposits which firms, individuals and other bodies place with them. This money is then lent to industry, individuals, and governments. Others, such as insurance companies, pension funds and unit trusts collect long-term savings which they then invest in a variety of stocks and shares with the aim of obtaining the best possible return on their investment and to ensure that their returns are not dependent on any single company. In this way, they spread the risk. If the share price of one of the companies in which they have a stake collapses, it will not cause significant damage to the finances of the pension fund, insurance company or unit trust.

> **⚠?⚠ Unit trusts** raise money from investors. The money is invested by the trust in a variety (called a portfolio) of different company shares. They are not listed on the Stock Exchange but their prices are advertised in the national press.

Now carry out an activity to explore for yourself the nature, importance and size of the financial sector. This gives rather surprising results. You need a copy of the *Financial Times*.

STRUCTURE OF THE FINANCIAL
SECTOR

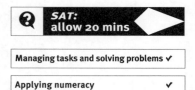

Managing tasks and solving problems ✓

Applying numeracy ✓

ACTIVITY 2

As we have seen, the financial sector consists of banks, unit trusts, building societies, insurance companies, and pension funds.

This activity asks you to explore the nature of the financial and non-financial sectors of the economy, and helps you get a picture of their relative importance.

Use the London share service section of the *Financial Times* to find answers to the following questions.

1. You may have heard of the big four High Street banks – Barclays, Midland, Lloyds and National Westminster. Approximately how many other retail banks are quoted on the London Stock Exchange?

   (Midland is now listed under the initials of its new owner – The Hong Kong and Shanghai Bank Corporation (HSBC).)

2. Write down the names of each kind of financial institution listed – not the names of individual organisations but the names of different types, e.g. retail banks, insurance ...

3. The *Financial Times* lists roughly 24 companies in each 5 cms of column space. Write down approximately how many non-financial companies are listed, i.e. companies classified under other headings like building materials, household goods, transport.

4. Estimate the number of financial institutions listed, the number of unit trusts, and the number of insurance companies. Now find the ratio of financial institutions to non-financial companies.

Commentary...

Only approximate answers were asked for, so your answers
and those below may not be exactly the same.

1. Some 35 retail banks are listed.

2. The different types of financial institution listed are:
    merchant banks, retail banks, insurance, investment
    trusts, investment companies, life assurance and other
    financial institutions.

3. By measuring columns and counting names of
    companies, we calculate that roughly 3,600 non-financial
    companies are listed.

4. We estimate that there are about 1,200 financial
    companies, unit trusts and insurances. (This excludes the
    off-shore insurances.) So the ratio of financial institutions
    to non-financial companies is approximately 1:3.

Of course, this is a very crude way of exploring the significance
and structure of the financial sector, but it does give you an
impression of its size and importance. We do things a bit more
scientifically from now on.

The financial sector has grown very rapidly in the post-war period
compared to other sectors of the economy. Do the next activity to
explore the growth and the change in this sector.

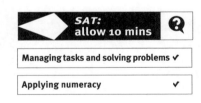

Managing tasks and solving problems ✔

Applying numeracy ✔

ACTIVITY 3

**Table 3.1 shows the sizes of different parts of the financial sector in
1982 and 1992 respectively.**

	£ billion 1982	% change 1992
Banks	560	1,379
Life assurance and pension funds	142	674
Building societies	75	258
Total for all institutions	834	2,653

Financial assets include lending to banks, securities in UK
companies, bank deposits with other banks and British
government securities.

Source: CSO, United Kingdom National Accounts, 1993, tables 12.4, 12.5, 12.6, 12.7.

TABLE 3.1: *Total financial assets UK*

STRUCTURE OF THE FINANCIAL
SECTOR

Complete table 3.1 by calculating the percentage change of each part of the financial sector. Use this information to answer these questions:

(a) Which was the largest element in the sector in 1992?

(b) Which part of the financial sector has grown fastest over the decade?

(c) Which controls more assets: all the building societies together or British Telecom? (The market capitalisation of British Telecom is £23.4 billion.)

Commentary...

The complete table should look like this:

| | £ billion | | |
	1982	1992	% change
Banks	560	1379	146
Life assurance and pension funds	142	674	374
Building societies	75	258	244
Total for all institutions	834	2653	218

You should notice that although the banks still have the greatest assets, growth has been greater in other parts of the financial sector.

The total financial assets of the sector increased more than threefold from £834 billion in 1982 to £2,653 billion in 1992. Banks alone account for more than half of the assets, but they are growing at a slower rate than life assurance companies, pension funds and building societies. Building societies control more assets than British Telecom.

The growth of the financial sector has also been reflected in their employment levels. In the early 1980s, there were around 1.7 million people employed. By 1994, the figure had risen to 2.7 million (*Employment Gazette*, June 1994).

THE CLEARING BANKS

> **\?/** **Clearing bank:** a bank that is involved in the operation of the money transmission system. The term has become somewhat confusing as the money transmission services are now used by other institutions such as building societies which are competing more and more directly with the clearing banks.

The **clearing banks** such as Barclays, Lloyds, Midland (owned by Hong Kong and Shanghai Bank) and National Westminster dominate **retail banking**. They were joined in 1989 by Abbey National, the UK's second largest building society, when it became a listed bank. Other clearing banks include TSB, Standard Chartered, Royal Bank of Scotland, Bank of Scotland, Clydesdale Bank and Yorkshire Bank (both owned by National Australia Bank).

> **\?/** **Retail banking:** usually refers to those financial institutions which offer current and deposit accounts and advance loans and overdrafts. These accounts are usually relatively small hold sums on short-term deposit. Examples of institutions include the clearing banks such as Barclays and National Westminster banks but also building societies, finance houses which offer a hire purchase facility, the National Savings Bank, and some foreign banks involved in credit card business.

These retail banks have more than 11,000 branches between them and dominate the banking sector. Barclays and National Westminster, in terms of assets, are more than double the size of their nearest competitor, Midland (see table 3.2). Between them they employ nearly 200,000 people.

	Total assets £ billion	Pre-tax profits £ million
Barclays	138.1	533
National Westminster	122.6	110
Midland	59.4	36
Lloyds	51.3	645
Royal Bank of Scotland	32.2	58
TSB	25.8	(47)
Standard Chartered	23.5	205
Bank of Scotland	23.9	104
Totals	476.8	1,644

Source: Price Waterhouse, *International Banking – London*, 1992, p14.

TABLE 3.2: *British Retail Banks (1991)*

THE BUILDING SOCIETIES

Building societies form another very important group of financial intermediaries. In 1993, there were 83 societies with nearly 6,000 branches, over 100,000 employees and total assets amounting to £278 billion (table 3.3). They accounted for 61 per cent of all mortgages and 47 per cent of savings, serving 32 million customers. The building society sector is dominated by a handful of very large societies. The Halifax has a 19 per cent share of the market for mortgages and with assets of £67 billion is by far the largest society being almost twice as big as the second largest, Nationwide. (The major competitor for Halifax is the former building society, Abbey National, which also holds a 19 per cent share of the mortgage market.)

	Total assets (£ billion)	Profit after tax (£ million)
Halifax	67.3	574
Nationwide	35.0	250
Woolwich	25.1	137
Leeds Permanent	19.5	127
Alliance & Leicester	18.1	132
Cheltenham & Gloucester	17.7	132
Bradford & Bingley	13.9	87
National & Provincial	12.6	80

Source: The Building Societies Association, *The Independent*, Thursday 4 August 1994.

TABLE 3.3: *British Building Societies (1993)*

Building societies do not work primarily towards commercial objectives because of their legal status. They are supposed to operate for the benefit of their members, i.e. their depositors. Despite this, the activities of the societies have come close to resembling that of the retail banks. The societies compete fiercely with each other and with the banks for deposits and in the provision of loans. They are as enthusiastic as other financial institutions in their pursuit of reduced costs, increased income and growth.

ACTIVITY 4

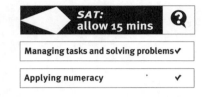

SAT: allow 15 mins

Managing tasks and solving problems ✓

Applying numeracy ✓

The previous activity concerned the size and growth of different parts of the financial sector. In this activity, you compare the size of different institutions and how that might change through merger and take-over. Use tables 3.2 and 3.3 to answer the following questions.

1. Which is the biggest bank and which is the biggest building society as measured by assets?

2. Approximately how many times larger is the bank?

3. The Halifax wishes to expand its chain of branches so as to compete more effectively against the big banks for personal customers. Consequently, a merger has been proposed between the Halifax and Leeds Permanent building societies. How will that change the relative position of the biggest bank, and the two building societies once they have merged?

4. Lloyds, as part of its growth strategy, wishes to diversify into the building society sector. It has proposed a take-over of the Cheltenham & Gloucester building society. How will that affect Lloyds' ranking compared with the other big retail banks?

Commentary...

The biggest bank is Barclays; the biggest building society is the Halifax. Barclays' assets are a bit more than double those of the Halifax. The combined assets of the Halifax (£67.3 billion) and those of the Leeds (£19.5 billion) will be £86.8 billion. That means that Barclays will be less than one and a half times bigger than the merged building society. Adding the assets of Lloyds (£51.3 billion) to those of the Cheltenham & Gloucester (£17.7 billion) gives a total of £69 billion. That moves Lloyds up one place in the rankings from 4th to 3rd ahead of Midland but still a long way behind Barclays and National Westminster.

If you have time, you could do a similar comparison of the size of assets between the Prudential, the largest insurance company, and Barclays and the Halifax.

Insurance companies and pension funds

Life assurance and pension funds are the most important form of personal savings. By 1992, their assets accounted for £674 billion, i.e. more than half of the financial assets of the personal sector.

There are more than 600 general insurance companies in the UK employing more than 250,000 people. The top ten insurance companies earn 52 per cent of total premium income for the industry (see figure 3.2). Like building societies some insurance firms, such as Norwich Union, are mutual companies. They have no shareholders but are owned by the policy holders. Others, the proprietary companies, are run for the benefit of their shareholders.

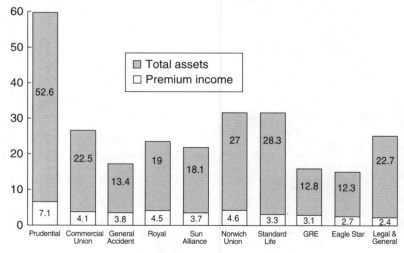

Source: Hudson, Brian, "The UK's Largest Insurance Companies", in *Insurance Trends*, Association of British Insurers, 1994.

FIGURE 3.2: *Top 10 insurance companies, 1992 (£ billion).*

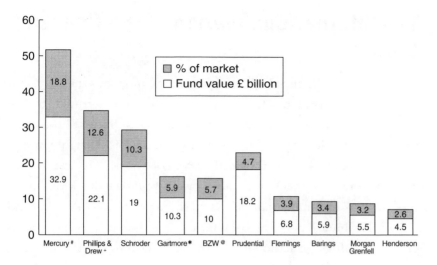

Source: Based on data from *Investors Chronicle*, 24 September 1993; *The Economist*, November 27th 1993.
\# controlled by S.G. Warburg, a merchant bank
+ owned by the Union Bank of Switzerland
* controlled by Banque Indosuez, a French investment bank
@ owned by Barclays Bank

FIGURE 3.3: *Top 10 pension fund management companies (end of 1992).*

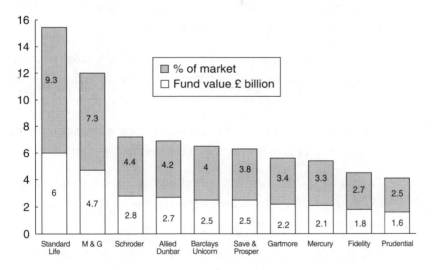

Source: Based on data from the *The Economist*, November 27th 1993.

FIGURE 3.4: *Top 10 unit trust companies, 1992 (£ billion).*

In terms of pension funds there has been a trend towards the big three fund management companies – Mercury, Schroders and Phillips & Drew. They dwarf their rivals regarding the value of the funds at their disposal. Together they control over 40 per cent of the market (figure 3.3). Concentration is not so high in the unit trust market (figure 3.4). Some companies such as Gartmore, Mercury and Schroder, operate both pension funds and unit trusts.

The internationalisation of the financial system

Increasingly the financial system is becoming more international and financial markets across the world more closely integrated. British institutions have established branches and subsidiaries abroad and foreign companies have set up operations in the UK. This integration means that events in the financial system of one country can have a major and rapid impact on others. For example, the Stock Exchange crash of 1987 had immediate effects on share prices on Wall Street and Tokyo. The interdependence of international financial markets poses great difficulties for national governments wishing to control them, for financial institutions can simply move assets between countries to avoid controls.

More than a third of Barclays' business and nearly one half of National Westminster's is undertaken abroad. Trading in shares quoted on foreign stock exchanges has increased significantly: more than 25 per cent of UK pensions funds are invested overseas. And there has been enormous growth in the eurocurrency market.

London has about 700 separate banking establishments; more than 520 of these are foreign banks, the majority being from Japan and the US. It has a leading position as an international banking centre.

Internationalisation of the finance sector has been spurred on by the quest for profits and growth. Specific reasons are now outlined.

- To finance the increase in international trade – as foreign trade expands, flows of finance directly associated with trade automatically expand too.

- The multinationalisation of their industrial and commercial customers has caused the banks to follow suit in order to retain their client base.

- Industrialisation in developing nations in South East Asia and Latin America in particular has led to an increased demand for financial services in those countries.

- It hoped to avoid regulation by the monetary authorities – one reason for the creation of the eurodollar market was that dollars were being deposited in London-based banks to avoid American interest rate restrictions.

⦿ The falling cost of, and advances in, communications technology made possible 24-hour financial trading. Institutions are able to move funds around the world to markets in different time zones. Where to deposit funds and in which form of financial asset, is determined by the return available and any expected currency appreciation/depreciation. New technology has, according to *The Economist*, helped financial institutions to 'by-pass international frontiers and create a global whirligig of money and securities' (*The Economist*, 3 October, 1992).

⦿ The large increase in the price of oil in 1973 led to OPEC countries having very big trade surpluses. On the other hand, large oil-consuming countries had deficits to finance. At the same time, governments in the Third World and in Eastern Europe were seeking finance for economic development. International syndicates of banks were formed to channel the enormous sums of money from the OPEC countries to the borrowing nations.

⦿ Financial institutions internationalised to take advantage of the single European market (SEM).

A CLOSER LOOK AT THE SINGLE EUROPEAN MARKET

The single market programme was designed to liberalise the movement of capital within the Community and to remove barriers to financial institutions operating outside their country of origin. Any institution authorised in one EU member state was allowed to operate in any other country – such institutions thus had a 'passport' to do business anywhere in the EU. The aim was to increase competition by opening up financial markets to a larger number of firms and by allowing those firms to choose the most cost-effective means of supplying services to a particular market. Banks and insurance companies would be free to sell their financial products without restriction and securities would be quotable on all stock exchanges and issuable in all EU countries. Increasing competition, it was argued, would force financial institutions to cut their prices and to increase their efficiency.

The financial services area was identified as one of the EU markets with most to gain from the liberalisation proposed in the 1992 programme. Prices in this sector differed by over 50 per cent in some instances. It was expected that highly competitive UK banks and insurance companies would be major beneficiaries as the single market measures would permit their entry into lucrative markets which had previously been protected from competition.

Whether the single market programme will provide the predicted benefits is open to question. The retail financial market is one where competition is most lacking. But the high costs of entry into EU markets, such as those associated with establishing extensive branch networks and a good reputation, make it unlikely that competition will increase. As a result the anticipated cut in the costs of banking services for businesses and individuals may not happen.

Financial institutions have responded to the single market by restructuring within and across national boundaries. The Bank of England recorded 247 cross-border alliances between 1987 and 1993 in the form of full or partial acquisitions, or joint ventures. Some examples are: the take-over of Hoare Govett, the UK stockbroker, by the Dutch bank ABN-AMRO; the conclusion of co-operation agreements between TSB and Cariplo, Italy's biggest savings bank, and between Lloyds and Banco Bilbao Vizcaya in Spain; and the acquisition of Morgan Grenfell by Deutsche Bank (*Bank of England Quarterly Bulletin*, August 1993). The result of this restructuring could be that the increased competition envisaged by the single market programme does not happen.

The strategies of internationalisation have been made possible by the removal of certain government controls on financial institutions and markets:

- removal of controls on the export of capital

- relaxation of exchange controls

- deregulation of the banks.

The trend towards internationalisation will be further boosted by the Uruguay round world trade agreement of 1993 which requires the signatories to open their financial markets to foreign firms. This will provide UK financial institutions with market opportunities particularly in the developing world.

ACTIVITY 5

This activity tests whether you have understood some of the main points relating to the internationalisation of the financial sector.

1. Give three reasons why UK banks have set up abroad.

2. Explain one way in which the UK government and the EU have each made internationalisation easier.

3. Does it look as if the trend towards internationalisation will slow down or accelerate? Give two reasons for your answer.

SAT:
allow 10 mins

| Communicating | ✓ |
| Managing tasks and solving problems | ✓ |

Commentary...

There are at least eight reasons given in the text:

- the quest for profits and growth

- growth in international trade

- the multinationalisation of industry and commerce

- the industrialisation of developing countries

- to avoid regulation

- improvements in communications technology

- the increase in the price of oil

- the single European market.

The internationalisation of the financial sector has been made easier by the UK government's liberalisation of the movement of capital and by the creation of the single European market.

The trend to internationalisation will accelerate. Products are now made for a world market. Liberalisation of trade is sought by the World Trade Organisation and Organisation of Economic Co-operation and Development (OECD). Protectionism does still exist but it is being driven out by the globalisation of the economy.

Concentration and competition

Now we consider how financial institutions have moved from providing a narrow to a broad range of financial services.

In the 1960s, the financial services sector was relatively uncomplicated. Financial institutions such as retail and **wholesale banks**, and building societies had their own particular market niche. Customers had to go to the institution specialising in the service they required. Considerable change, however, has occurred over the last 30 years.

> **¡?¡ Wholesale banks** These banks, sometimes called merchant banks, provide a full range of banking services but with emphasis on the corporate sector. They depend on deposits of relatively large amounts from large firms and financial intermediaries. Examples include the merchant banks such as Rothschilds, Schroders, and BZW, a subsidiary of Barclays.

Banking, along with the insurance, pension fund, and building society sectors has become highly concentrated with a few large firms accounting for a significant proportion of the market.

The number of British-based banks, building societies and insurance companies has been declining, often as a result of mergers, takeovers, and alliances leaving the biggest institutions with, apparently, a more powerful market position.

Paradoxically competition has increased for these organisations. Competition has become more intense due to changes in economic circumstances and political pressures: the competitive strategies pursued by the big domestic institutions; the influx of foreign companies; deregulation, and the changes in the regulatory framework.

Many financial institutions in their quest for profits and growth diversified into other areas of the finance sector and consequently have become less specialised. The big clearing banks appear to see their future as financial supermarkets selling a range of financial products and services – this is often referred to as 'bancassurance' where a single company provides a full range of banking and insurance services. Banks now offer mortgages thus competing directly with building societies. They are also involved in the provision of pensions and life assurance products through:

- Barclays Life

- Black Horse (owned by Lloyds)

- Natwest Life

- TSB Pensions

- Midland Life.

The logic underlying bancassurance is that by selling extra financial products through established branch networks to existing customers, financial companies can offer a low cost high-productivity method of distribution.

**RECALL:
allow 10 mins**

Test your understanding of this session by listing the objectives of lenders and the objectives of borrowers.

CONCENTRATION AND
COMPETITION

Growth in the financial sector results from the strategies and policies pursued by the institutions themselves, i.e. on the supply side and also as a result of changes in the market, i.e. on the demand side. The government has also played a large part, directly and indirectly, in boosting the growth of the financial sector.

SUPPLY-SIDE FACTORS

> **\?!** **Cartel:** is where organisations co-operate to follow commonly agreed policies, e.g. on interest rates to be charged. The clearing banks used to operate such an arrangement whilst the building societies used to agree on the mortgage rate and the interest to be paid to depositors.

In the financial sector, competition has grown and this has caused the market to expand.

The banking and building society **cartels** which set interest rates have disappeared. The building societies were given more flexibility by the Building Societies Act (1986). They are competing more fiercely for deposits by offering current accounts, cash cards, personal loans, credit cards, travellers' cheques, and foreign currency. Many, such as the Halifax and National & Provincial, have moved into insurance, unit trusts, and the buying and selling of shares for customers. In other words, they are joining the ranks of the bancassurers.

Competition has also increased as the lower cost of computers has allowed retailers to offer their own charge cards and consumer loans while companies such as General Motors have launched new credit cards. Marks and Spencer customers can get loans, buy unit trust shares, and arrange pension schemes and life assurance.

In October 1986, the Stock Exchange was liberalised with the 'Big Bang'. Price competition was introduced through the abolition of the system of minimum commissions charged by stockbrokers for buying or selling shares, and competition increased after the decision to allow large financial institutions like the clearing banks and foreign financial institutions to operate on the Stock Exchange.

Innovation Financial institutions, facing more intense competition, have become more responsive to the demands of their customers providing a wider variety of financial products and services, e.g. the introduction of automatic teller machines (ATMs), electronic funds transfer at point of sale (EFTPOS), touch-tone telephone services, and the direct provision of car and home insurance (e.g. by Direct Line) and banking services via the telephone (e.g. by First Direct, a Midland Bank subsidiary).

\?/ **Electronic funds transfer at point of sale (EFTPOS)** is an electronic payments system using magnetically striped cards which transfers funds from the cardholder's account to the account of a retailer.

Financial institutions have been very clever in developing business outside the regulated area where there are profits to be made. Thus when the retail banks were forced by government in the 1960s to ration loans, the system responded by offering loans through non-bank financial intermediaries.

Information technology Advances in technology and its falling price have made it easier to do simple things quickly and accurately. It has reduced the costs and accelerated the speed of transactions. New systems allowed the banks to handle more business. This has made the services offered by financial institutions more attractive.

The development of the Euromarkets In the late 1950s, the USA was running a balance of payments deficit. Suppliers of goods and services to the USA were prepared to accept payment in US dollars. Increasingly, large amounts of dollars were available abroad. Rather than put those dollars on deposit in the US where interest rates were low, holders put them where a higher return was obtainable. London became the leading financial centre for the eurodollar market. In 1992, bank assets in eurocurrencies totalled a massive $5,805 billion.

DEMAND-SIDE FACTORS

Growth of demand for financial services was caused by several factors.

- Increasing discretionary income levels led to an increased demand for financial services such as mortgages, insurance and assurance policies, and pensions.

- Economic growth: the expansion in output by industry and commerce have increased the demand for financial services.

- International trade and investment has grown at an unprecedented rate in the post-war period. This has increased the demand for export/import and investment finance.

- To reduce costs employers prefer to pay employees' wages and salaries directly into a bank or building society account. Consequently, the proportion of adults holding a bank account has increased. In 1993, more than four out of five adults had bank accounts, a rise of 50 per cent over 1986.

- Removal of controls on the movement of capital: until October 1979, UK residents were unable to purchase foreign currency unless authorised and financial institutions were restricted in their positions in foreign exchange. The controls also limited the ability of UK residents to buy foreign securities. To comply with EU directives and in line with its preference for the free market, the government removed these controls, thus freeing profitable opportunities for UK financial institutions.

- The government through its extensive privatisation programme – the selling-off of nationalised industries – has encouraged individuals to buy shares. This has benefited financial institutions in three ways:

  1. Merchant banks received very substantial fees for advising the government on privatisation.

  2. Many financial institutions, banks and building societies among them, have earned commission income from the buying and selling of shares in the privatised industries.

  3. To the extent that the shares were sold at low prices, institutions were able to make capital gains as the value of the shares rose after flotation.

- Tax incentives and reliefs were given by the government on life assurance premiums encouraging an increased demand for life policies. More recently it has given tax advantages to individuals as an incentive to opt out of state earnings related pension scheme (SERPS).

The importance of the financial sector

This section looks at how the financial sector has an important impact on the operations of businesses and government.

The output of financial services accounts for about a quarter of UK gross domestic product (GDP), and employs one out of every eight workers. The financial system plays a vitally important role in the external environment of organisations in both the public and the private sectors.

THE POWER OF FINANCIAL INSTITUTIONS OVER BUSINESS

The big financial institutions wield a great degree of power over business. The fees and charges they set, their willingness to lend, the interest rates they charge on loans, and their buying and selling of shares can all have considerable effects on business.

One particular area of controversy has been the relationship between the banks and small and medium-sized business. Businesses with sales of £1 million or less account for more than 95 per cent of all UK enterprises and a third of the non-government workforce. The big four banks – National Westminster, Barclays, Midland and Lloyds – are especially important to the fortunes of Britain's three million or so small businesses as 80 per cent of them rely on the banks for short-term finance. In 1992, small businesses had more than four million accounts with the banks and they were borrowing nearly £44 billion. The complaints made by small firms about banks concern excessive charges, the difficulties of getting loans, especially long-term loans, the premature calling-in of overdrafts which has forced some firms out of business, and the failure to pass on reductions in interest rates to small businesses (see *Bank of England Quarterly Review*, February 1993).

FINANCIAL INSTITUTIONS AND SHARE OWNERSHIP

Another important issue for public quoted companies, is that their shares have become increasingly concentrated in the hands of financial institutions. In the 1950s, individuals held nearly 70 per cent of shares. By the early 1990s, that figure had fallen, despite the extensive privatisation programme, to less than 20 per cent. Financial institutions now own more than one half of shares, of which pension funds hold almost a third and insurance companies a fifth (table 3.4).

**THE IMPORTANCE OF THE
FINANCIAL SECTOR**

Beneficial owner	1963	1969	1975	1981	1989	1993
Pension funds	8.4	9.0	16.8	26.7	30.6	34.2
Insurance companies	10.0	12.2	15.9	20.5	18.6	17.3
Unit trusts	1.3	2.9	4.1	3.6	5.9	17.3
Banks	1.3	1.7	0.7	0.3	0.7	0.6
Investment trusts + other institutions	11.3	10.1	10.5	6.8	2.7	3.1
Individuals	54.0	47.4	37.5	28.2	20.6	17.7
Other personal	2.1	2.1	2.3	2.2	2.3	1.6
Public sector	1.5	2.6	3.6	3.0.	2.0	1.3
Industrial and commercial sector	5.1	5.4	3.0	5.1	3.8	1.5
Overseas	7.0	6.6	5.6	3.6	12.8	16.3
TOTAL	100	100	100	100	100	100

TABLE 3.4: *Beneficial ownership: percentage of total equity owned, 31 December*

This gives them great potential power over those organisations in which they own shares. If they are unhappy with the policies and performance of a company in which they own shares, they could sell up, the share price would plummet and the company would be left vulnerable to take-over. Company managements, obliged to please their powerful institutional shareholders, may feel constrained to make decisions that boost short-term profits so as to keep their share price up. Financial institutions can also use their power to get involved directly in company management decision making.

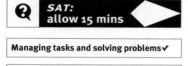

**SAT:
allow 15 mins**

Managing tasks and solving problems ✔

Applying numeracy ✔

ACTIVITY 6

This activity helps you to appreciate the increasing importance of financial institutions in the owning of shares between 1963 and 1993.

Using table 3.4, calculate and compare the growth in the proportion of shares held by pension funds, insurance companies, and banks.

Explain in about 50 words why banks hold such a low proportion of shares.

Commentary...

Pension funds have increased their share of total equity by a factor of four; insurance companies by almost double; the banks has fallen by just more than one half.

The banks buy and sell shares on behalf of their clients. However, traditionally, they have avoided holding shares on their own account. They much prefer to use their customers' money to give overdrafts, personal loans to businesses and individuals as well as lending to the government by buying government bonds and treasury bills.

THE FINANCIAL SYSTEM AND GOVERNMENT

The financial sector is very important to the government to the extent that it can contribute to, or frustrate, the achievement of its economic objectives. Since 1945, governments have generally aimed to achieve:

- increased economic growth

- low inflation

- a healthy balance of payments

- high levels of employment.

Governments have aimed to provide the stable macro-economic framework necessary for the attainment of these objectives through the pursuit of monetary, fiscal and exchange rate policies. Governments would find it impossible to meet their objectives if banks were unstable and insecure. People would not trust banks with their money and they would be reluctant to borrow. As a result, the government would not be able to use the banks to implement its money, credit and interest rate policies effectively (See *Bank of England Quarterly Bulletin*, May 1993).

An important activity of the banks that can have a major effect on the economy is their ability to create credit. Banks take deposits from organisations and individuals. Banks know from experience that they will not normally be expected to pay back deposits all at once. This enables them to lend most of their deposits to borrowers (or to buy financial assets such as government bonds). Credit is created whenever a bank makes a loan to a customer and credits his or her account with the amount of the loan. Except for the need to maintain an adequate level of liquidity, banks can continue creating credit as long as people have confidence in the acceptability of their cheques as payment for goods and services.

If banks lend excessive amounts, this can lead to a very high demand for goods and services. This can have two adverse effects for government policy.

- ● Sellers, finding that their customers are clamouring for their goods, could take advantage by increasing prices and this could cause inflation.

- ● Consumers are likely to buy more cars, CD-players, and freezers made abroad, causing balance of payments problems.

On the other hand, too little lending can lead to insufficient demand for goods and services and an increase in the unemployment rate. In short, bank lending policies can contribute to economic boom and recession thereby frustrating the traditional aims of post-war governments.

Similarly, it would be difficult for the government to pursue its desired policies on public expenditure if financial institutions are unwilling to lend the authorities money by purchasing government bonds. In this event, the government either has to cut public expenditure, or raise taxes, or print more money.

Financial institutions, by their decisions to buy or sell sterling, can also frustrate government exchange rate policies. For example, in September 1992, the authorities raised interest rates by 5 per cent to give holders of sterling a higher return on their money in an attempt to persuade them not to sell pounds. The government also tried to maintain the level of the pound by spending £5 billion of foreign reserves buying sterling. These efforts proved unsuccessful as the pound was forced to leave the exchange rate mechanism (ERM).

The financial services sector is also important for the balance of payments. The City undertakes a large share of the world's commercial, banking and financial operations. In 1992, financial institutions earned £18.8 billion abroad, with banks and insurance companies accounting for more than two thirds of this total. London is the leading centre for international lending, ahead of Japan. It stands head and shoulders above other European financial centres. It has the biggest foreign exchange and equity markets, the greatest concentration of insurers and pension funds and the largest number of foreign banks. The sector has become increasingly important both in terms of output and employment to the whole economy.

Note that institutions can also aggravate the balance of payments problem through their purchases of shares overseas (portfolio investment). In 1992, total portfolio investment abroad was £33 billion, an almost fivefold increase over ten years.

Finally, given its important role in allocating credit, the financial sector can have a major impact on the performance of the economy. If lending policies result in funds being channelled to efficient firms then economic performance can be improved. On the other hand, if financial institutions restrict their lending to short-term, high-return, low-risk projects then the growth prospects for the economy can be damaged.

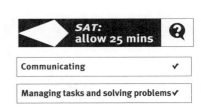

SAT:
allow 25 mins

Communicating ✓

Managing tasks and solving problems ✓

ACTIVITY 7

Try the following exercise to see if you have grasped the main points.

1. Decide which of the following statements are

    T = True, or more True than False

    F = False, or more False than True

    (a) Banks exist to help small businesses.

    (b) Complaints from small businesses against banks are fairly uncommon, and when they occur are usually due to misunderstanding.

    (c) Following privatisation of gas, water and electricity, the proportion of shares held by individuals has increased from about 20 per cent to 70 per cent.

    (d) Pension funds own about a third of the shares of British companies.

    (e) It makes little difference to a company whether its shares are owned by many individuals or a few large insurance companies or pension funds.

2. In terms of government policy, which is the odd one out in the following list?

    ○ increase economic growth

    ○ keep inflation low

    ○ maintain high levels of employment

    ○ internationalisation

3. Match the following to form sentences:

    (You may need to use (a)(b)(c) or (d) as an answer more than once – or not at all.)

    (i) Banks could slow economic growth ...

    (ii) Banks could increase inflation ...

    (iii)Banks could increase unemployment ...

    (iv)Banks could worsen the balance of payments ...

    (a) by increasing lending.

    (b) by decreasing lending.

    (c) by calling in overdrafts.

    (d) by buying computers from Japan.

4. You are employed as a management trainee at a bank. As part of your training, you and the other trainees have been asked to produce a pamphlet on the financial sector. The group of trainees decide to divide the work between them. You have agreed to write a section, of up to 100 words, explaining why the financial sector is important. Prepare a draft of your section. (This is an individual task.)

Commentary...

Banks exist to provide services that make profits for their shareholders. Recently, small businesses have complained bitterly about how banks treat them.

The number of complaints has been increasing. They are mostly due to the heavy-handedness of banks trying to protect their interests at the expense of small businesses.

About 70 per cent of UK company shares are held by financial institutions. Pension funds own about a third of the shares of British companies.

When the shares of a company are distributed among many individuals, no one of them has much power to influence the company. When the shares are held by a few then those owners can be very influential. Today, the financial institutions own the majority of shares and can be very influential.

The financial sector is important because its lending can affect the rate of inflation and employment. Its credit policies can make or break businesses and can have a major influence on the competitiveness of the economy.

By investing abroad, the financial sector adversely affects the balance of payments when the investment is made initially but improves it when the dividends come in.

Financial services provide a large number of jobs in the UK and make a major contribution to the balance of payments through overseas earnings.

The regulation of the financial system

We now look at regulation and supervision of financial institutions. The regulators are an important element in the financial sector's operating environment because of the effect they can have on sales turnover, costs and profits.

Businesses and individuals dealing with financial institutions have an interest in those institutions being effectively regulated and supervised. Regulation is necessary not simply to protect the interest of customers but also to ensure the stability of the whole financial system. As David Goacher argues in his book, *The Monetary and Financial System* (The Chartered Institute of Bankers, 1990), regulation must be more than the 'protection of the naive from their own ignorance and the inept from their own greed'.

**THE REGULATION OF THE
FINANCIAL SYSTEM**

Regulation of financial institutions is carried out the Department of Trade and Industry (DTI), the Bank of England, by agencies such as the Personal Investments Authority and by a number of other bodies. In the main, the financial institutions have traditionally been self-regulating rather than legally controlled by government.

THE GOWER REPORT

The Gower Report in 1984 on the regulatory framework for investment businesses drew a number of disturbing conclusions:

- the quality of supervision varied significantly in different areas of the financial sector

- regulation was frequently too complicated, uncertain, and inequitable

- there were too many regulators and regulations.

Overall, the framework was inadequate and inefficient: it neither protected the investors' interests nor the position of the UK as a major international financial centre. The report led to the Financial Services Act (1986) which sought to improve the system of regulation by strengthening the self-regulation process.

We now consider two of the most important regulators, the Bank of England and the Securities Investment Board.

THE BANK OF ENGLAND

The Bank of England, as agent of the government, has a major responsibility for the supervision of the financial markets. The Banking Act (1987) protects depositors by holding the Bank of England responsible for ensuring that deposit-taking companies conduct themselves prudently with regard to:

- capital adequacy

- liquidity

- provisions for bad debts

- keeping records

- internal management controls.

The Bank of England aims to ensure that institutions can meet their obligations to depositors and borrowers when they fall due. Deposits, with some exceptions, may only be taken by institutions authorised by the Bank of England which supervises the system by looking over the shoulder of management rather than by a rigorous system of inspection. It monitors information supplied by the institutions and holds regular meetings with their senior management and auditors. Although the Banking Act has very few formal sanctions, the Bank of England can revoke the authorisation to take deposits if, for example an institution is supplying false or misleading information, or in the case of the bankruptcy/insolvency of the institution. This sanction is rarely used. The Bank of England aims to identify problems at an early stage and to agree a solution with the institution concerned.

Building societies are not supervised by the Bank of England. This role is undertaken by a government body, the Building Societies Commission. The insurance industry is regulated by the Department of Trade and Industry. It protects insurance company customers from company failure and from being sold unsuitable insurance policies.

THE FINANCIAL SERVICES ACT (1986)

The Financial Services Act (1986), concerned with the honesty and competency of suppliers of financial services, established a system of self-regulatory organisations (SROs):

- the Life Assurance and Unit Trust Regulatory Organisation (LAUTRO)

- the Financial Intermediaries Managers and Brokers Regulatory Association (FIMBRA)

- the Investment Management Regulatory Organisation (IMRO) which regulates pension funds

- the Securities and Futures Association (SFA) which regulates dealers in securities and futures contracts.

> **\?/** **Futures contracts:** volatility in the price/value of financial assets such as shares or foreign currency can create considerable risk for their holders. Futures contracts allow those wishing to avoid risk to do so, at a price, by passing the risk on to those willing to accept it.

The SROs were set up under the auspices of the Securities and Investments Board (SIB) which is responsible to the Treasury (see figure 3.5). Note that the retail functions of both LAUTRO and FIMBRA have been taken over by a single SRO, the Personal Investment Authority (PIA) set up in 1993.

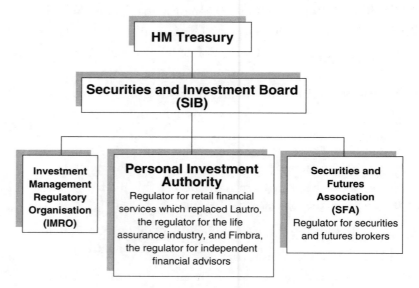

FIGURE 3.5: *'The Regulators'.*

The SIB, a private company, has ultimate responsibility for protecting the investor through regulation of financial institutions involved in:

- the buying and selling of securities

- investment fund management

- the marketing of life assurance and pensions

- the provision of investment advice.

Any firm wishing to carry out any of these investment activities must be authorised by an SRO set up under the Financial Services Act. Each approved firm must undergo an annual check, have a full independent audit and be regularly inspected by the supervisory agency.

The Act distinguishes between independent financial advisors, i.e. those who are free to recommend to their customers the products of any financial institution, and advisors who are tied to recommending the products of the institution to whom they are linked. In all cases, advisors are supposed to be well informed about the products available, to explain the nature of the product to the client, and to give advice appropriate to the particular circumstances of each client.

WEAKNESSES IN THE REGULATORY SYSTEM

Despite the changes in the law and the activities of the new regulators, the financial sector remains prone to scandal and upset. This is not surprising because often highly complex products are being sold to relatively unsophisticated customers who find them difficult to understand.

All forms of regulation need:

- an effective monitoring system

- a set of sanctions that are appropriate to the scale of the wrong-doing

- sanctions that act as a deterrent to others

- sanctions that are effectively enforced.

The current regulatory framework has been criticised for failing to provide an effective monitoring system and for failing to impose appropriate sanctions against malpractice. Widespread concern continues to be expressed about inadequacies in the protection provided for the investor. In 1992, the Bank of England, for example was strongly criticised in the Bingham Report after the collapse of the Bank of Commerce and Credit International (BCCI) in 1991. About $10 billion went missing at the expense of several hundred thousand depositors.

Some critics have argued that the Bank of England faces a conflict of roles.

- It is supposed to supervise financial institutions.

- At the same time, it acts as the ultimate supplier of liquidity to those same institutions, i.e. when money is short, the Bank of England provides liquidity and reduces the risk of a banking collapse by guaranteeing certain institutions immediate access to its funds. In other words, it bales out the institutions at risk.

- It is also a voice of those institutions to the government.

So the Bank of England is expected to police the institutions, support them when they have liquidity problems and also act as their representative with the government.

A second area of concern involves financial institutions that have not been scrupulous in selling private pension schemes and insurance policies. Furthermore, the pensions industry was assailed by criticism after the misappropriation of Mirror Group pension funds by Robert Maxwell.

There are a number of other weaknesses in the system of regulation.

- The system of self-regulation fails to give the investor an adequate level of protection against unscrupulous sellers of financial services.

- Some regulators have been captured by the financial institutions they are supposed to regulate. They have been too willing to take on trust what the financial institutions tell them. As a result, the system of monitoring and inspection has been lax and, when standards have been breached, the offenders have not been pursued with sufficient vigour.

- The system is fragmented. There are too many regulatory agencies dealing with supposedly distinct parts of the financial sector. But the once clear distinctions between financial institutions are becoming blurred. This means that the regulatory bodies need to co-ordinate their supervisory activities much more closely so as to ensure that breaches of standards are not undiscovered because they fall between the various regulators. The establishment of the Personal Investment Authority (PIA) could be seen as a response to this criticism.

- The internationalisation of financial markets has made effective control by one government virtually impossible.

Some progress has been made on international supervisory co-operation and harmonisation of regulatory standards. The Basle Committee on Banking Supervision, comprising representatives of the major industrialised countries, agreed the division of supervisory responsibilities and set minimum standards for the supervisory responsibilities and powers of home and host countries. The Basle Capital Accord (1988) set a minimum of eight per cent ratio of capital to assets, with banks expected to observe this ratio by the end of 1992.

The relevant EU Directives correspond closely to the requirements of the Basle proposals. In addition to the protection afforded to customers by the establishment of EU minimum standards in each financial area, the EU is also in the process of creating more safeguards for depositors and investors. An example of this is through the Deposit Protection Directive which makes a rather messy distinction between the responsibilities of the countries where a bank is based and the responsibilities of the countries where the bank does business. Generally, the home state takes responsibility for the safety and the soundness (the prudential supervision role) of the institution and all its branches while the host state is largely responsible for the conduct of the bank's business with its customers (See *Bank of England Quarterly Review*, February 1993).

IMPROVING THE REGULATORY SYSTEM

The authorities face a number of dilemmas regarding regulation. Increased regulation could damage London's position as one of the dominant international financial centres while too little regulation could frighten customers away. The Bank of England has argued for a middle way on depositor protection:

> **Banking systems in which no bank can be allowed to fail and depositors face no risk of loss lack the vital ingredient of market discipline and breed management and depositor recklessness. At the other extreme, systems which rely only on market discipline court unnecessary bank and possibly, systemic failure and avoidable loss to depositors. Somewhere between these extremes lies the right balance.**

> (*Bank of England Quarterly Bulletin*, May 1993)

Critics argue that the system of regulation has shown itself to be ineffective in protecting the investor. And the regulatory framework in its present form is unlikely to be able to deal with the growing complexity of supervision caused by:

- the internationalisation of financial markets

- the increased use of computers and telecommunications technology by financial institutions which means that the buying and selling of financial assets can take place instantaneously across national boundaries

- the development of even more sophisticated financial instruments, e.g. the cross-border trade in futures contracts.

It can be argued that some of the inadequacies made in the Gower Report persist. The failure to put an effective framework in place arises from the hostility of the financial institutions themselves. They argue that more regulation will push up costs, make London uncompetitive and result in a loss of business. This position has also tended to gain support from the government. Thus, the recommendations made by the Goode committee in 1993 to tighten up pension fund regulation after the Maxwell scandal were:

- a new pensions regulator with wide-ranging powers

- minimum solvency requirements for pension schemes

- compensation to protect against fraud and theft.

These aroused opposition from the industry and gained little sympathy from the government.

Critics argue that a statutory system combined with a move to the more rigorous and systematic US system of supervision is required. The fragmentation should be dealt with by reducing the number of regulators and by having a more unified system of regulation. More co-ordination of the supervisory function is also needed between countries.

summary

▶ The financial sector has grown very fast in terms of output and employment and has become highly internationalised.

▶ The industry has come to be dominated by a small number of very large diversified companies.

▶ The big financial institutions have become very powerful actors in the UK economy.

▶ Their activities are vital for the effective functioning of the economy and the decisions they make have major implications for organisations, individuals and government.

▶ Because of their size, the extent of their diversification and internationalisation, and their ability to innovate new financial products, they continue to pose great challenges to the regulatory authorities.

Economic policy

Objectives

After participating in this session, you should be able to:

▶ state the objectives of government economic policy

▶ explain in your own words the meaning of unemployment, economic growth, inflation and the balance of payments

▶ describe the performance of the UK economy in the post-war period

▶ explain the meaning of monetary and fiscal policy

▶ put forward solutions to problems concerning economic growth, inflation, unemployment and the balance of payments.

In working through this session, you will practise the following BTEC common skills:

Managing and Developing Self	✔
Working with and Relating to others	✔
Communicating	✔
Managing Tasks and Solving Problems	✔
Applying Numeracy	✔
Applying Technology	
Applying Design and Creativity	

The objectives of economic policy

In the UK, the government tries to have some control over the way in which the economy behaves. And to be successful in business you need to understand how government affects business.

In this session, you discover how the interventions of government do just that; how it can sometimes create opportunities and at other times create problems. To start with, we study some of the main elements of the economy which the government tries to influence:

- economic growth

- inflation

- unemployment

- the balance of payments.

We see how attempts to influence these factors affect businesses. For example, raising interest rates to reduce inflationary pressures in the economy increases the cost of finance to business. It also raises the cost of borrowing to consumers and increases the cost of some existing loans (e.g. mortgages) thereby reducing the overall level of spending.

The government has at its disposal three sets of policies it can use to try to control the economy:

- monetary policy

- fiscal policy

- direct policies.

MONETARY AND FISCAL POLICIES

> **!?!** **Monetary policy** seeks to influence economic activity by adjusting the amount of money and credit available in the system.

Monetary policy can be pursued:

- directly, by controlling the supply of money, i.e. by controlling the amount of money in circulation in the economy, or

- indirectly, by controlling the demand for money. If the government wishes to reduce the demand for money it can increase interest rates. This reduces the amount of loans people take out and therefore reduces the supply of money.

!?! **Fiscal policy** seeks to influence economic activity through control of government revenue and expenditure. The government can adjust its own spending if it wishes to change the level of economic activity and/or alter taxation to adjust individual spending.

Direct and indirect policies Monetary and fiscal policies are both examples of indirect policies in that they do not directly target the variables they hope to affect, i.e. prices, employment, the balance of payments and growth. Direct policy, on the other hand, does. Prices and incomes policies might be used to control prices and incomes directly; regional policies may offer grants to firms to locate in a certain area; import controls might be used to restrict imports.

A SIMPLE MODEL OF THE ECONOMY

To understand the effect of different policies, it helps to have an idea of how the economy operates. We start with a diagram (figure 4.1) in which we are more concerned with the flows between the different units of the economy rather than the operation of the markets.

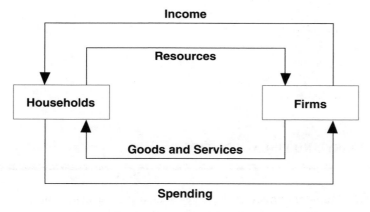

FIGURE 4.1: *Flows in the economy.*

Households supply resources (labour) to firms in return for payment. There is, then, a flow of resources from households to firms and a flow of income from firms to households. Households use their income to purchase the goods and services produced by the firms. There is now a flow of goods and services to households and a flow of income in the opposite direction.

The income of households represents the costs (including profits) that the firms incur. It follows that there should be sufficient income

THE OBJECTIVES OF ECONOMIC
POLICY

to buy all that is produced as prices would be made up of the various costs.

This situation would not last for long as some consumers would not spend all their money – they would save.

❓ SAT:
allow 5 mins ▶

Communicating ✔

Managing tasks and solving problems ✔

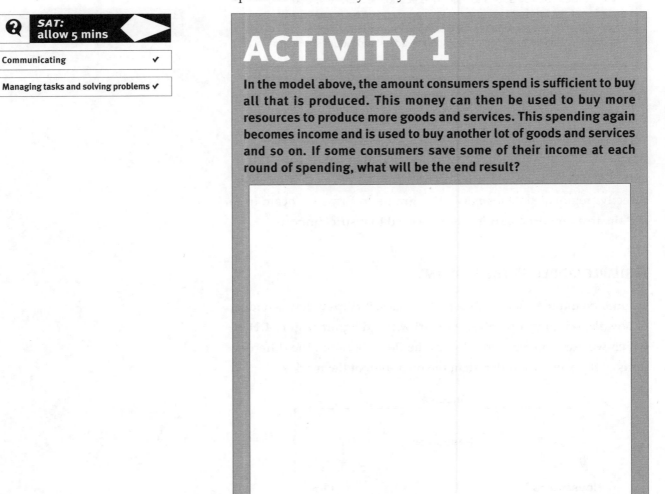

ACTIVITY 1

In the model above, the amount consumers spend is sufficient to buy all that is produced. This money can then be used to buy more resources to produce more goods and services. This spending again becomes income and is used to buy another lot of goods and services and so on. If some consumers save some of their income at each round of spending, what will be the end result?

Commentary...

If consumers save some of their income then there will not be sufficient spending to buy all that is produced. Firms will be left with stocks of goods and services. They will cut back on production and make some people unemployed. Incomes will fall and therefore, in the next round, spending will be reduced. If saving takes place again, spending will be even lower and output will be cut again. Eventually, if this process continues, output will fall to zero.

Fortunately, in the real economy, consumers are not the only people who spend money. In our simple model (figure 4.1) firms also spend money on other firms' products. Some firms produce machinery and tools (capital equipment) for sale to other firms, so that the shortfall in spending can be made good by a firm's investment in capital equipment.

SAT: allow 8 mins

Managing tasks and solving problems ✓

ACTIVITY 2

1. When consumers save some of their income, spending on goods and services is reduced. Write down two other ways in which the amount consumers spend on goods produced in the UK is reduced.

2. In Activity 1, the reduction in spending caused by savings is made up by an investment. Write down two sources of additional spending which can compensate for the reduction in consumer spending in goods and services.

Commentary...

When consumers buy goods produced in other countries (i.e. imports) the spending on UK goods and services is reduced. The government also takes a proportion of people's incomes through taxation.

Just as we spend money on goods and services made in other countries, so people in other countries spend money on our goods and services. So the one answer is exports. Another is government, which as you saw in Session 2, is also a big spender.

INJECTIONS AND LEAKAGES

Our simple model of the economy can now be expanded to add leakages from the system (savings, imports and taxation) and injections (investment, exports and government spending).

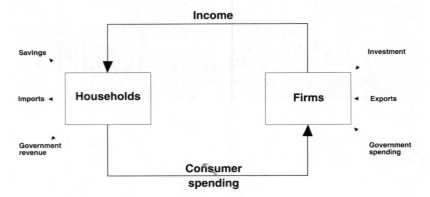

FIGURE 4.2: *Leakages and injections.*

The important points to note about the model are listed below:

- Income flows from firms to households and back. These income flows are matched by the flow of goods and services and resources.

- Output and employment are determined by the amount of expenditure in the economy.

- Total demand for goods and services is made up of demand from consumers, government, business investment and overseas spending on exports.

THE POLICY OBJECTIVES

In the post-war economy, there was general agreement, or consensus, between the major political parties that the objectives of government economic policy should be:

- full employment

- reasonable stability of prices

◉ a satisfactory rate of economic growth

◉ balance of payments equilibrium.

There was also broad agreement that the means of achieving these objectives should be through the management of overall demand by both fiscal policy (deliberate manipulation of government revenue and spending) and monetary policy (control of the supply and cost of money). The basic Keynesian argument is that the amount of goods produced is determined by the total demand for them. As the volume of production determines the level of income and employment, these variables could be affected by varying the level of demand (demand management).

If you look back to figure 4.1, it is perhaps easier to understand the Keynesian argument. Here, it is total spending in the economy that determines how much is produced and how many people are employed. When the government manages the economy it has to ensure that total spending is sufficient to meet its objectives of full employment and economic growth. But, the government also has to be careful not to increase spending too much because if firms cannot produce sufficient goods to satisfy demand, imports and/or prices will rise.

Similar fiscal and monetary policies were pursued by post-war Labour and Conservative administrations. There were some differences in that the Labour governments of 1964–70 and especially 1975–79 were much more interventionist in terms of public ownership, negotiations with both the Trades Union Congress (TUC) and the Confederation of British Industry (CBI) and prices and incomes policies.

SAT:
allow 5 mins

Managing tasks and solving problems ✔

ACTIVITY 3

Post-war governments broadly agreed on the aims of economic policy and also on the means for achieving these aims.

Which of the following list of aims were not economic aims agreed by all the parties?

(a) Maintain the same number of people in work.

(b) Increase standards of living.

(c) Squeeze inflation out of the system.

(d) Encourage spending on goods from Europe.

Commentary...

Maintaining the same number of people in work and encouraging spending on goods from Europe were not aims of the government. Keeping as many people in work that wanted to be in work was the objective. Encouraging imports from Europe would cause balance of payments problems.

THE END OF CONSENSUS

This consensus on both objectives and policies was abandoned with the election of the Conservative government in 1979. Stable prices replaced full employment as the main objective to the extent that unemployment was allowed to rise to levels only experienced in the 1930s in order to keep inflation down. Incomes policies were abandoned and labour laws toughened. A programme of privatisation was introduced, attempts were made to cut state spending and some taxes were reduced. There was much greater reliance on monetary policy (particularly interest rates) to control the level of demand.

There was also a much greater emphasis on the 'supply side' of the economy: those elements that contribute to production, i.e. labour and capital and the way in which they are organised. Supply-side policies provide incentives to increase the supply of labour and capital and improve the way in which they are organised. This was thought to be done best by introducing market forces to more areas of the economy and increasing incentives to work and invest. Hence Conservative administrations made reductions in taxes on incomes, cut some welfare benefits and introduced policies to make the labour market much more flexible.

Previous (Keynesian) policies were criticised for concentrating on the demand side and producing disappointing growth rates. Demand had been increased to encourage production but the supply side had failed to increase production sufficiently.

SAT:
allow 10 mins

Managing tasks and solving problems✔

ACTIVITY 4

Put the policy initiatives listed below into a table according to whether they are most likely to be used to affect the supply side or the demand side of the economy.

For example, factors influencing the price and availability of labour affect the supply side of the economy: so the provision of training (which affects availability) goes in the first column, under the heading supply side.

(a) improved training provision

(b) increases in taxation

(c) the introduction of special savings schemes

(d) increased government spending

(e) cuts in local authority spending

(f) investment in new road schemes

(g) reductions in welfare benefits

(h) abolition of minimum wage legislation

(i) reduction in taxation

(j) privatising British Rail

(k) imposing import taxes

Commentary...

Supply side	Demand side
improved training	increases in taxation
special savings schemes	government spending
	cut local authority spending
reduction in welfare benefits	investment in new roads
abolition of minimum wage	imposing import taxes
reduction in taxation	
privatisation of British Rail	

Economic growth

> **!?!** **Economic growth** is the growth in a country's capacity to produce goods and services. This should result in growth in the total volume of goods and services available for people to consume.

If we equate living standards with the volume of goods and services available then clearly economic growth is the key to raising the standard of living. Many people, and you may be one of them, think that other things are equally important. For example, people value good working conditions, increased leisure time, liberty, the countryside, freedom from pollution, congestion and stress. All of these might be threatened by economic growth.

Economic growth is important to governments because the increase in personal incomes increases the amount of money they receive through taxation. They can then spend more on schools, hospitals and other public sector activities without increasing tax rates.

Economic growth in the UK You have probably read that growth rates in the UK have been worse than in other countries. This does not mean that the UK is getting poorer. Indeed, because the economy has continued to grow (even though slowly) people in the UK today are better off (on average) than their parents and grandparents.

Some countries (such as Germany and France) have grown so much more rapidly than the UK over the past 40 years that, although they started from a lower base, they now enjoy higher standards of living than the UK.

Economic growth is usually measured in terms of increases in the total output of the economy, i.e. in increases in gross domestic product (GDP). Strictly speaking, growth only occurs when the productive capacity of the economy increases. If an economy has substantial unemployed resources then an increase in total output may be achieved by employing some of the unemployed resources without increasing the productive potential of the economy.

Two more factors have also to be taken into account. The first is that GDP can increase if the prices of goods and services increase. For there to be a 'real' increase in GDP, the physical total produced must increase. Therefore when measuring growth, price changes must be taken into account.

The second factor relates to GDP as a measure of living standards. For there to be an increase in living standards, account must be taken of changes in population. If total real GDP increases at 3 per cent and population increases by 3 per cent then on average nobody is better off. Therefore to measure changes in living standards, GDP per head in real terms must be measured.

What **a 'good' rate of growth** is, is difficult to define. In the 1950s, R.A. Butler then Chancellor of the Exchequer promised a doubling of living standards every 25 years. This implied a growth rate of less than 3 per cent per annum but subsequently has been criticised and abandoned as being over ambitious. One view might be to grow as fast as possible but at least as fast as your major competitors. Others may point out that growth does have its costs in terms of the externalities talked about in Session 1 (e.g. pollution and congestion) and the exhaustion of the world's finite resources.

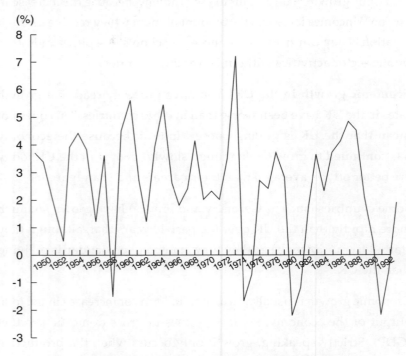

FIGURE 4.3: *UK annual rate of economic growth (1950–92).*

	1950–73	1973–79	1979–90
USA	3.7	2.4	2.6
Japan	9.4	3.6	4.1
Germany	5.9	2.3	2.0
France	5.1	2.8	2.1
UK	3.0	1.5	2.1
Italy	5.5	3.7	2.4
Total EC	NA	2.5	2.2
Total OECD	NA	2.7	2.7

Source: OECD Historical Statistics 1960–90 cited in Buxton T., Chapman P., and Temple P., 1994, *Britain's Economic Performance*, Routledge.

TABLE 4.1: *Comparison of growth rates (average annual percentage growth)*

	1950	1960	1970	1980	1990
USA	148	135	139	141	136
Germany	65	98	110	119	116
France	74	84	106	114	111
Japan	27	44	91	95	112
UK	100	100	100	100	100

Source: OECD Historical Statistics 1960–90 cited in Buxton, T., Chapman, P. and Temple, P., 1994, *Britain's Economic Performance,* Routledge.

TABLE 4.2: *Comparative levels of GDP per head (UK = 100)*

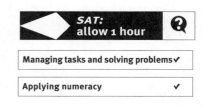

SAT: allow 1 hour

Managing tasks and solving problems ✓

Applying numeracy ✓

ACTIVITY 5

Study table 4.2 which shows the level of GDP per head in various countries compared with the UK and how it changed from one decade to the next. To make the comparison we call the GDP per head of the UK 100 in each of the years chosen. You can see that in 1950 the USA was almost 150. What this means is that each person in the USA was on average nearly 50 per cent better off than each person in the UK. Japan's GDP per head was only 27, so on average each person in Japan had less than a third of the income of someone in the UK.

1. Since the USA is the world's richest economy, it is not surprising that the UK lags behind. But has the difference between the UK and USA increased between 1950 and 1990, or decreased?

2. Making use of tables 4.1 and 4.2, describe in your own words what has happened to the gap between the UK and France, and between the UK and Germany over the same period.

3. Many people speak of Japan as having undergone an economic miracle. What was the gap between the UK and Japan in 1980?

4. Given that the Japanese economy has grown spectacularly since 1950 the answer to the previous question surprises many people. Provide a brief explanation.

5. Draw graphs showing the comparative levels of GDP for each country against that of the UK.

   When you have drawn your graph you might like to compare it with the one drawn in figure 4.4

   On your graph, examine the gap between the GDP per head of the USA, France and Germany from 1970 to 1980 and from 1980 to 1990.

   Do you think the gaps have closed? Would you regard this change as evidence of an economic miracle in the UK?

   Now examine the gaps between the GDP of the UK and Japan over the same periods.

Have the gaps closed? Would you regard this as further evidence of an economic miracle in the UK?

Look at table 4.1. On the whole, other countries have been growing faster than the UK. What has happened to the size of the advantage achieved by these countries between 1950 and 1990?

6. Now study table 4.3.

Percentage change in:					
	Output per worker	Employment	Output	Real earnings	Product wage
USA	29.8	−6.3	21.6	−3.9	17.3
Japan	52.2	6.7	62.4	13.4	51.9
Germany	16.5	−7.5	7.6	10.4	9.9
UK	37.8	−27.5	0.0	25.8	28.8

Source: Rowthorn, B., 1984, The Thatcher revolution, in Green, F., *The Restructuring of the UK Economy,* Harvester/Wheatsheaf.

TABLE 4.3: *Changes in manufacturing industry 1979–87*

What was the percentage change in manufacturing output between 1979 and 1987 for the USA, Japan, Germany and the UK?

Some politicians claim that the UK has undergone a miracle in the 1980s and the process of relative decline has been reversed. In a few sentences, explain what you feel is the case, and give reasons.

Summarise your findings in the box below.

Commentary...

The graph in figure 4.4 was produced on a spreadsheet. The key points to notice are that the GDP per head of Japan increased very rapidly and overtook that of the UK in the early 1980s.

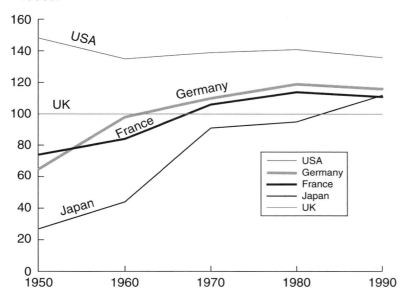

FIGURE 4.4: *GDP per head 1950–90 (UK=100).*

The GDP per head of the other countries had overtaken the UK by the late 1960s, but the difference between our GDP per head and theirs has fallen in recent years.

Tables 4.1 and 4.2 demonstrate clearly how the UK's performance has lagged behind that of our major competitors and the effect that this has had on our relative GDP per head. The gap between ourselves and the USA has been closed from 48 per cent to 36 per cent but that is still a big gap. From being 54 per cent ahead of Germany, 35 per cent ahead of France and 270 per cent ahead of Japan in 1950 we were, by 1980, 19 per cent and 14 per cent behind Germany and France respectively and only 5 per cent ahead of Japan.

Many claims have been made by politicians that the UK economy has undergone a miracle in the 1980s and that this process of relative decline has been reversed. Much depends on the period used to measure changes in GDP. If you wish to exaggerate the growth record then you simply measure growth from the low point of the cycle to the next high point, e.g. 1981 to 1990. A more accurate reflection would measure growth between two peaks in the cycle, e.g. 1979 and 1990. If these years are chosen, as in table 4.1, then a close inspection of the figures shows that it is growth in the other economies that has slowed rather than any increase in growth in the UK. At just over 2 per cent per annum this was better than the period 1973–79 but worse than for the 1950s and 1960s.

Between 1979 and 1981, the economy suffered two years of falling output but this was followed by several years of continuous growth culminating in the boom of 1987–89. The economy then entered another recession (1990–92) but now appears to be growing once again and the Treasury predicts this to continue at 2–3 per cent per annum until at least 1996.

The 1979–81 recession was particularly severe on manufacturing when approximately 20 per cent of manufacturing capacity was lost. Manufacturing output did not achieve 1979 levels until 1987 and at the peak of the cycle in 1990 was only 12 per cent higher. It fell back in the 1991 recession and is now only just ahead.

It would appear that the significant productivity improvements in manufacturing made between 1980 and 1986 ('the economic miracle') were the result of considerable shedding of labour (see table 4.3) with no increase in output; these were easy once and for all gains. Between 1979 and 1991, 32 per cent of jobs in manufacturing disappeared. Output did increase at the end of the decade but future increases in productivity will require higher levels of investment and training at both shop floor and management levels.

Inflation

> **\?/ Inflation** is usually defined as a continuous increase in the general level of prices or as a continuous decline in the value of money.

There are two important points to note about this definition.

- The price rise is continuous.

- The price rise refers to the general level of prices. As with the figures on GDP this is an average; some prices may well be falling while the average is increasing.

MEASUREMENT OF INFLATION

The Central Statistical Office produces a number of different measures of price inflation, all of which are constructed as an index number calculated as a weighted average of the relevant prices. The most well known is the retail price index (RPI).

The RPI is based on what it costs to buy a typical basket of goods and services. This is often referred to as the 'headline' rate of inflation. This index reflects changes in the 'cost of living'. It is the indicator which is generally referred to when negotiating wage rises.

The government uses the same index stripped of the effects of mortgage repayments as an indicator of the underlying rate of inflation. Mortgage repayments were not included because increases in interest rates were being used as a weapon to reduce inflation. The effect was that the increasing interest rates actually increased this measure of the rate of inflation.

Companies might also be interested in an index showing changes in the prices of fuel and raw materials as these might be important elements in the cost structure of the business. An index of 'factory gate prices' (i.e. the price of the product as it leaves the factory) is also calculated and this, together with the index of materials and fuels, gives the government an early indication of any likely increases in final retail prices. This assumes that businesses are in a position to 'pass on' these cost increases to customers.

THE RECORD ON INFLATION

Figure 4.5 shows the annual percentage rate of inflation from 1949 to 1994.

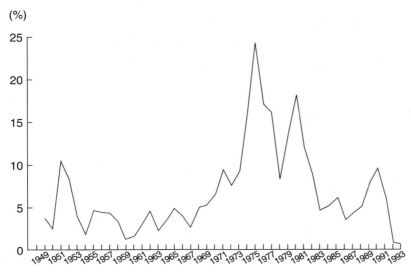

FIGURE 4.5: *UK annual inflation 1949–93.*

INFLATION

Managing tasks and solving problems ✓

Applying numeracy ✓

ACTIVITY 6

One of the objectives of government economic policy has been to achieve reasonable stability of prices. Using the information in figure 4.5, make a note of the years in which the government has achieved this target.

Commentary...

You probably started by asking yourself what is meant by 'reasonable stability of prices'. At the time of writing, the government's target range is between 1 and 4 per cent. If we take under 5 per cent as a measure of stability, the period from 1953 to 1969 would be termed successful. After that, the mid-1980s and 1994 would be the only successful years.

THE EFFECTS OF INFLATION

In the early 1950s, inflation reached 10 per cent as a result of the combined effect of a devaluation of sterling in 1949 and the Korean war (1950–51). The average throughout the 1950s was about 3 per cent and in the 1960s about 4 per cent. The 1970s were the most inflationary period of the twentieth century averaging 13 per cent and reaching record levels of 24 per cent in 1975. After rising to 18 per cent in 1980, inflation fell to 3.4 per cent in 1986 but then rose to 9.4 per cent in 1990. It has since fallen to around 2 per cent in 1994, well within the government's target range of 1–4 per cent.

Inflation can cause some serious economic and social problems. Inflation affects incomes in several ways.

- Those on fixed incomes (e.g. pensioners and students) will see the real value of their incomes falling. Some pension schemes may be index-linked but most private sector schemes are not.

- Those in weak bargaining positions may find that they are unable to negotiate rises to protect themselves from inflation.

- If the money value of incomes rises with inflation then some individuals will move into higher tax brackets.

- The real value of savings may fall. This will depend on what form of savings are held and on the level of interest rates. Cash holdings earning no interest will fall in value but savings held on deposit attracting interest will fall in value only by the difference between the rate of interest and the rate of inflation and may even rise in value if the latter is lower than the former.

- The value of debts falls. All those people with large mortgages would see the real value of their mortgages and mortgage payments fall. No doubt all those now suffering negative equity would be delighted to see a surge in inflation which boosted the money value of their homes and returned them to positive equity (assuming their wages also grew in line with inflation). Conversely the people or institutions to whom money is owed (creditors) lose out as they will receive less in return (in real terms) than they anticipated.

There are important effects on output and employment.

- Inflation may lead to unemployment through a loss of international competitiveness. If UK inflation is higher than our competitors' then the increase in export prices will lead to a loss of overseas markets and subsequently reduced employment.

- As UK goods become expensive relative to overseas goods it is likely that UK consumers will be attracted to relatively cheaper foreign imports which will take the place of domestically produced goods. This import penetration may ultimately lead to the closure of many domestic businesses.

● High interest rates and increased uncertainty about future returns may also lead to reduced investment which again may lead to reduced employment.

● In competitive situations, or where trading conditions are difficult, employers may be less willing to pass on cost increases (wage or other) to customers and may pay for any increases in costs by reducing employment.

● If rising prices lead to rising wages and these increased costs are passed on by employers this may well lead to what is known as a wage–price spiral in which both prices and wages follow each other continuously.

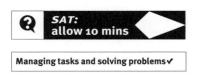

SAT:
allow 10 mins

| Managing tasks and solving problems✓ |
| Applying numeracy   ✓ |

ACTIVITY 7

Imagine you own a small business producing machine parts mainly for the domestic market but part of your output is exported to Germany and France. List four problems that high rates of inflation might cause.

Commentary...

Increases in prices may mean lost orders in Germany and France if our inflation rates are higher than theirs. This may also mean a loss of domestic orders to cheaper imports. If interest rates rise to combat inflation then this would increase the cost of loans/overdrafts. A more uncertain future may encourage workers to ask for higher wages causing more increases in costs.

THE CAUSES OF INFLATION

Economists offer two broad explanations of why prices tend to rise continuously. There are those who look to the supply side of the economy and blame increases in costs and those who analyse the demand side of the economy and explain rising prices by the presence of excess demand. The two sets of explanations are known respectively as 'cost-push' and 'demand-pull' inflation.

Cost-push inflation Cost-push theorists point to the fact that most firms set their prices by calculating their average costs of production and adding a mark-up which is their profit. It follows from this that any increase in costs is likely to be passed on to a firm's customers in the form of increased prices. The main cost pressures are likely to come from increases in wages, raw materials or fuel or from companies attempting to raise their profit margins irrespective of demand conditions.

Demand-pull inflation Demand-pull theorists tend to fall into two camps: the Keynesians and the monetarists.

The Keynesian view looks at the relationship between the level of employment and the level of demand in the economy. If the economy is operating at or near full employment, any increase in the spending plans of businesses, consumers, government or overseas buyers will lead to an increase in prices because these spending plans cannot be met by increases in output. Keynesians explain that this excess demand will lead to employers attempting to increase output but as resources are already fully employed, the price of these resources – labour and raw material – would rise. These cost increases then lead to price increases.

Let us look at this illustration. If a building firm which is already fully occupied building houses is offered a new order to build a school, then it needs to engage more tradespeople – bricklayers, carpenters and electricians. If they are already employed, the firm can get more workers to the site only by poaching them from other employers. The traditional method of doing this is to offer higher wages, and so wages rise. As wages rise, the cost of building the school rises and the building firm has to charge a higher price.

In practice, this can be very difficult to distinguish from cost-push inflation and this has been the subject of much debate between economists. 'Cost-pushers' have pointed to the power of trade unions, especially in the 1970s, being able to secure wage rises even when there was substantial unemployment and little, if any, increase in productivity. They have also pointed to rapid increases in import costs, like the quadrupling of oil prices in the 1970s.

The monetarist school puts the blame for inflation on an over-expansion of the money supply. Money like any other commodity is subject to the forces of supply and demand and like any other commodity, if there is excess supply, the value will fall. If the supply of money is increased by 10 per cent and the volume of goods and services does not increase, then ultimately the average price of goods and services will rise to absorb the increase in the supply of money. The government, which is responsible for the supply of money in the economy, is blamed because it borrows money to finance its own expenditure plans and it is this borrowing that leads to an expansion of the money supply.

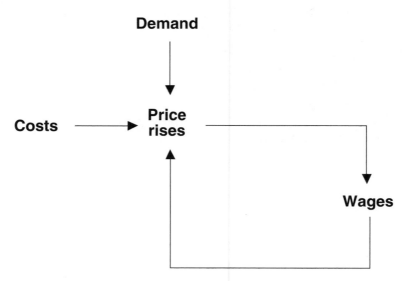

FIGURE 4.6: *The wage–price spiral.*

Whatever the cause, once inflation takes hold, people try to protect themselves by demanding higher wages or by increasing prices. A spiral as shown in figure 4.6 may begin to operate. This can only occur if the government expands the supply of money to accommodate the price increases. If prices rise by 10 per cent, total spending on the same volume of goods must rise by 10 per cent. This can only happen if the money supply rises to accommodate the price rise. If it does not, then some of the goods will remain unsold. This would lead to cuts in output and employment much as happened in the early 1980s when inflation was brought down from 18 per cent but at great cost in terms of lost output and jobs. This policy was eased in the mid-1980s when credit was much easier to obtain. Demand increased but the capacity of the economy could not meet the increase in demand which resulted in inflation rising to 9.4 per cent and a deteriorating balance of payments as imports rose to fill the domestic output gap. Demand was subsequently squeezed by successive hikes in interest rates which curbed the excess demand and eventually brought inflation down to the current very low figures.

Managing tasks and solving problems ✔

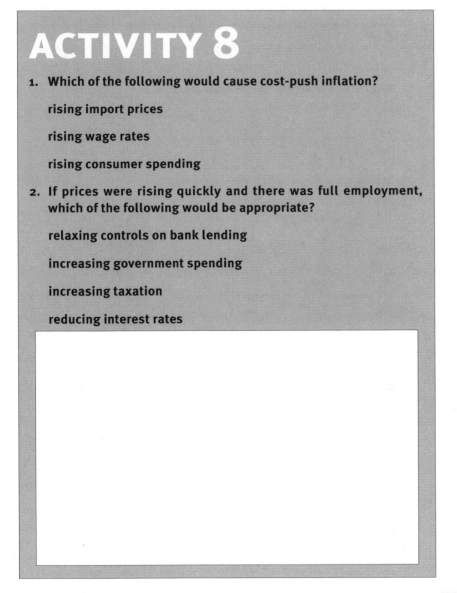

ACTIVITY 8

1. **Which of the following would cause cost-push inflation?**

    rising import prices

    rising wage rates

    rising consumer spending

2. **If prices were rising quickly and there was full employment, which of the following would be appropriate?**

    relaxing controls on bank lending

    increasing government spending

    increasing taxation

    reducing interest rates

Commentary...

Rising import prices and rising wage rates are both examples of causes of cost-push inflation.

Increasing taxation would reduce spending power in the economy and help to reduce inflation. The other measures would all add to inflationary pressures.

Unemployment

Labour is our most important asset yet in September 1994 2,470,200 people or 9 per cent of the workforce were unemployed according to the Department of Employment. Full employment had been a major policy objective for much of the post-war period but this policy objective was abandoned in the 1980s. Many people who never envisaged the threat of redundancy had to face up to the possibility and for many it became a fact. Having the right skills, qualification and experience has never been more important in what is now a very competitive jobs market.

> **!?!**   The **unemployed** can be defined as those people who would like to work but are unable to find a job.

This is not the definition used in arriving at the monthly unemployment figures provided by the government. This figure (called 'the claimant unemployed') counts only those people who are claiming unemployment related benefits at employment service local offices. It therefore excludes all those who are seeking work but are not claiming benefit but includes those who are receiving benefit but are not looking for work. There have been a number of changes to the methods of calculating unemployment figures since 1979 (30 according to the Unemployment Unit, eight of any significance according to the government), all but one of which reduced the recorded figure. The Unemployment Unit estimated that on the 1979 basis of calculation, unemployment in July 1990 would have been 900,000 higher than the official estimate. The changes make comparisons over time difficult. Nevertheless, figure 4.7 gives a rough estimate of the rate of unemployment since 1953.

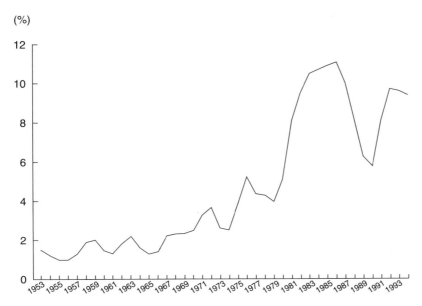

FIGURE 4.7: *UK unemployment rate (1953–94).*

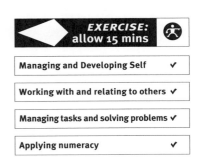

EXERCISE:
allow 15 mins

Managing and Developing Self	✔
Working with and relating to others	✔
Managing tasks and solving problems	✔
Applying numeracy	✔

ACTIVITY 9

Divide into groups of four and complete the following task.

You have already read that there was a major change in the priority of objectives with the election of the Conservative government in 1979. Employment levels in the 1980s were left increasingly to the market.

Study figure 4.7.

Look in particular at what happened to levels of unemployment after the change of government policy in 1979. Compare this period with the previous decades.

Some of the following statements are consistent with the data represented in the graph and some are not.

Discuss which statements are consistent with the graph and which are not and write down your conclusions.

(a) The free market mechanism tends to maintain more stable rates of employment than those produced by direct government influence or control.

(b) Between 1953 and 1968 unemployment rates were both low and relatively stable.

(c) The government which took office in 1979 with the slogan, 'Getting Britain Back to Work', succeeded in reducing the level of unemployment over the next 15 years.

(d) Prior to 1979, unemployment rates were moving upwards.

UNEMPLOYMENT

Commentary...

From 1979, the government was less concerned with maintaining full employment and less interventionist than previous governments. So, the market mechanism had greater influence after 1979. During this period, the graph begins to rise more steeply until 1985, then it plunges to almost the level it was when the government took office. It then soars again between 1989 and 1991. Comparing this with previous years, the change in levels of unemployment were far more marked. Therefore rates of unemployment were less stable. Statement (a) is inconsistent with the graph.

Between 1953 and 1968, unemployment was never above 2.3 per cent and never less than 1 per cent. Whether this is low or not depends on how 'low' is defined. As the economy is constantly changing and people are moving from one job to another, there will always be some unemployment so full employment – zero unemployment – is not achievable. These levels must be counted as low and certainly, compared with later years, they are very low. Statement (b) is consistent with the graph.

The level of unemployment actually rose after the government took office, so it was not successful in getting Britain back to work.

Look carefully at the graph for the period 1953–79. Notice that there is a fairly consistent trend of increasing unemployment. The rate of increase seems to accelerate after 1974. Statement (d) is consistent with the graph.

KEYNESIAN VIEWS ON UNEMPLOYMENT

There are a number of different ways of classifying unemployment. One method, associated with Keynesians, is as follows:

- **Frictional unemployment** refers to those people who are in the process of moving from one job to another as they look for jobs better suited to their skills and hopes. From January 1993 to June 1994 about an average of 350,000 were leaving the unemployment register every month with a slightly lower number coming on to the register.

- **Structural unemployment** refers to those people who are unemployed because of long-term changes in the structure of the economy, i.e. as some industries go into decline and others emerge. The 32 per cent loss of jobs in the manufacturing sector since 1979 has left many people with skills which are no longer in demand and/or in locations where jobs do not exist. People tend to adjust slowly to new situations and this period of adjustment is likely to increase as the skill content of jobs increases; it will take longer to retrain and update skills. The Association of British Chambers of Commerce reported that, in the second quarter of 1994, 44 per cent of service firms were having difficulties in recruiting staff. This, at a time when the level of unemployment is still very high, indicates that the unemployed do not always have the right skills for the jobs available and/or they are in the wrong geographic area.

- **Demand-deficient unemployment** or **cyclical unemployment** occurs when there is insufficient demand for goods and services in the economy. The effect of demand can be seen clearly in the behaviour of the economy since 1979. The period 1979–81 was one in which the government manufactured a severe 'credit crunch' with interest rates at record levels. Unemployment eventually rose to over three million. From 1986 onwards, monetary policy was eased and there was a 'credit explosion', with unemployment falling to 1.7 million. As inflation accelerated, interest rates were once again raised causing the level of demand to fall and unemployment to rise.

The usefulness to policy makers of this approach is that it gives an indication of what needs to be done in order to reduce unemployment.

MONETARIST VIEWS ON UNEMPLOYMENT

Monetarists tend not to be concerned with this type of analysis but treat the labour market just as any other market. In product markets, excess supply exists when sellers cannot sell their goods. The only way to get rid of their surplus stocks is to reduce prices. Unemployment is treated in just the same way – it is an excess of supply over demand in the labour market. Workers are refusing to work at the 'going rate' or in other words they are pricing themselves out of work. The answer is for workers to accept lower wages; then employers will increase employment.

Full employment would be a situation in which the number wanting a job at the market wage equalled the number employers wished to hire at that wage. Any excess supply of labour would be caused by workers asking for too high a wage. Even if workers did accept lower wages there would still be some unemployment (frictional and structural) as the economy is in a constant state of change but this could be reduced to a minimum if labour markets were more flexible. The residual unemployment could be reduced by improving the supply side of the economy, i.e. removing imperfections in the labour market which acted as obstacles to employment. This might include improving occupational mobility by increasing the skills base of the labour force, improving geographic mobility, reducing the power of the trade unions, improving job information and adjusting income differentials, especially between those in work and those out of work.

THE INCIDENCE OF UNEMPLOYMENT

ACTIVITY 10

The chances of becoming unemployed are not evenly spread throughout the economy. Study the tables 4.4 and 4.5 and figure 4.8 and then list which groups of people are likely to suffer the highest rates of unemployment.

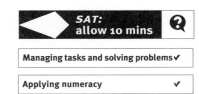

SAT: allow 10 mins

Managing tasks and solving problems ✔

Applying numeracy   ✔

United Kingdom	Percentages			
Males	1986	1991	1992	1993
16–19	21.8	16.5	18.7	22.0
20–29	15.7	12.3	15.3	16.4
30–39	9.4	7.8	10.4	10.3
40–49	7.8	5.8	7.8	8.8
50–64	9.3	8.4	10.4	11.9
65+	9.3	5.9	4.9	4.6
All males 16+	11.7	9.2	11.5	12.4
Females				
16–19	19.8	13.2	13.8	16.0
20–29	14.4	9.4	9.4	10.2
30–39	10.1	6.9	7.2	7.0
40–49	6.7	4.9	5.0	4.7
50–59	6.1	5.1	5.0	5.6
60 and over	5.1	4.4	3.1	3.9
All females 16+	10.7	7.2	7.2	7.5

Source: Social Trends, 1994.

TABLE 4.4: *UK unemployment rates: by sex and age*

United Kingdom	Percentages				
	1989	1990	1991	1992	1993
North	10.7	8.6	10.6	11.2	11.2
Yorkshire	8.0	6.8	9.1	9.9	9.8
East Midlands	6.0	5.1	7.8	8.7	9.0
East Anglia	3.8	3.8	6.2	7.1	8.3
South East	3.1	3.9	7.4	9.4	10.3
South West	4.8	4.5	7.7	9.1	9.2
West Midlands	6.9	5.9	9.0	10.7	11.6
North West	8.8	7.5	9.9	10.1	10.9
Wales	7.9	6.6	9.2	8.9	9.5
Scotland	9.8	8.0	9.2	9.5	10.1
Northern Ireland	15.4	13.7	14.1	12.1	12.5

Source: Social Trends, 1994.

TABLE 4.5: *UK unemployment rates by region*

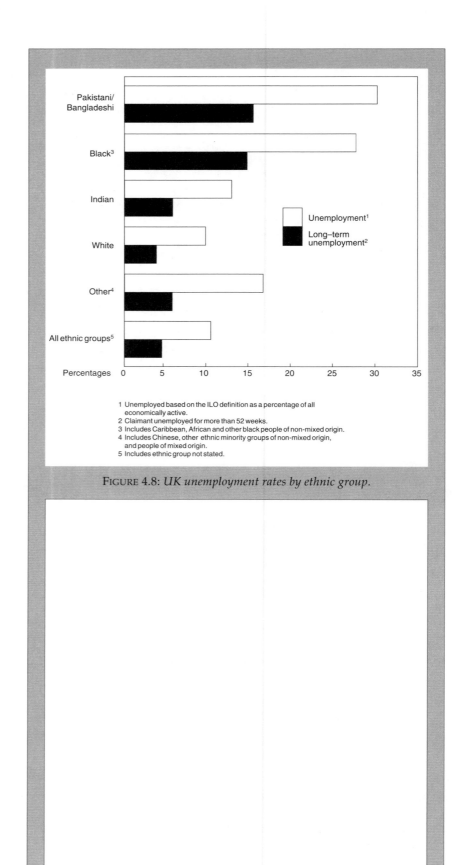

FIGURE 4.8: *UK unemployment rates by ethnic group.*

Commentary...

Age – From the tables it is clear to see that in terms of age the young are the most likely to suffer unemployment, especially young males with 22 per cent of 16–19-year-olds seeking work being unemployed in 1993.

Ethnic group – Pakistani/Bangladeshi and Afro-Caribbean people seem to suffer very high rates of unemployment with around 30 per cent unemployed for some time and around 15 per cent unemployed for more than one year.

Region – Here the disparities in unemployment are not so wide as they used to be. In 1989, Northern Ireland was suffering unemployment rates of 15.4 per cent when the rate in the South East was 3.1 per cent. By 1993, Northern Ireland still had the highest rate at 12.5 per cent but the rate in the South East had increased to 10.3 per cent.

Another group to suffer above average unemployment rates (not shown in the tables) is manual workers, especially unskilled manual workers.

EFFECTS

The effects on the individual are well documented (White, 1991, *Against Unemployment*, Policy Studies Institute). The most obvious and pressing problem is lack of money but divorce, boredom, sickness, sleeplessness, isolation, anxiety and loss of self-confidence are all commonly reported effects of both short-term and long-term (i.e. over 52 weeks) unemployment.

For the economy, it is a waste of resources (in terms of lost output): it puts pressure on social services; it increases public expenditure and reduces revenue (lost taxes and national insurance); and increases crime and general health problems.

Where a region is particularly dependent on an industry, the closure or run down of that industry can have severe multiplier effects on the region.

The multiplier effect means that any initial increase or decrease in spending will bring about a much greater increase or decrease in total spending. For example, the closure of many of the coal mines has hit members of those communities other than the miners. Many local business will have been suppliers to the pit. Miners' wages will have been spent locally, generating income for other businesses. Thus the closure of one large business can ultimately cause the closure of many more. This can work in reverse. A large investment in an area can generate many jobs. Initially, jobs are created in the one firm but as the increased spending power of workers filters through to other businesses, many more jobs can be created.

It can be argued that there are some benefits for business from a large pool of unemployed workers. It makes it relatively easy for firms to find new workers although finding workers with the right skills may not be easy. It also means that, generally, workers are in a weak bargaining position in relation to conditions of work (including wages). As a consequence, firms will be able to hold down wage costs and gain a competitive edge over overseas competition.

The balance of payments

> **\?/** **The balance of payments** is a record of all the transactions between the UK and the rest of the world.

These transactions are generally of two types. One is the exchange of goods and services and the other is the exchange of capital. The account is divided up into two main parts reflecting these different flows.

The **current account** records the flows of money associated with trade in goods and services. The balance between exports and imports of goods is called the **visible balance** or the **balance of trade**. The transactions in services such as banking, insurance, tourism and transport together with interest, dividends and profits on overseas holdings are known as **invisibles**. The sum of the visible and invisible balance is called the **current balance**.

The other section records all currency flows related to capital items. This includes direct investments by companies setting up subsidiaries, portfolio investment (purchase of shares) government borrowing and lending, and inter-bank dealings in sterling and foreign currency. The balance between the inflow and outflow of funds each year is shown in the change in official reserves.

The balancing item includes unrecorded or under-recorded transactions.

Visible	exports	107,047	
	imports	120,453	
	balance		−13,406
Invisibles	exports	108,438	
	imports	103,652	
	balance		4,786
Current balance			−8,620
Transaction in UK assets and liabilities			
UK external assets		−84,976	
UK external liabilities		93,295	
Net transactions			8,319
Balancing item			301

TABLE 4.6: *The UK Balance of Payments, 1992 (£ million)*

EQUILIBRIUM IN THE BALANCE OF PAYMENTS

One of the objectives of economic policy is to achieve equilibrium in the balance of payments. If imports exceed exports, this is referred to as a deficit. If, on the other hand, exports exceed imports, this is referred to as a surplus. The traditional pattern for the UK is that there is a deficit of visible trade and a surplus on invisible trade. The sum of the two balances gives the current balance and it is this balance which is the important indicator of external performance.

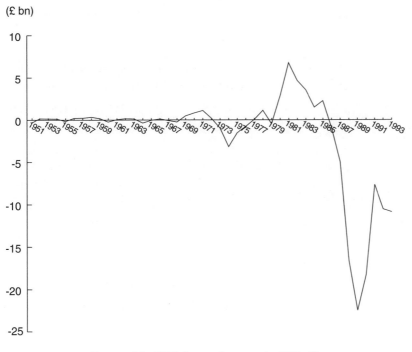

FIGURE 4.9: *UK balance of payments 1951–93.*

Figure 4.9 shows that the current account has usually been in deficit since 1985. This is important for two reasons.

1. The deficit has to be financed in some way which may mean higher interest rates and reduced investment.

2. A persistent deficit shows that a country's expenditure is exceeding its income and this can only go on by continued borrowing, to which there is a limit.

The persistent deficit also indicates a weakness in the UK economy. Since the Second World War, there have been few years in which the UK has not had a deficit in visible trade but this, more often than not, has been made up for by a surplus on invisible trade. In 1980, the UK actually had a trade surplus of £1.357 billion but by 1989, this had been transformed into a deficit of £24.683 billion. The invisible surplus in that year was only £2.171 billion. The surplus in the early 1980s was due to the effect of north sea oil but the combined effect of high exchange rates, inflation and domestic recession decimated the UK manufacturing sector. When there was a surge in domestic demand in the later part of the decade, domestic manufacturers were unable to satisfy the demand for goods and, as a consequence, the gap was filled by overseas producers.

RESTORING BALANCE OF PAYMENTS EQUILIBRIUM

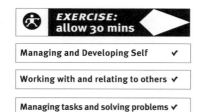

EXERCISE: allow 30 mins

Managing and Developing Self ✔

Working with and relating to others ✔

Managing tasks and solving problems ✔

ACTIVITY 11

A persistent deficit in the balance of payments can have serious consequences for the country's people: inflation, unemployment and hardship. But what can the government do to bring about a change in this situation which has been in existence for much of the past 20 years?

Divide into groups of four and brainstorm how you would deal with a persistent balance of payments problem. Write down your ideas and present them to the rest of the class.

Commentary...

You probably hit on one or two good ideas, but for every suggestion there is probably some factor that makes it unsatisfactory in some way. Let us look at some of the ideas you may have come up with, and the problems associated with them.

- Reducing domestic expenditure by deflationary policies, e.g. raising interest rates and/or increasing taxes may reduce expenditure on imports and increase the price competitiveness of domestic manufacturers *vis-à-vis* overseas competition as relative inflation falls. This may, however, lead to quite severe reductions in output and employment as happened in the early 1980s.

- Import controls, either by directly limiting imports or by increasing import duties, do not attack the underlying causes of the deficit and may invite retaliation from competitors. Because we are a member of the EU and GATT (General Agreement on Tariffs and Trade), attempts to impose tariff barriers may not be an available option.

- You might have considered devaluation of the currency. A fall in the rate at which a country's currency exchanges with others has the double effect of reducing the foreign currency price of UK exports and increasing the sterling price of UK imports. This should encourage exports and discourage imports.

The long-term answer is of course for UK manufacturing industry to adopt strategies which give it a competitive advantage over its overseas competitors. There is a fundamental and continuing dispute between economists and politicians over the extent to which a government can and/or should intervene in markets to aid this process.

Post-war economic performance

The period since the Second World War can, in terms of economic policy, be divided into two periods: pre-1979 and post-1979. Economic policy pre-1979 was dominated by the thinking of Keynes irrespective of whether the government was Conservative or Labour. During the periods when Labour was in office, there was much greater consultation between government and representatives of labour and business (i.e. TUC and the CBI). This is often labelled as **corporatist** by political scientists.

The post-1979 period was initially inspired by monetarism and, in particular, by the ideas of **Milton Friedman**. This was superseded by what is termed the **new classical macro-economics** and this term is now usually used to refer to the theoretical underpinning of policy since 1979. This latter school emphasises the role of markets in allocating resources efficiently and claims that government intervention as advocated by Keynes is counter-productive.

PRE-1979 POLICIES

In the period to the mid-1970s, the major role for government economic policy was to secure full employment. Keynes had provided the analysis which showed that full employment, and economic growth, could be achieved by increasing the level of demand in the economy. In other words, he identified a deficiency in demand as the major cause of unemployment. If the level of demand was increased this would lead to an increase in production which in turn would require more employees. More people in employment would generate more income and hence more spending and so on. Thus a virtuous circle of production and employment growth would be created (figure 4.10).

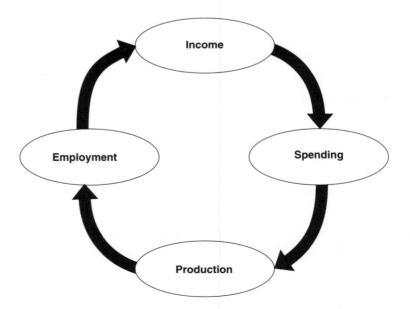

FIGURE 4.10: *The virtuous circle of production and employment.*

A stop-go economy One view held that the government should take responsibility for controlling the economy through its own spending. This policy was pursued throughout the 1950s and 1960s and some way into the 1970s. It was not however without its problems. The economy tended to follow a familiar pattern which became known as 'stop-go'. Demand would be stimulated in order to reduce unemployment. The economy would begin to grow and unemployment would fall. As the economy reached full employment and total demand for goods and services exceeded the total supply of goods and services, inflation would start to accelerate (demand-pull inflation). In addition, as the domestic economy could not satisfy the increased demand, imports would increase causing a balance of payments problem. This would be a signal to government to reduce the level of demand. The balance of payments would improve, inflation would fall but growth would slow and unemployment would begin to rise. The cycle would start again, hence 'stop-go'.

The 1970s saw more severe crises. Unemployment began to rise to what were then unacceptable levels and traditional Keynesian remedies seemed to have little effect. Eventually the government was faced with rising unemployment, rising inflation and zero or low growth – a situation dubbed 'stagflation'. Periods of rising unemployment were usually associated with periods of falling inflation and policy was seen as a trade-off between the two. Now both were rising and the traditional Keynesian cure for one would have made the other worse. It seemed that Keynesian policies had no answer to the problem. This impasse created the conditions for a different approach to policy.

POST-1979 POLICIES

In 1979, a Conservative government was elected with Margaret Thatcher as prime minister. This brought to an end the consensus on macro-economic policy which had existed for the previous 30 years. The Conservatives believed a radical new economic agenda was needed to transform the economy after years of relative decline. No longer was the economy to be managed by Keynesian demand management as government intervention was thought to be de-stabilising.

What was needed, it was argued, was a government committed to ridding the economy of job-destroying inflation and a return to market forces as the main resource allocator. Monetary and fiscal policy were now to be used to maintain price stability by controlling monetary growth. The 'supply side' of the economy was to be transformed by removing the shackles of government intervention and control and opening up the economy to the power of market forces.

Now we will see how successful the new policy was.

CONTROL OF INFLATION

The 1980s' record on inflation could hardly be called a success. At first, inflation increased. It has never been less than 3.4 per cent. By 1990, it was 9.5 per cent and throughout it was higher than our major competitors'. A long recession brought inflation down to historically low figures in the early 1990s, but it will be interesting to see whether the government can keep it under control as the economy comes out of recession and at what cost.

	1982–6	1987	1988	1989	1990
United States	3.8	3.7	4.1	5.0	5.4
Japan	1.9	0.1	0.7	2.6	3.1
Germany	2.6	0.3	1.2	3.0	2.7
EU	5.0	3.1	3.3	4.9	5.1
OECD	5.0	3.2	4.0	5.2	5.3
Britain	5.5	4.1	4.9	7.7	9.3

Source: Healey, N., 1993, *Britain's Economic Miracle: Myth or Reality*, Routledge.

TABLE 4.7: *Consumer price inflation around the world (annual average percentage)*

The monetarist experiment required the government to be able to control the supply of money. Crucial to this process of monetary control is the ability to measure the stock of money. This is not quite so easy as it sounds. If you think for a minute how much money you have, what would you include? Cash and current bank accounts certainly, but what about deposit accounts, building society accounts, post office savings which are all withdrawable on demand? Would you include all the deposits which require notice of withdrawal? If we are concerned with the level of spending, should we include credit cards?

The government did not attempt to control the supply of money directly but chose to operate on the demand for money which it assumed would lead to changes in the supply. The tools of control were reduction in government borrowing and interest rate adjustments. Interest rates were raised to record levels (16 per cent in October 1981) and public expenditure was squeezed, in order to reduce the public sector borrowing requirement (PSBR). While the monetary indicators were indicating otherwise the government was, without realising it, managing to engineer a severe 'credit crunch' causing the decimation of manufacturing output and employment.

High interest rates and a squeeze on public expenditure managed to reduce inflation to the relative low of 3.4 per cent by 1986 but a 'credit explosion' towards the end of the decade saw inflation rise once more to double figures. This was countered by another hike in interest rates and a tightening of fiscal policy; the government budgeted for a surplus of £14 billion in 1989–90. As in 1980, this resulted in recession with unemployment exceeding three million.

This may seem very familiar: the pattern of economic activity is not dissimilar to the pattern in the 1950s and 1960s. Some critics argue that the increase in interest rates and the squeeze on public spending has been nothing more than a typical Keynesian deflationary package (i.e. a deliberate reduction in the level of demand in the economy) albeit more severe in that its objective was the eradication of inflation. Moreover the severity of the deflation may well have accelerated the structural changes taking place in the economy. The shift from manufacturing to services which was taking place accelerated in the 1980s. Many workers suddenly found themselves unemployed, with the wrong skills for the jobs that were becoming available. They had little time to adjust to the new situation. Many of the unemployed are now in the long-term category, unskilled and with low educational attainment.

SUPPLY-SIDE REFORMS

Monetarists criticised Keynesian polices because they considered only the demand side of the economy. So if there was unemployment, Keynesian remedies were to increase the level of demand. But what if firms were not in a position to respond? Perhaps there was insufficient labour, or labour without the right skills. In this case, if firms are unable to respond to the increases in demand, all that happens is that the gap between supply and demand increases. In other words, the policies implemented to cure inflation will actually increase it.

One of the major problems with the labour market was seen as the power of trade unions, who by clinging to traditional ways of working (restrictive practices) created inefficiency. By exercising their bargaining power they also maintained unrealistically high wages. A series of legislative acts were introduced in order to:

- reduce union power

- restore to management the power to manage (management's 'right to manage').

With managers back in the driving seat, it was hoped that there would be a move to greater efficiency in the workplace. These new laws, coupled with the fact that trade union membership has declined with the demise of manufacturing industry, did in fact reduce union power. (Cynics might also say that the creation of three million unemployed was a deliberate move designed to undermine trade union power.) Whether these changes are to have positive consequences remains to be seen.

A second set of policies attacked the disincentives to work that were said to exist. One concern was the difference between those in work and those out of work. Low wages meant that some people were better off (in monetary terms) receiving unemployment benefit than working. If the difference between being in work and being out of work was small or even negative, those out of work would have little incentive to take a job.

Additionally 'over-generous' welfare payments, it was argued, had created a 'dependency' culture which undermined individual responsibility. As a consequence, the extent and scope of income support measures has been restricted.

Another concern was the supposed disincentive effect of direct taxation. Consequently, income taxes have been substantially reduced in order to encourage enterprise, effort and innovation while indirect taxes have increased. These changes have increased income inequality but it is argued that this is justified in terms of the extra incentives it provides.

Other changes have been made in an attempt to stimulate savings and increase investment. The best known measure is the privatisation programme. In addition home ownership, the self-employed and small businesses have all been encouraged.

The overall aim of these supply-side changes was to bring about a change in the general business culture. The welfare state had created a dependency culture (which many blamed for the decline of the UK) and the aim was to change this to an enterprise culture. The emphasis was to be on individuals taking responsibility for their own actions and being encouraged to take risks, work harder and become more self-reliant.

ACTIVITY 12

The four broad objectives of government economic policy during the period 1950–79 were:

1. full employment

2. stable prices

3. economic growth

4. balance of payments equilibrium.

Using the data previously provided, judge how far governments were successful in achieving each objective.

Use a scoring system like this:

5 = very successful

4 = partly successful

3 = partly successful/partly unsuccessful

2 = unsuccessful

1 = very unsuccessful

For example, if you think the government in 1950–59 was very successful in maintaining full employment, you would put '5' in the first box.

Complete the table according to your own judgements, based on the data provided in this session.

Objective	1950–59	1960–69	1970–79	1980–89	1990–95
Full employment					
Stable prices					
Growth					
Balance of payments equilibrium					

Commentary...

In terms of achieving the main economic objectives, it would appear that the 1950s and 1960s were fairly successful years. Inflation and unemployment were relatively low, growth was steady but small (very low relative to our major competitors) and the current account was roughly in balance. In the 1970s, things started to go wrong. Inflation reached record heights, unemployment increased, economic growth slowed and the current balance went first into surplus and then into serious deficit. The 1980s started with increasing inflation and unemployment and a major recession but with a large current account surplus. As the decade proceeded growth increased, inflation fell but unemployment continued to increase and the current balance went into deficit. The decade finished with a 'boom' with high rates of growth, falling but high unemployment, rising inflation and record current account deficits. This was followed by yet another recession from which the UK economy is still emerging.

summary

▶ The objectives of government economic policy are:
economic growth
low inflation
employment
a positive balance of payments.

▶ Government economic policy can be direct or indirect.

▶ The major policies at the government's disposal are monetary, fiscal and direct.

▶ A widely used model of the economy is one that uses a circular flow of resources.

▶ This simple model needs to recognise leakages (savings, imports and taxation) and injections (investment, exports and government spending).

▶ In the post-war period, there was a broad consensus on economic policy based on Keynesian demand management.

▶ In the 1970s, monetarism-based supply-side economics replaced Keynesian economics.

▶ The two schools of economics — Keynesian and monetarist — offer different solutions to an economy's problems. Each school places different emphasis on different policy objectives. Keynesian economics seems to be more concerned with employment, monetarist economics with inflation.

▶ The success of government economic policy has been mixed in the post-war period.

Industrial policy

Objectives

After participating in this session, you should be able to:

> ▶ describe the aims and objectives of industrial policy

> ▶ explain the impact of industrial policies on business

> ▶ describe the attitudes of business to industrial policies

> ▶ explain how business influences industrial policies

> ▶ describe the impact of business on industrial policies.

In working through this session, you will practise the following BTEC common skills:

Managing and Developing Self	✔
Working with and Relating to others	✔
Communicating	✔
Managing Tasks and Solving Problems	✔
Applying Numeracy	
Applying Technology	
Applying Design and Creativity	

Industrial policy objectives

In this session, we look at UK policy towards industry and commerce. Industrial policy includes all those policies that have a direct impact on the structure, behaviour or performance of business. Privatisation policy, for example can affect the structure of ownership and control; regional policy can influence the location of business; agricultural policy can have an effect on how farmers perform, e.g. in terms of productivity and profits.

Industrial policy has rarely been coherent, consistent, or co-ordinated. Policy has comprised a number of separate elements introduced at different points in time to deal with specific issues or with particular problems as they arose. The chopping and changing of industrial policy can pose problems for organisations wishing to plan their long-term strategies, e.g. with regard to decisions on investment, location, research and development (R&D), product development, mergers and acquisitions. The *ad hoc* nature of UK policy has been further complicated by the increasing powers of the EU to intervene in areas such as regional, public procurement and competition policies.

There have been tensions both within and between the major political parties over the extent to which governments should intervene directly in the economy. To a large extent, these divisions reflect different explanations of Britain's relative industrial decline and the remedies recommended for dealing with that decline. Conservative governments since 1979 have supported the case for a free market economy arguing that excessive government intervention has been a major cause of Britain's economic problems. Consequently they set out to cut intervention. Conversely, the political centre and left contend that government action has been insufficiently interventionist particularly with regard to the manufacturing sector and with respect to investment, R&D, new technology, and the skills levels of the workforce.

The fact that all post-war governments, irrespective of their political hue, have pursued industrial policies, indicates a recognition that decisions can not be left wholly to the operation of the market, i.e. to the choices of individuals and organisations. Governments realise that a complete abandonment of intervention in industry would be unpopular with the electorate.

Policy towards industry covers a wide variety of policy areas that have impacts on firms, industries, industrial sectors or regions. Industrial policy includes:

- privatisation and nationalisation

- agricultural policy

- R&D and technology policy

- regional policy

- public procurement policy, i.e. the purchase of goods and services by state bodies

- competition policy.

SAT:
allow 20 mins

Managing tasks and solving problems ✔

ACTIVITY 1

1. Read the statements below. Insert the name of an appropriate policy at the beginning of each statement.

   _____ policy changes who owns the business.

   _____ policy could give businesses money grants for research and development.

   _____ policy could determine the prices farmers get for their produce.

   _____ policy could lead to changes in the level of sales for producers of arms.

   _____ policy could determine the prices food manufacturers pay for agricultural products.

   _____ policy may subsidise businesses for locating in certain areas.

   _____ policy could make it difficult for firms to merge.

   _____ policy could reduce interference by politicians in the running of businesses.

2. Which governments have blamed the UK's industrial decline on excessive government intervention?

3. In the light of your answer, explain why there might be disagreement on industrial policy between Michael Heseltine, President of the Board of Trade (who favours intervention), and other members of the cabinet? Write about 30 words on this.

4. Which political viewpoints argue for more government intervention to deal with industrial decline?

Commentary...

Privatisation (or nationalisation) policy changes who owns the business.

R&D and technology policy could give businesses money grants for research and development.

Agricultural policy could determine the prices farmers get for their produce.

Public procurement policy could lead to changes in the level of sales for producers of arms.

Agricultural policy could determine the prices food manufacturers pay for agricultural products.

Regional policy could subsidise businesses for locating in certain areas.

Competition policy could make it difficult for firms to merge.

Privatisation policy could reduce interference by politicians in the running of businesses.

Conservative governments since 1979 have blamed the UK's industrial decline on excessive government intervention. They have been hostile to intervention. Michael Heseltine is quoted in *The Economist* (30 April 1994) as favouring it. This could be a source of conflict with some of his cabinet colleagues. The political centre and left argue for more intervention.

The impact of industrial policy on business

Industrial policy can affect an organisation in numerous ways. The structure of the industry in which it operates, the decisions it makes, its ownership and control, and its performance can all be influenced.

Industry structure The number of firms could be reduced and their size increased by the government allowing mergers to take place. On the other hand, the number of firms could be increased by making it easier for organisations to enter a particular market through liberalisation/deregulation policies. The deregulation of the bus industry, for example led to the entry of new competitors on some routes, and Mercury was permitted to enter the market for telecommunications previously monopolised by British Telecom.

Organisational decision making Governments can influence firms' policies in important areas such as pricing, advertising and sales promotion, investment, location, merger and acquisition, R&D and training. Conduct can be altered by the offer of 'carrots' such as subsidies. Thus British Aerospace was given financial inducements by the government to buy the Rover Group. Nissan, Toyota, and Samsung have all located factories in the UK financed in part by large regional assistance grants. The government can also use 'sticks' to promote what it sees as desirable company behaviour. For example, the restrictive practices laws make it illegal for businesses to collude in certain ways, e.g. by agreeing to charge the same prices or to share out the market between them.

Ownership and control Governments can change the structure of ownership and control through privatisation or nationalisation. Senior managers in privatised industries such as British Steel and British Airways are now free to set their own objectives and pursue them without the intervention of civil servants and government ministers. (These companies now have what is sometimes called commercial freedom.) Other privatised businesses, such as gas and water, have been given more commercial freedom but, unlike British Steel and British Airways, remain subject to controls by their regulatory bodies.

Performance Government policy can have important implications for business performance. For example, action by the Office of Telecommunications (OFTEL) over prices can have a major impact on British Telecom's profits; merger policy might frustrate a firm's achieving growth and market share objectives by refusing it

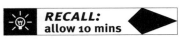

RECALL:
allow 10 mins

Give examples of industrial
policy having an impact on
business.

1. List four areas of
    business which industrial
    policy can affect.

2. Name one way in which
    liberalisation affected
    Mercury.

3. What method did the UK
    government use to attract
    investment by Nissan to
    the North-East?

4. Name one benefit
    privatisation gave to the
    management of British
    Airways.

5. How can OFTEL affect
    British Telecom's profits?

permission to acquire another firm in the same market; and an
increase in public investment on the roads could lead to a big rise in
sales and profits for construction companies.

The attitudes of business to industrial policy

The attitudes of business to industrial policy vary depending on how
their interests are affected. Firms view favourably policies which help
them to achieve objectives such as growth or profits and they are
unhappy with policies which hamper them.

Nissan and Samsung, for example, happily accepted government
grants to set up in the North-East (see Resource 1 at the back of the
book). Rival firms may see those grants as an unfair subsidy to already
very strong competitors.

Similarly, a firm facing a hostile take-over bid might be grateful for
competition policy that protects it from the predator. But the predator
firm may see merger policy as operating against its interests.

The rescue of a 'lame duck' firm by government may be welcomed by the firm itself, its suppliers and customers. Its competitors, on the other hand, might prefer to see their rival going bankrupt. They might then be able to buy the lame duck's factories cheaply and/or gain its customers, thereby increasing sales and market share.

Organisations that are dependent for a significant proportion of their business on contracts from the public sector, may have mixed feelings about the EU Directives on public procurement. They give UK firms more opportunities to compete abroad. But they result in more competition from abroad for UK government contracts.

As these arguments illustrate, it cannot be assumed that private industry is automatically hostile to industrial policy. In a survey of chief executives of the UK's largest 100 industrial companies, approximately 90 per cent of respondents felt that the government had no clearly defined industrial policy and that what stood for policy was not effective for UK industry. Senior managers desired the government to define an industrial policy, adopt an interventionist stance, raise the money to finance new investment through higher taxes on spending, and to invest heavily in the infrastructure (*Management Today*, May 1993).

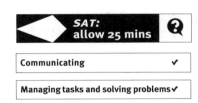

SAT:
allow 25 mins

Communicating   ✔

Managing tasks and solving problems ✔

ACTIVITY 2

Use the article from the *Financial Times* on Samsung locating in Wynyard, Cleveland (see Resource 1 at the back of the book) to help you complete this activity. You can also use the information in table 5.1.

	Average gross weekly earnings (full-time) (£) April 1992		Unemployment rate % (January 1993)
	Males	Females	
United Kingdom	340.1	241.1	10.8
Cleveland	320.7	223.3	15.4

Source: *Regional Trends*, 28, 1993.

TABLE 5.1: *Earnings and Unemployment 1992–93*

You are an employee in the information office of the local authority in Cleveland. The local authority asks you to write a press release to the local media on the 'good news'.

THE ATTITUDES OF BUSINESS TO
INDUSTRIAL POLICY

Write a 200-word press release which:

- **includes a brief description of the company and what it is going to do at Wynyard**

- **explains the important role played by central and local government, and the other regional organisations involved**

- **explains why it will be good for the economy and the residents of Cleveland.**

Summarise your findings in the box below

Commentary...

Here is a sample press release:

Samsung, the Korean manufacturing giant today announced plans to invest £450 million in building a new factory at Wynard in Cleveland. The scheme will eventually create 3,000 new jobs in the area, where unemployment is currently more than 40 per cent above the national average.

Initially, Samsung intends to produce 25,000 microwave ovens and more than 19,000 computer monitors every week at the site. Production facilities for making personal computers, facsimilie machines and semiconductors will be added in the future.

When the plant reaches full production in 1999, it will generate £1.2bn in turnover, about half of Samsung's total European sales.

John Bridge, chief executive of the Northern Development Company, said: 'This is a major boost for the area. Samsung has shown its faith in the local workforce. High quality skills and a good industrial relations record helped us win the deal for the North East.'

Samsung is to receive £58 million in government grants and loans from regional development funds. The plant is to be built on the new industrial zone, guaranteeing low-cost fixed business rates for five years.

The investment is expected to generate further new jobs in the area through investment by other companies in related areas such as plastic injection moulding, metal casing manufacture and wiring systems production. Construction firms and service suppliers will also benefit.

How organisations influence policy

Organisations are not simply the passive subjects of domestic government or EU policy. Big business has the power to prevent government achieving its economic objectives (in relation to employment, growth, inflation, and balance of payments). Business can increase prices so that inflation rises. It can reduce investment and cut the growth rate. It can relocate abroad causing an increase in the level of unemployment. So governments need to keep business sweet by maintaining economic and political conditions that allow profits to be made. They are often reluctant to create hostility in the profit-seeking business community. Governments listen to, and frequently canvass the views of, business on policy. Business organisations in this way are able to participate in the policy-making process through their influence on ministers, civil servants and members of parliament.

Industries dominated by a small number of large firms have a great potential to influence government policy. The bigger the firm, the easier it is to get direct and extensive contact with government ministers and senior civil servants. To quote the managing director of a large construction company:

> **It is not uncommon for ministers to send for the leaders of the larger companies to get their views. In this field it is the big boys who have the muscle and are therefore listened to by the government.**

(Grant & Marsh, *The CBI,* Hodder and Stoughton, 1977, p56)

**HOW ORGANISATIONS INFLUENCE
POLICY**

Industries characterised by large numbers of small and relatively powerless firms, on the other hand, are unlikely to be heard in Whitehall unless they band together to form an effective pressure group.

Organisations use a variety of methods to influence government policy. This influence can be used to:

- encourage the government to introduce a new policy

- bring about changes in a policy proposal at the consultation stage, for example, in response to a Green Paper

- change an existing policy.

Even if organisations fail in their attempts to reverse or to modify a policy significantly, they may still be able to gain important concessions.

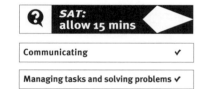

**SAT:
allow 15 mins**

| Communicating | ✓ |
| Managing tasks and solving problems | ✓ |

ACTIVITY 3

1. **List three reasons why governments are reluctant to cause hostility in the business community.**

2. **Explain in around 50 words why it is easier for big firms to influence government than small firms.**

3. **Explain how small firms might go about influencing government policy.**

Commentary...

Governments are reluctant to cause hostility in the business community because business could prevent their achieving:

- economic growth

- full employment

- a healthy balance of payments

- a low rate of inflation.

It is easier for big firms to influence government because they have much more economic power. If big firms decide to raise prices, cut investment, lay people off, import rather than export, they could make it very difficult for the government to achieve its objectives.

Small firms' decisions do not have the same macro-economic effects and so they are not so important for government.

Small firms need to band together in pressure groups in order to influence government.

Large organisations have the resources to influence policy on their own account. The alternative is to operate collectively through a trade association like the Engineering Employers' Federation, the Society of Motor Manufacturers and Traders, or bodies such as the Confederation of British Industry (CBI). The influence exerted by firms on policy is diluted when they do not speak with one voice – in other words, where they have not been able to identify a common set of priorities or where they have contradictory interests. Some commentators claim a division of interests between the finance sector and manufacturing industry. For example, the banks obtain more income when interest rates are raised but high interest rates increase manufacturers' costs and may cause a fall in demand for their products. In such circumstances, it would be surprising if the two sectors speak to the authorities with one voice. Another example is the small and medium-sized enterprise sector. They promote their views through a variety of different bodies such as the National Federation of Self-Employed and Small Businesses which has 50,000 members, the Forum of Private Business with over 17,000 members, the Association of Independent Businesses, the Union of Independent Companies, and the Small Business Bureau which is affiliated to the Conservative Party. As a result, the message received by government from the small firm sector is fragmented.

In addition to direct contact with ministers and civil servants, business organisations lobby MPs either through their own public relations departments or their trade associations. Bigger firms such as Cadbury Schweppes, Coca Cola, British Gas and British Steel often use the services of specialist lobbying organisations which monitor the parliamentary process for policy proposals and decisions likely to have an impact on their client's interests. They inform the client and advise on how best to influence political processes.

Many organisations pay MPs as advisers or consultants or offer them positions as a non-executive director. Nigel Lawson, who was Chancellor of the Exchequer, subsequently became a non-executive director of Barclays Bank. Norman Tebbit, another former minister, took non-executive directorships with British Telecom, Blue Arrow and became honorary adviser to the chairman of British Aerospace. Ex-ministers are not alone for many other MPs are also involved. In 1994, Sir Archibald Hamilton, a backbench conservative MP, held directorships in seven companies, was a consultant to five others, and provided services to a variety of others (table 5.2).

Registered interests of Sir Archibald Hamilton	
Paid directorships in:	Saladin Holdings (security sector)
	Woodgate Farms Dairy
	Siam Selective Growth Trust
	First Philippine Investment Trust
	James R. Glass (insurance brokers)
	Crownridge Industries (property developers)
	TPS Training and Project Services
Consultant to:	W. S. Atkins (engineering consultants)
	Merrill Lynch Europe (investment bankers)
	Litton Industries
	United States Defence Manufacturers
	Charles Barker (PR consultants)
Provides services for:	Customers of Charles Barker
	The Biscuit Cake Chocolate and Confectionary Alliance
	The British Videogram Association

Source: Register of Members' Interests, reproduced in *The Independent on Sunday*, 30 October 1994.

TABLE 5.2: *The registered interests of an MP*

ACTIVITY 4

Form into groups of four and complete the following tasks.

1. **Present the case for MPs having outside interests.**

2. **Present the case against MPs having outside interests.**

EXERCISE:
allow 30 mins

Managing and Developing Self ✓

Working with and relating to others ✓

Commentary...

Outside interests keep MPs in touch with the world of business and help them to support organisations they approve of. MPs gain a lot of useful information through these contacts. Some MPs argue that they need to supplement their parliamentary salary. It is also agreed that placing a ban on outside interests would deter many successful business professionals from entering politics

Outside interests raise the possibility of a conflict of interest. MPs may be given financial inducements to support various policies. They may be given biased information. Many argue that the democratic process should be above all suspicion of corruption. MPs are paid a good salary to repesent their constituents; that should be a full-time job.

Organisations may also provide MPs with free goods and services such as travel and accommodation. In 1994, Boeing, the giant US aerospace company paid for MPs to visit its manufacturing facilities in Philadelphia. Ford and 3M sponsored a trip to the USA for MPs connected with the Roads Campaign Council. British Gas took members of the Parliamentary Energy Group to Tunisia.

Advertising campaigns can also be used as an indirect method of influencing the political process although some firms use this approach only after others have failed. Thus the brewers ran, in part successfully, a £2 million campaign in the national press to dissuade the government from implementing the recommendations contained in the Monopolies and Mergers Commission Report of 1989.

Organisations can also attempt to influence the policy process by putting evidence to select committees and through representation on government advisory bodies and quasi autonomous non-governmental organisations (quangos). Quangos are non-elected public bodies operating outside the civil service but funded by the government. Their members are appointed by ministers. They include a wide range of bodies whose decisions could be important for many business organisations. Some examples of quangos are given below:

- the Development Agencies for Scotland and Wales
- the Urban Development Corporations
- the Arbitration Conciliation and Advisory Service (ACAS)
- the Health and Safety Commission
- the Training and Enterprise Councils (TECs)
- the National Health Trusts
- the Equal Opportunities Commission.

According to government figures there are about 1,400 quangos spending over £18 billion in 1994. (This spending is about three times higher than in 1979.) Other estimates, which include bodies such as National Health Trusts and TECs, put the number of quangos much higher at around 5,500, with 73,000 members appointed at the behest of the government, spending more than £46 billion of public money.

Another possible channel of influence arises when firms temporarily exchange managers for civil servants. This gives firms the opportunity to put the business point of view to civil servants and their ministers.

Finally, many firms make donations to political parties. The Conservative Party is the chief beneficiary of company donations to political parties (see table 5.3).

	£
United Biscuits	1,004,500
Hanson	852,000
Taylor Woodrow	837,362
British & Commonwealth	823,560
George Weston Holdings	820,000
P&O	727,000
Western United Investment	620,900
Glaxo	600,000
Trafalgar House	590,000

Source: The Guardian, 14 April 1994.

TABLE 5.3: *Major company donations to the Conservative Party, totals for 1979 to 1992*

Organisations justify their donations on the grounds that the Conservative Party is the only political party committed to providing a favourable economic and political environment for private enterprise.

The Nolan committee was set up to investigate MPs' outside interests, appointments to quangos and the like. Its first recommendations were being considered in Parliament in May 1995.

RECALL:
allow 10 mins

Name five ways in which business organisations can influence government policies.

summary

▶ Industrial policy has rarely been coherent, consistent or co-ordinated.

▶ There are disagreements between the political parties on industrial policy. The Conservative party tends to be less interventionist than the other parties.

▶ Industrial policy covers a wide variety of policy areas.

▶ Industrial policy affects an industry in many ways through industry structure, decision making, ownership and control and performance.

▶ The attitudes of business organisations towards industrial policy depends on how their industry will be affected by it.

▶ Business organisations have an influence on industrial policy and can have close links with politicians.

Environmental Factors Affecting Business Activities

Social stratification

Objectives

After participating in this session, you should be able to:

- interpret data describing social stratification and outline their significance for business

- describe the implications for business of the social structure in the UK

- describe the main social inequalities relating to gender and race and their importance to business

- explain the social position of older people and describe its significance for business.

In working through this session, you will practise the following BTEC common skills:

Managing and Developing Self	✔
Working with and Relating to others	✔
Communicating	✔
Managing Tasks and Solving Problems	✔
Applying Numeracy	✔
Applying Technology	
Applying Design and Creativity	

Occupations and income distribution

This session examines the social framework within which business operates. From our own experience we know that people differ from one another in all sorts of ways. We know that people come from different social backgrounds and that what they are like and how they behave is partly a matter of how they have been shaped by the society in which they live. For those working in business, an appreciation of this social framework is helpful in understanding:

- the problems encountered in managing the different kinds of people which make up a workforce

- the social factors which influence patterns of household consumption

- the importance of race, gender and age differences

- the kinds of life-styles which exist in our society

- the communities in which people live

- the aspirations people hold and the opportunities, constraints and problems that confront them in their everyday lives.

> **\?!** The term **social stratification** is used to describe the way in which societies are divided into a series of strata or layers.

In our kind of industrial society, these **strata** or layers involve economic differences. Some people have higher incomes and/or substantial wealth. Others have much lower incomes and often no wealth at all. Between these two extremes, many people have moderate incomes and small holdings of wealth, usually a house and some personal savings.

These strata are normally known as **classes**. A class consists of all those households in occupations at a similar level taking into account their income, skill, security and general standing in the community. Since occupation is currently seen as the basis of class, then the place we hold in the world of business is what places us in our particular location in the class system.

The system of social stratification in different societies can vary substantially.

- The stratification system can be 'open' or 'closed' as shown by the amount of **social mobility**, i.e. the movement of individuals between the classes. In an open system people are able to achieve the position that their energy and talents merit. In a closed system, the social positions people hold are largely fixed by their social background. (This is discussed more fully on page 180.)

- The class to which people belong may depend on individual achievement or it can come from being born into a particular class.

- Membership of a class may exercise a major or a small influence on the opportunities open to people.

- The system of stratification can be widely accepted or it can be the subject of serious political disagreement.

So far as social stratification in Britain is concerned, there is disagreement between experts on all these issues. One purpose of this session is to present the different viewpoints which are held so that you have a clear basis for formulating your own views.

Social stratification is an important feature of most societies. It is important to be aware that, even without studying the subject, we are likely to know a great deal about it – simply through being a member of a society. For example, if you look around you, you will notice social differences between people. Some people are more highly regarded than others; some are better educated; some dress more expensively, have more possessions and so on. People are different; and some of these differences are not genetically determined (they are not inborn) but are acquired through interaction with people and society.

Now look more closely at these differences. If men (and to a smaller extent women) are well educated, it is more likely that they will be in well-paid jobs, possess more goods, be respected by other people in society. That is to say, there are a cluster of characteristics that go together. Test this out for yourself in the following task.

ACTIVITY 1

Read the following description of one person, Mr Fotheringay-Smedley. Pick out the elements in the description which do not seem to belong and say why.

SAT:
allow 10 mins

Managing tasks and solving problems ✔

OCCUPATIONS AND INCOME
DISTRIBUTION

Mr Fotheringay-Smedley is a retired army officer, and is well respected by the other residents of his nearest village. He is a company director and a member of the Church of England. He votes Labour. He watches cricket, and attends Church every Easter. He runs a large farm and owns a flat in London. He is black. He reads *The Daily Telegraph* or *The Times*, keeps two large dogs and a horse. He drives a Range Rover. He is concerned about the well-being of travellers.

Commentary...

The way you answered this question depends not only on your experience of life, but also on the mental pictures or stereotypes you have formed from your experience, as well as pictures you have formed from information given by the media, your parents and teachers. Stereotypes may be inaccurate, but often they represent a summary of what people believe to be generally true of other groups of people.

You probably realised that most of the descriptions of Mr Fotheringay-Smedley – from his name to the kind of car he drives – describe a kind of person we call 'upper class'.

It is unusual that he votes Labour and very unusual that he is black. You would expect him to be less concerned about the well-being of gypsies and 'new age travellers' than he is about the well-being of his farm and life-style.

It is true that Mr Fotheringay-Smedley could read the *Sun* and drive a Mini, as well as answering most of the other descriptors. But social research into characteristics of people finds that there is a tendency for some factors to go together.

In our society the most common indicator of the class we belong to is our occupation. Occupations are used by government statisticians to divide the population into classes. The **Registrar General's classification** groups occupations into a six broad categories known as 'social classes'. This classification is used in official sources of data such as the Census or the General Household Survey. These are often used by businesses, e.g. to describe the kinds of people who purchase their products.

Occupational class	IPA	Men	Women	Total
I Professional occupations	AB	6.5	1.8	4.5
II Intermediate occupations	AB	26.2	26.5	26.3
III (N) Skilled occupations: non-manual	C1	10.5	37.5	22.0
III (M) Skilled occupations: manual	C2	30.7	6.9	20.5
IV Partly skilled occupations	D	14.7	16.1	15.3
V Unskilled occupations	E	5.1	7.0	5.9
Armed forces and inadequately described		3.5	2.1	5.5
Total		100.0	100.0	100.0
Total number		14.91m	11.14m	26.05m

Source: OPCS, (1993), *1991 Census*, Report for Great Britain, table 91, p417.

TABLE 1.1: *Occupational class structure, 1991 (percentages)*

Versions of the Registrar General's classification are also used by those providing information for business such as market researchers. The occupational categories used in the table are sometimes indicated on a scale A to E which was originally developed by the Institute of Practitioners in Advertising (IPA) for the purpose of classifying social groups for marketing purposes. The IPA classification is as follows:

AB   (professional and managerial)

C1   (white collar)

C2   (skilled manual workers)

D   (semi-skilled)

E   (unskilled and unemployed)

There are a number of reasons why it is convenient to measure social class in terms of occupation:

- it is linked to income

- it is linked to educational achievements

- it is related to life-styles and consumption patterns

- it is a handy measure for research.

Occupation is also a useful indicator of status. Status is the general esteem in which an occupation is held in the community. In most occupations, status and income are closely related. High status occupations also tend to have high incomes. There are some exceptions: nurses have high status but relatively low incomes; estate agents may have high incomes but a low status.

One major weakness involved in using occupation as an indicator of class is that about half the population does not have one. This includes those who:

- are too young to work

- are retired

- are unemployed

- are full-time housewives

- own substantial income-earning assets.

These problems are usually dealt with by assuming that all members of a household belong to the same class. Those people who do not have an occupation, such as children and some housewives, are assigned to the class of the main earner in their household. The unemployed and retired are usually classified as belonging to the class in which their former occupation would have put them.

INCOME DISTRIBUTION

The term **distribution of income** refers to the way in which incomes are allotted to the different groups in society. It is often measured by comparing the proportion of the national income going to particular groups in society. The bigger the difference, the greater the inequality in the distribution of income. The distribution of income affects business since it influences purchasing patterns and living standards.

Income inequalities are substantial with very large incomes at one end of the scale and people with almost no income at all at the other. There have been some changes in the distribution of pre-tax income in the last few decades. Inequalities have worsened with the poor losing out due to the high levels of unemployment. Despite examples of redundant professionals and executives, unemployment is closely related to social class and the unemployed are drawn disproportionately from those previously earning low wages.

Changes have been taking place in the sources of people's incomes. Since the mid-1970s, the proportion of national income paid out in wages and salaries has dropped from 69 per cent of all pre-tax income in 1975, to 60 per cent in 1985. Income from the ownership of wealth, such as renting property, investing and saving has risen. Income from benefits has also gone up, due mainly to rises in the numbers receiving unemployment benefit.

Tax cuts since the change of government in 1979 have favoured the rich. While income tax plus national insurance contributions increased for most wage and salary earners in the 1980s, they fell for high earners.

Fringe benefits produce further inequalities. Fringe benefits are economic benefits from employment which are not paid in the form of money, e.g. a company car, or free private health insurance. For those earning £50,000 a year or more, the taxable value of fringe benefits averaged £3,375 every year in the years 1979–87. Very high earners, including those in top executive jobs and company board members have also increased their salary levels. As a result, the top five per cent have increased their share of net income and there has been an increase in the number of poor people in Britain.

SAT:
allow 10 mins

Managing tasks and solving problems ✔

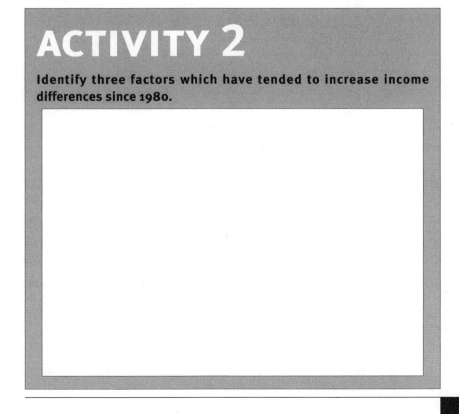

ACTIVITY 2

Identify three factors which have tended to increase income differences since 1980.

Commentary...

Below are some of factors you might have identified.

Tax changes have benefited the rich, particularly the reduction in the higher rates of income tax paid by very high earners. The shift to indirect taxation, e.g. VAT, has fallen more on the poor as a proportion of their income.

Increased unemployment from the decline in manufacturing has led to the loss of many working-class jobs. The unskilled, who had low incomes when in work, were also the most likely to become unemployed.

Fringe benefits have risen, but mainly for the relatively well-paid.

You may have raised some other points. Whatever you came up with, there is little doubt that the 1980s was a time of growing income inequality.

Class

Our knowledge of class comes firstly from our own experience. We learn early on in life that there are people who are our social equals – 'the same as us' – and others who may be higher or lower than us in the social scale. As we become more aware of our society through exposure to newspapers and television, we also develop an awareness of people living in social environments far from our own circumstances, though often our knowledge of them is based on stereotypes and distorted images.

The term **social stratification** is used as a shorthand to refer to the various classes and the relationships between them. Over time this structure can change as the composition and character of classes change. Over a longer historical period new classes can emerge and older classes may decline and even disappear. For example, as a result of the industrial revolution a new class of industrial workers and a new class of industrial capitalists emerged. Similarly, over a long period, the peasantry, a class of small independent landholders, has disappeared.

In modern Britain, it is usual and useful to identify three main classes – the working class, the middle class and the upper class. In order to give you an initial overall picture, their characteristics are summarised in figure 1.1.

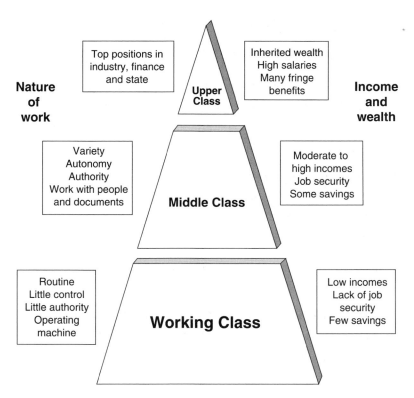

FIGURE 1.1: *Social stratification in Britain.*

THE WORKING CLASS

We are all familiar with the term 'working class' and we may hold images of the characteristics of its members, whether or not we belong to it. The working class principally comprises all employees and their families who normally carry out manual work whether this is skilled, semi-skilled or unskilled. In addition, we would also include routine non-manual workers such as clerks or secretaries, because their income and opportunities are generally similar to, or below those of skilled manual workers. Many routine non-manual workers are women who are often married to manual workers. However, some sociologists assign all 'white collar' workers to the middle class.

Most members of the working class are born into it and remain in it throughout their lives. The chances of moving out of the working class and into the middle class are greatest for the children of skilled manual workers and routine non-manual workers.

The jobs performed by working-class people are likely to have a number of distinguishing characteristics:

- ⦿ a high element of routine

- ⦿ little control by the worker over the pace and methods of work

- little authority exercised over others

- few educational requirements

- work involving operating a machine.

Those who perform these jobs are likely to have:

- low incomes

- few fringe benefits

- few educational qualifications

- a below-average chance of good health and a long life.

Members of a class have a tendency to hold similar views. Most people classified as working-class would describe themselves in this way. Many working-class people belong to trade unions and support the Labour Party. However, there are also important differences within the working class including:

- status differences between skilled and non-skilled workers (skilled workers may view themselves as superior)

- status differences based on race and ethnic background

- cultural divisions between people who live in different types of community (Northerners may look down on Southerners or vice versa)

- differences based on attitudes towards union membership

- differences resulting from the size of the firms in which people work (workers in some small firms may have a much closer identification with management than employees in large enterprises).

THE MIDDLE CLASS

The middle class, as its name suggests, refers to those found mid-way between the top and the bottom of the class structure. This is a very varied class and some authors refer to it in the plural as the 'middle classes' and go on to distinguish the different groups within it.

The middle class may be divided into three segments according to the source of income. Middle-class income may come from:

- fees for professional or other services or work performed

- profits from entrepreneurial activity

- salaries from managerial, administrative or professional employment.

Middle-class incomes are normally higher than those found in the working class. Most members of this class are born into it. Certainly most children of middle-class parents become members of the middle class as adults. However, because the class is expanding due to changes in the occupational structure and because of its relatively low average family size, the middle class also recruits members from the working and upper classes. Middle-class occupations are likely to have the following characteristics:

- some degree of autonomy

- some control over the pace and methods of work

- some authority in the workplace

- educational requirements

- work involving dealing with people and documents.

Educational levels vary, with the highest average levels found among the professionals, both salaried and self-employed. Doctors, lawyers, accountants and architects, all have to undergo a prolonged education to acquire the requisite professional knowledge.

The greatest range of incomes is found among the entrepreneurs and the self-employed. Some small-scale entrepreneurs and self-employed workers have very low incomes but stay in their line of work because they have no alternative or because they greatly value their independence. Within the middle class, the highest incomes are found among the entrepreneurs, although a few self-employed professionals, such as leading lawyers, may also be highly paid. The range of incomes of salaried employees is generally rather less.

Important differences in status also exist. The professions – occupations requiring a specialised academic training – tend to have a high status. Status is highest for members of the 'old' professions such as doctors or lawyers. The 'new' professions such as teachers, social workers and nurses have a moderately high status even if, as with nurses, the level of income is relatively low. Non-professional self-employed workers such as plumbers, tend to have a low status because of their association with manual work. Non-professional salaried employees such as general managers tend to have a status related to the size of their incomes as do entrepreneurs.

In view of the considerable diversity within this class, the members exhibit a surprisingly high degree of similarity in their political views, which are often Conservative. They are also likely to perceive themselves as middle-class. Self-employed professionals normally belong to professional associations as do some employed professionals and managers. Entrepreneurs often belong to trade associations of various kinds. Other members of the middle class may belong to trade unions. This is particularly true of public sector employees among whom larger numbers of non-Conservative voters are to be found.

? *SAT:* allow 15 mins

Managing tasks and solving problems ✔

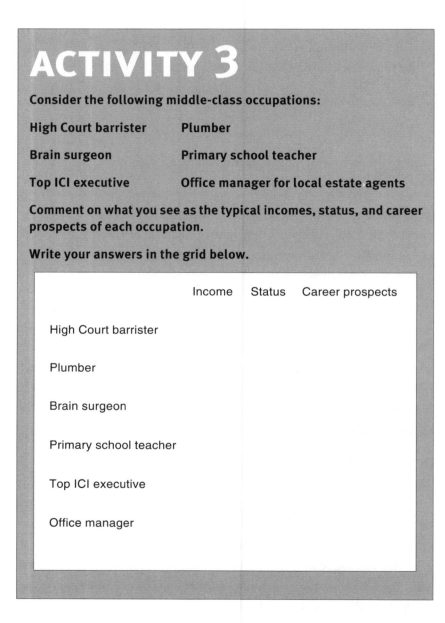

ACTIVITY 3

Consider the following middle-class occupations:

High Court barrister	**Plumber**
Brain surgeon	**Primary school teacher**
Top ICI executive	**Office manager for local estate agents**

Comment on what you see as the typical incomes, status, and career prospects of each occupation.

Write your answers in the grid below.

	Income	Status	Career prospects
High Court barrister			
Plumber			
Brain surgeon			
Primary school teacher			
Top ICI executive			
Office manager			

Commentary...

We filled in the grid as shown to show very clearly the range of circumstances found within the middle class.

	Income	Status	Career prospects
High Court barrister	High	High	Good
Plumber	Moderate	Low	Poor
Brain surgeon	High	High	Good
Primary school teacher	Moderate	Moderate	Moderate
Top ICI executive	Very high	High	Good
Office manager	Moderate	Moderate	Moderate

THE UPPER CLASS

Most of us have little direct experience of the upper class though we may have some knowledge of it through press and TV interest in the rich and the aristocracy. The upper class consists of those who own considerable wealth and who are therefore not substantially dependent on income from their own labour even though they may have a job.

The wealth owned may be land, housing, financial assets, industrial and commercial capital, or some combination of these. The upper class recruits new members from very high earners in top positions in business who accumulate substantial wealth. Full membership of this class, however, is not simply a matter of money but involves acquiring a particular life-style.

The majority of members of the upper class are born into it. This is particularly true of landowners, some of whom belong to families whose wealth has been established for centuries. A section of the hereditary aristocracy, which is largely found in this group, has special political privileges including membership of the House of Lords.

Members of the upper class share a number of characteristics. They tend to:

- have been educated at fee-paying schools

- marry members of the same class

- find work in a limited number of occupations

- hold Conservative political views.

An important minority of the very rich live solely from their income from property and adopt the life-styles of a leisure class. In this they are sometimes joined by top entertainers or sports stars. However, the majority of members enter business, the professions or the public service. Those who enter business tend to be found more in the financial sector than in manufacturing. Those who enter the professions and public service tend to be found in the church, the law, the armed forces and the civil service.

The upper class plays an important role in our society – certainly far more influential than their numbers alone would suggest. The majority of those in leading positions in business, commerce, finance, the church, the army and the judiciary are from upper-class backgrounds.

AN 'OPEN SOCIETY'?

> **!?!** A **meritocracy** is a society where leading positions are held on merit rather than on other grounds, such as possession of inherited wealth or belonging to well-connected families.

An issue which often arises in discussions of social stratification is the extent to which we live in an open society. This depends on the degree to which opportunities for social and economic advancement are available to all. This is best indicated through an assessment of the extent of social mobility. This is of crucial importance for business since it affects the kinds of people who will occupy positions of leadership and control. It also affects the career opportunities open to those from lower positions in the class structure.

Social mobility may be either horizontal or vertical. **Horizontal social mobility** implies a movement laterally within the same level such as a receptionist becoming a clerk. **Vertical social mobility** implies a movement up or down the stratification hierarchy such as a postal worker becoming a teacher. **Upward mobility** can be taken as a measure of the openness of a society with opportunities for individual achievement. However, high rates of upward mobility can also result from:

- the expansion of higher level occupations which increases the number of top jobs and the opportunity for upward mobility

- low fertility rates in higher social classes which increase opportunities for lower social groups to rise to fill higher level posts.

Whether or not Britain can be considered a meritocracy depends, in part, on whether the education system provides equality of opportunity for all. The evidence is that it does not and that children from better off homes have considerable advantages which enable them to enjoy a better education and to convert this into better career chances.

There is not much **downward social mobility**. This suggests that higher class people are able to pass on their advantages to their children. In particular, inherited wealth helps to transmit class membership from one generation to the next.

ACTIVITY 4

Form into groups of four and complete the following task.

It is often claimed that giving everyone a chance to improve themselves will benefit society as a whole by increasing economic prosperity. Give some reasons why high rates of upward social mobility might improve the efficiency of business.

Write up to 60 words.

EXERCISE: allow 15 mins

Working with and relating to others	✔
Communicating	✔
Managing tasks and solving problems	✔

Commentary...

Those with talents are not prevented from using them. Firms benefit through drawing on a greater range of talents and abilities. In general, people may be more ambitious and work harder knowing that opportunities are available for those able to perform well. Those who reach the top will be the best available and so should run things more efficiently.

Of course, there can be negative results as well. People may become over-competitive. Those who fail to advance may be disappointed. Selfishness may increase.

Women in society

The position of women in our society is changing.

- More women now enter the workforce, and many of the new jobs created in the last few decades have gone to women.

- In the view of some commentators, the workplace has been 'feminised'. Many employers put a high value on qualities believed to be more common among women. These include adaptability, dexterity and teamwork.

- There has been a change in women's values. Work and career have become more central. Traditional roles including that of wife and mother are no longer so popular. More women are choosing to establish their careers before starting a family.

- Women have gained more than a foothold in some professions where they were previously largely excluded.

PERSPECTIVES ON WOMEN

People hold very different views about the proper role of women (and men) in our society. Some of these views are described below.

Traditional view This rests on a 'traditional' view of the family. The proper role of women is to act as wives and mothers, rearing children and looking after the home. Since women's proper place is in the family, they should not be encouraged to have careers. Many feminists see this as a form of sexism as supporting forms of discrimination which put women at a disadvantage to men.

Modern view This view believes that women have been unfairly treated in the past and that further moves towards full equality with men are needed. Holders of this view believe that a combination of state action – making sex discrimination an offence, and the provision of facilities such as nurseries – can help women to achieve equality. Those who hold this view also emphasise how society as a whole will benefit from the increased participation of women in the labour force. This widens the pool of talent from which those occupying positions of leadership in business and government are drawn.

Radical left view This approach relates the position of women to the operation of the capitalist system. It claims that women perform 'domestic labour' (i.e. housework) which is essential to the continuation of capitalism. The work done by women in the home helps capitalism and the private businesses which make it up, by 'reproducing' labour power (i.e. feeding and caring for the current generation of workers).

Marxists also point out that women often have a distinctive place in the workforce. They form part of a 'reserve army of labour' helping to maintain flexibility in the use of labour. They are taken on by businesses during periods of labour shortage but when labour surpluses develop they are forced out of the workforce and back into the home.

WOMEN AND WORK

The proportion of women in the workforce has risen, with the increase in the number of working married women being particularly marked. Women now constitute 45 per cent of all employed people. However, their position in the labour force is distinctive.

- They are more likely to be in occupations where pay is low.

- They are often paid less than men in similar jobs.

- They are more likely than men to have a discontinuous or two-phase working life.

- They are most often found at the less skilled or junior levels within both manual and non-manual occupations.

- They are found mainly in a restricted range of occupations conventionally viewed as 'women's work' especially those which are the business equivalent of domestic tasks such as cooking, cleaning and caring for others.

● They are more likely to work part-time particularly if they have small children.

Spring 1987	Numbers employed		('000s)
	Full-time	Part-time	Total employed
Women with youngest dependent child:			
Under 5 years	299	697	1,000
5–9 years	255	731	988
10–15 years	487	865	1,354
Women without dependent children under 16 years	4,603	2,317	6,952
All women	5,634	4,610	10,294

Source: CSO (1990) *Social Trends*, p.72.

TABLE 1.2: *Part-time and full-time employment of women with and without dependent children*

In recent years, the barriers to women taking paid work have been reduced due to:

● the growth in employment in social services

● the increasing number of office jobs

● smaller families

● the availability of labour saving household devices

● changes in values emphasising women's rights and opportunities.

THE ROLE OF THE STATE

The state has played a part in improving the prospects for women in the workplace. In the 1970s, a number of Acts were passed which were designed to provide greater opportunities for women.

The Equal Pay Act (1970) came into force in 1975. It was designed to provide for equal pay for women if they did the same or like work as men. If a woman does not receive equal pay in such circumstances, she can take her case to an industrial tribunal. However, very few cases are upheld each year at tribunals and despite the legislation women's weekly earnings are still about 30 per cent less than men's.

The Sex Discrimination Act (1975) seeks to promote equal opportunities for women through outlawing both direct discrimination, where a woman is treated less favourably than a man because of her sex or marital status, and indirect discrimination, where a condition is imposed that more men than women can comply with, e.g. height or age limits.

From the end of July 1994, women have some maternity rights under the Trade Union Reform and Employment Rights Act (1993). All employees (including part-timers) are entitled to a minimum of 14 weeks' maternity leave, irrespective of their length of service or the number of hours they work. If they have been in a job for two years they are entitled to return to their job after a maximum of 40 weeks off to have a child.

SAT: allow 15 mins

Managing tasks and solving problems ✔

ACTIVITY 5

What economic, social and political changes have made it easier for women to obtain employment over the last 50 years? Write a few notes under each of the three headings:

- ◐ **Economic change**

- ◐ **Social change**

- ◐ **Political change**

Write about 60 words.

Commentary...

You may have some of these points and quite possibly some others as well. Putting them down all together like this gives you an idea of the substantial forces for change which are operating in our society.

- **Economic change:** growth of white-collar work, more part-time jobs, decline of heavy industry

- **Social change:** decline in support for traditional female role, rise of feminism, smaller families

- **Political change:** expansion of welfare state (more teaching, nursing and caring jobs), legislation to improve women's employment rights

Race

In social science, a **racial group** is one that is socially defined on the basis of physical characteristics, such as colour or facial appearance. An **ethnic group** is one which is defined on the basis of cultural criteria, such as language, diet, dress or accent or some other aspect of its life-style.

Racism involves a negative view of a group based on its perceived physical characteristics. Racism has deep and strong roots in British history. These go back at least as far as the slave trade where black people were treated as commodities to be bought, sold and worked for profit.

Ethnic group	GB	Percentage
White	51,843	
Black – Caribbean	499	
Black – African	207	
Black – Other	179	
Indian	841	
Pakistani	476	
Bangladeshi	160	
Chinese	158	
Other – Asian	197	
Other – Other	290	
All minorities	3,007	
Total population	54,860	

Source: Owen, 1993.

TABLE 1.3: *Ethnic group composition of the population in 1991 (thousands of persons)*

ACTIVITY 6

Complete table 1.3 by calculating the proportion of each group as a percentage of the population.

List some of the products for which a knowledge of ethnic groups would be useful for businesses marketing consumer goods and services.

SAT:
allow 20 mins

Managing tasks and solving problems ✔

Applying numeracy   ✔

Commentary...

Ethnic group	Percentage
White	94.50
Black – Caribbean	0.91
Black – African	0.38
Black – Other	0.33
Indian	1.53
Pakistani	0.87
Bangladeshi	0.29
Chinese	0.29
Other – Asian	0.36
Other – Other	0.53
All minorities	5.48

It is useful to remember that an ethnic group is one that is characterised by its distinctive life-style. So businesses marketing 'life-style products' might want to understand more about the purchasing patterns of different ethnic groups.

This is our list:

Food

Clothing

Kitchen utensils

Home furnishings

Newspapers and magazines

Holidays.

PERSPECTIVES ON RACE

Many people believe that race relations problems can be solved by carefully planned state action. Since the mid-1960s, British policy on race issues has been based mainly on this view. The key assumptions of this approach are as follows:

- **Discrimination,** in which a person is treated unfairly because of their race, is seen as the main problem.

- Discrimination is seen as based on **racial prejudice** which is an unthinking belief in the inferiority of people of a particular race.

- The roots of racism are the beliefs held by prejudiced people.

- Racism can be effectively combatted by education and legislation.

This view assumes that discrimination can, eventually, be overcome. The experiences of earlier immigrant groups, such as Irish and Jewish immigrants, who were initially rejected but are now largely accepted, are sometimes used as parallels.

Some people think that racism is rather more deep-rooted. They see racism built into the operation of major social institutions and organisations. They call this **institutional racism**. Racism is seen as more than just a matter of personal motivation. It has deep roots in the dominant culture: it is not an aberration. It can only be removed by radical policies. Those who hold this view emphasise the importance of actively 'challenging' racist behaviour and attitudes and of rigorous 'anti-racist' training.

WORK AND RACE

During the late 1940s and the 1950s, some sectors of British industry experienced labour shortages. To overcome these, and also perhaps to keep a cap on wages, the government encouraged large-scale immigration from Commonwealth countries such as Jamaica and India. Although a few blacks immigrants worked in medicine as professional and semi-professionals, the vast majority were concentrated in the least-sought-after, low-paid jobs in industries like textiles. Many members of ethnic minorities also worked in low-paid jobs in the public sector, e.g. in the health service and in public transport. The concentration of ethnic minority employees in particular occupations and areas of business produced what has been termed a 'racial division of labour'.

Most immigrants found it difficult to buy houses due to their low incomes. They also experienced difficulties obtaining council housing due to long waiting lists and to discrimination. As a result, many found themselves living in rented housing in inner city areas. This resulted in a concentration of people suffering from poor housing, poor jobs, high unemployment, discrimination in the allocation of housing, and sometimes police harassment.

Racism, in the form of prejudice and unequal treatment, increased during the late 1950s and 1960s. As the labour shortage of the early post-war decades eased, government began to restrict further immigration, starting with the Commonwealth Immigrants Act (1962). The main government response in the 1960s and 1970s was to legislate against open discrimination and to make some special provision for the children of immigrants in schools. The Race Relations Act (1976) legislated against discrimination in employment. However, although many appeals to the industrial tribunal have been made against discrimination, few of these applications have been upheld.

	White	West Indian/ Guyanese	Indian	Pakistani/ Bangladeshi
Men				
Non-manual occupations	48	32	59	40
Manual occupations	52	68	41	59
Women				
Non-manual occupations	68	63	62	64
Manual occupations	31	37	38	36

Source: Adapted from Amin, K. and Oppenheim, C., 1992, *Poverty in Black and White*, CPAG/Runnymede Trust, London.

TABLE 1.4: *Employment by occupation, ethnic origin and sex; average, Spring 1989–91: persons in employment aged 16 and over, GB, percentages*

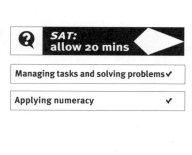

SAT: allow 20 mins	
Managing tasks and solving problems	✔
Applying numeracy	✔

ACTIVITY 7

Study table 1.4.

Does the data in the table confirm or contradict the opinion that there is discrimination in employment?

Which groups diverge most from the employment patterns of white people?

Quote figures from the table to support your view.

Write up to 80 words.

Commentary...

This is a difficult question because the data only gives a very broad overview with little detail. It gives no indication of relative unemployment rates.

It is not possible to be sure about the existence of discrimination on the grounds of either race or sex simply from the data in the table. The differences may simply represent differences in skill and educational levels. The table certainly shows that men with an ethnic background from the West Indies are more likely to be employed in manual occupations than their white co-patriots. However, Indians have a higher likelihood than whites of being in a non-manual job. There are more women than men in the non-manual category for all ethnic groups compared with whites. However, it is likely that most of these women are in relatively junior non-manual jobs.

The ethnic group which differs most from the white population in these general employment terms is the West Indians. The differences are greater for men than for women. Indeed a feature of the table is the similarity of the position of women in all groups.

Age

Another social factor that we have to recognise is age. In all societies, people are treated differently according to their age.

> **\?/   Ageism** is a form of prejudice linked to discrimination on the basis of age. It occurs when an age group is treated less favourably than others.

In modern Britain, ageism is most commonly viewed as affecting the old, though it can be experienced by other age groups as well. Older people form an important group in our society. The proportion of people in the over-65 age group rose from 5 per cent in 1901 to 16 per cent by the end of the 1980s. Old age also represents a significant social division.

Misunderstanding between the generations can be a source of tension in families and at the workplace. Old and young people do not mix very much except where they are members of the same family. Elderly people may sometimes unfavourably contrast the views and behaviour of young people with those current when they were young. The young may see the old as out of touch and living in the past.

Old people constitute a distinctive group.

- Their life-style may be restricted in scope.

- They are largely excluded from the world of work.

- Many activities are closed to them for economic reasons.

- They require high levels of state financial support through pensions.

- They have above-average requirements for health care.

However, while old people have these things in common, they also differ substantially, especially in terms of their incomes. The inequalities of social class are magnified after retirement since those who had high earnings when in employment tend to have disproportionately high pensions.

There is plenty of evidence of ageism. Older people do not have a positive image in our society. Negative stereotypes abound and old people can justifiably claim that in some areas they are treated unfairly. However, there are some special provisions made for the old including concessionary fares on public transport and admission to some entertainment facilities at a reduced price. At the same time, many old people suffer poverty, poor housing, a limited diet, ill-health and lead very restricted lives with few treats or luxuries.

There are differing views on how to account for the position of old people in our society. Some authors believe that the old are not discriminated against. They see old age as a gradual process of voluntary withdrawal from life. However, critics of this view would argue that the reduced social participation of old people is more likely to result from their deliberate exclusion from normal social and economic opportunities rather than from choice.

Others claim that the unfair treatment of old people takes place because they do not have a permanent place in the labour force. They will be called on to work only when labour is in short supply. In these periods, they are likely to be viewed favourably. They may be viewed as exercising a 'steadying influence' over younger workers. Conversely, when there are not enough jobs to go round, the old may be pushed out of the workforce through schemes for early retirement.

In these circumstances, they are likely to be portrayed as 'keeping younger people out of a job'.

'Retirement' in the sense of a final and permanent withdrawal from the labour force is now the normal situation for the old. Before the Second World War, the majority of men over 65 years old still worked. Even by 1951, the proportion of men over 65 still in work was 31 per cent. During the relative labour shortages of the 1950s, little attempt was made to discourage older workers from finding employment.

However, unemployment began to increase substantially in the mid-1960s and older workers were disproportionately affected. From 1967, their rate of unemployment has been rising above the average for all workers and their prospects for part-time work have almost disappeared. State policy has accelerated this withdrawal from the labour force through:

- the Redundancy Payments Act (1965), which increased inducements to older workers to leave their jobs

- the encouragement of additional provision of severance pay for redundant workers

- early retirement schemes, especially in the state sector

- the use of the 'earnings rule' for those over pension age – whereby pensioners returning to work had their earnings over a certain limit deducted from their pensions.

It is worth pointing out that while ageism is most strongly experienced by the old, it can also affect the middle-aged. In periods of reduced employment opportunities, the middle-aged may also suffer from discrimination and a negative social image. Especially in times of rapid social and technological change, the middle-aged may be viewed as possessing skills which are out of date. In addition, they may be seen as unable to adapt to new circumstances as easily as younger people. The phrase 'too old at 40' expresses this well. The denial of opportunities and the bestowal of a negative image appear to be recurrent features of the ways we treat some age groups.

FAMILIES AND HOUSEHOLDS

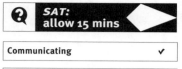

Communicating ✓

Managing tasks and solving problems ✓

ACTIVITY 8

What are the implications for business of the growing numbers of old people in society?

Write up to 100 words.

Summarise your findings in the box below.

Commentary...

The existence of a larger number of old people could affect businesses in a range of ways:

- higher costs – businesses may have to pay higher taxes to finance pensions and health care programmes

- new markets – there will be opportunities to produce goods and services specifically for older people

- new source of labour – firms may choose to employ older people – perhaps on a part-time basis – to meet their labour needs.

Families and households

The family is the major social unit in our society. Families, or at least some members of them, normally live together in a household. The household is of great economic significance. It is obviously a key element in consumption since many goods are purchased on behalf of, and consumed by, a family. Businesses need to take account of the different kinds of household that exist because this affects patterns of consumption as well as people's availability for work.

The family also plays a vital role in supporting business. It is within families that the existing generation of workers is fed, clothed, housed, and generally kept in a condition for the daily demands of work. It is also within the family that the next generation of workers is brought up, though of course other institutions, such as schools, play an important part here.

Our image of the typical family and household is often based on the stereotype of mum, who is a housewife, and dad, who works full-time, along with 2.3 children. However, in reality, many families and many households diverge from this pattern.

Great Britain	Percentages				
	1961	1971	1981	1991	1992
Living alone	3.9	6.3	8.0	10.7	11.1
Married couple, no children	17.8	19.3	19.5	23.0	23.4
Married couple with dependent children	52.2	51.7	47.4	41.1	39.9
Married couple with non-dependent children only	11.6	10.0	10.3	10.8	10.9
Lone parent with dependent children	2.5	3.5	5.8	10.0	10.1
Other households	2.0	9.2	9.0	4.3	4.6
All people in private households (= 100%) ('000s)	49,545	52,347	52,760	54,056	NA

TABLE 1.5: *People in households: by type of household and family in which they live*

The figures in table 1.5 show the proportions of the population in a range of types of household (not the percentage of different types of household).

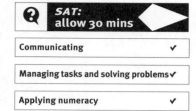

Communicating ✔

Managing tasks and solving problems ✔

Applying numeracy ✔

ACTIVITY 9

Study table 1.5. Identify three significant trends of change in the distribution of people between different types of household since 1961.

Write up to 50 words.

Assess the impact of changes in household structure over the last two decades on the demand for (a) housing, and (b) child care.

Write up to 100 words.

Use a separate sheet of paper to record your answers. Summarise your findings in the box below.

Commentary...

There have certainly been some significant changes over this period, as the figures indicate. The main trends of change in the distribution of household types since 1961 involve:

- a big increase in the number of people living alone

- a big increase in the number of single parent families

- a significant decline in the proportion of households conforming to the traditional pattern of two parents and dependent children.

Assessing the impact of these changes is rather speculative. However, the various changes affecting families with children evidently do have, and will probably continue to have, an influence on the kinds of housing and child care services ideally required.

(a) Housing – the increase in the number of people living alone may require more small housing units. The large number of relatively poor single-parent families require plenty of cheap family homes.

(b) Child care – the large and growing numbers of married women going out to work suggest a need for more child care. Similarly, the single parents may also have a need for child care but are probably in even less of a position to pay for it than the married couples.

ACTIVITY 10

Write a short report highlighting the possible implications for your employer of the changes that have taken place in the position of women over the last 20 years in:

(a) employment

(b) the social attitudes women face

(c) their legal rights

(d) household structure

(e) the demands of household labour.

Use a separate sheet of paper to record your answer. Summarise your findings in the box below.

**ASSIGNMENT:
allow 2 hours**

Managing and Developing Self	✔
Communicating	✔
Managing tasks and solving problems	✔

summary

▶ Social class inequalities are an important feature of British society which have a major impact on business.

▶ Important differences in income, wealth and status exist between the three main classes. These have an impact on the problems of managing the workforce and on consumption.

▶ Social inequalities of gender and race play a role in British society and affect work and consumption and their importance.

▶ The fact that Britain does not possess a fully 'open' society affects the quality of business management and can create problems in recruiting high-quality employees.

▶ Household and family patterns are changing in modern Britain and businesses have to adjust to this in marketing, management of the workforce and employment of labour.

▶ The social position of older people has implications for business.

Social welfare and state policy

Objectives

After participating in this session, you should be able to:

▶ interpret and summarise data dealing with the impact of state welfare policies on living standards, consumption and opportunities

▶ describe the organisational framework used in the delivery of social policies and show how it relates to business organisation

▶ give an account of different views of the impact of state welfare provision on the operation of business

▶ assess the extent of income redistribution and its significance for business

▶ explain the factors responsible for shifts in social policy and assess their implications for business.

In working through this session, you will practise the following BTEC common skills:

Managing and Developing Self	✔
Working with and Relating to others	✔
Communicating	✔
Managing Tasks and Solving Problems	✔
Applying Numeracy	✔
Applying Technology	
Applying Design and Creativity	

The welfare state

In our society, the state intervenes in all sorts of ways and this affects how well off we are. It requires us to pay taxes on our incomes and on much of our expenditure. It may subsidise some of the things on which we spend our money, such as housing (through tax relief on mortgage interest payments). It provides us with a range of cash benefits if we are unemployed or sick or retired. It provides us with services such as schooling and medical care. So far as business is concerned, the activities of the state in these areas have important implications for people in their roles as producers, consumers and citizens.

The ways in which business is affected by state welfare provision are often quite complicated. In Britain, child benefit is a weekly payment made to each family with school-age children. It is easy to see how a cut in child benefit affects families; however, it can also affect businesses. Employers often support cuts in government spending hoping for lower personal and corporation taxes. However, a cut in child benefit can increase demands for higher wages because of poverty among employees with larger families. Child benefits therefore might be a way of reducing pressure for higher wages. In addition, where family incomes are cut and their spending is reduced a company's goods and services are harder to sell and businesses suffer.

Businesses can be directly affected by changes in welfare provision and social policy:

- The efficiency and the loyalty of members of the labour force may be altered by social legislation affecting social benefits, wages and job security.

- Patterns of consumption may shift because of the redistribution of income and wealth.

- The social damage caused by poverty and crime may affect business and citizens alike.

This session looks closely at many of the ways in which government actions in the field of welfare affect business.

\?/ The term **welfare state** is used to describe an extensive system of state organised provision in the areas of:

- social security (cash benefits)
- education
- subsidies for housing
- health and welfare services.

SAT:
allow 10 mins

Managing tasks and solving problems✔

ACTIVITY 1

Explain how business might benefit from state-spending designed to:

- ensure incomes high enough to avoid extreme poverty
- improve housing standards
- provide workers with medical care when they are ill.

Write up to 60 words.

Commentary...

Adequate incomes might reduce conflict at work and increase working efficiency. Better housing standards might lead to a healthier workforce. Medical care for workers should reduce absence due to illness. Workers should feel more secure knowing that medical care is available when required.

Social security

> **\?/** The **social security system** organises the payment of cash benefits to individuals. These are usually paid to meet particular 'needs' such as sickness, unemployment or retirement.

The social security system which operated in Britain until the 1970s was established in 1948 on the basis of proposals formulated in the Beveridge Report (1942). Beveridge was a moderate reformer who wished to support private-sector business. He believed that free markets were desirable but that they could have undesirable side-effects. Beveridge wished to abolish 'want', i.e. poverty. He wished to increase business efficiency without undermining private ownership and individual responsibility. Central features of his scheme were designed to do this.

- The insurance principle, under which workers made contributions which helped to pay for their benefits, would reinforce the idea of self-help.

- Contributions by employers and the state would symbolise concern for employee welfare.

- Subsistence-level benefits would maintain work incentives and encourage thrift and private provision.

- Income redistribution from the better off to the poor would be kept to a minimum.

THE SHIFT TO NEW-RIGHT POLICIES

A substantial shift away from the principles of the Beveridge scheme started in the mid-1970s. This was in line with the growing influence of the ideas of the new right. The new right argued that welfare spending led to excessive taxation on businesses which reduced profitability. Business also suffered because the high levels of taxation necessary to pay for social services reduced personal incentives. As a result, economic and business efficiency was reduced. The solution was to reduce the volume of state intervention and to cut taxation.

New-right ideas began to influence policy as a result of a financial crisis in 1976. The Labour government responded to this by introducing wide-ranging expenditure cuts. These policies were continued and intensified after the Conservatives, under Mrs Thatcher, were elected in 1979.

During the 1980s, social security spending rose due to high unemployment. In an attempt to keep costs down, the government introduced a number of changes.

- The Social Security Act (1980) substantially reduced the scope for discretionary payments, leaving many claimants worse off.

- The earning-related supplement to sickness and unemployment benefits was abolished in 1981. The benefit system was also modified to penalise those involved in strikes.

- Payments to the unemployed were made subject to tax in 1982.

- In 1982, housing benefit was introduced to bring together under one scheme rent rebates, rent allowances and rate rebates. Council tenants have their rent and rates paid direct to their council's housing department by the Department of Social Security.

- The real value of child benefit was reduced because its annual increase was often below the rate of inflation.

- The Social Security Act (1988) introduced a range of new means-tested benefits. **Family credit** was used to provide regular payments to low income families with children. The **social fund** grant and loan system was employed for one-off payments for items such as furniture, clothing or a cooker. However, the government set 'cash limits' on the total amount to be paid out and in 1993–94 over 200,000 grant applications and a million loan applications were turned down solely due to lack of funds.

- The cost of the state earnings-related pension scheme (SERPS) was cut by giving a national insurance rebate to those transferring to private 'personal pensions'.

SOCIAL SECURITY

SAT:
allow 10 mins

Managing tasks and solving problems ✔

ACTIVITY 2

List two groups which have gained and two which have lost as a result of changes in social security policies over the last 15 years. Briefly mention any possible implications for business.

Write up to 50 words.

Commentary...

In our suggested answer, the implications for business are given after the dash.

Gainers:

Top income earners – they have greater incentives to work hard because of lower taxes.

Some low-wage earners – family credit allows the poor to go on spending.

Losers:

The unemployed – their benefits have been cut and so they have less to spend. High unemployment keeps wage levels down.

Large families – cuts in the value of child benefit reduce family spending.

Education

Another important area of social policy is education. Education is of crucial importance to business because it has a major impact on the skills and knowledge of employees. It also affects attitudes to work and the aspirations people hold about their careers.

State education dates from 1870. For working-class children, the state set up schools designed to do little more than habituate children to obedience and provide them with basic literacy and numeracy. By the early twentieth century, schooling up to the age of 13 was free and compulsory. Some middle-class children attended independent day grammar schools, while upper-class children were educated in the 'public schools' which were private fee-charging boarding schools.

Under the Education Act (1944), all children received compulsory secondary education until the age of 15. The Ministry of Education promoted a system of 'grammar', 'technical' and 'secondary modern' schools. Grammar schools were for those who would enter administrative or managerial jobs, technical schools for those who would enter skilled manual or technical occupations and secondary modern schools were for those who were destined to be semi-skilled or unskilled workers.

From 1944 to the mid-1970s, there was strong support for educational expansion from voters, political parties and business. Many people saw education as a means of creating equality of opportunity with a chance for all children to develop their capabilities through schooling. Business would benefit because educational expenditure and economic growth were seen as linked.

CONCERNS ABOUT EDUCATION

During the 1960s, there was concern about a number of educational issues many of which were linked to what was coming to be recognised as the relatively poor performance of British business compared to competing nations:

- a possible inability of business to meet the challenge of advanced technology because of the relatively low level of technical education compared to some competitor countries, such as Germany

- the wastage of ability caused by lack of opportunity for the many bright working-class children who, it was felt, achieved far less educationally than they might.

The problem was seen by many to lie with the system of 'selective' grammar, technical and secondary modern schools. At age 11, children were given an exam ('the 11+') and allocated to one of the three types of school on the basis of their results.

Comprehensive schooling appeared to offer a solution to these problems. These schools would be comprehensive in the sense of taking all children regardless of ability. The Labour government encouraged the comprehensive system from 1965 and legislative compulsion was used in 1976.

Higher education was also increasingly viewed as a means of developing the high level of scientific and technical skills needed by an advanced economy. In the 1960s:

- new universities were established

- some existing colleges of advanced technology were given university status

- polytechnics were set up.

However, in the mid-1970s, the education system increasingly came under criticism. A 'great debate' on education was launched by the Labour government of the time. It focused on issues raised by new-right critics of the state education system. The main concerns were: the curriculum, educational standards, teacher competence, progressive teaching methods and the effectiveness of schooling as a preparation for working life.

The Conservative government elected in 1979 brought in further significant changes. The Education Act (1980) required local education authorities (LEAs) to allow parents to state a preference for the school their child would attend. An assisted-places scheme was established to finance attendance at independent day schools, and provision was made for parents and teachers to be represented on school governing bodies.

THE EDUCATION REFORM ACT (1988)

The Education Reform Act (1988) passed by the Conservative government, was the most fundamental change to the education system since 1944. Its provisions were based on new-right ideas about the best way to run state services. There was to be an emphasis on business methods and managerial skills for headteachers and others making decisions in education. In addition, schools were to be forced to operate as if they were businesses competing in market through establishing a **'provider market'**.

A provider market exists where the suppliers of a public service are subjected to market 'disciplines' by having their revenues determined by the 'demand' for their services from consumers. In theory, they have to provide what the purchasers want or they will run short of funds and have to reduce the scale of their operations. Since this 'market' may not involve individual private consumers and producers, it is sometimes also known as a **'quasi market'**.

Parental choice of schools was introduced to force schools to compete for pupils. The income of the school was made to depend on the number of pupils recruited. Supporters of the market see competition between schools as a way to increase standards. Good schools will get more pupils (and more income) and expand, and poor schools will contract or even close.

In order to encourage a more business-like approach, the Act introduced a system known as **local management of schools (LMS)**. This involved a system of delegated budgets from the local education authority (LEA). Schools were run by governing bodies who were seen as the equivalent of a board of directors of a private business. LEAs have to delegate funds to the school on an agreed formula, mainly based on numbers and ages of pupils. Governing bodies can shop around for services such as school meals or cleaning, which were formerly provided by the LEA.

Competition is also encouraged by allowing schools to opt out of LEA control and become 'grant maintained', receiving funds directly from the government. These schools appear to be more generously funded than those run by the LEAs. The government has also encouraged the establishment of schools known as 'City Technology Colleges' (CTCs).

Government now controls what is taught in schools through the Schools Curriculum and Assessment Authority. A national system of regular testing has been introduced with the national curriculum. Schools are required to publish the results so that parents can evaluate how well they are performing.

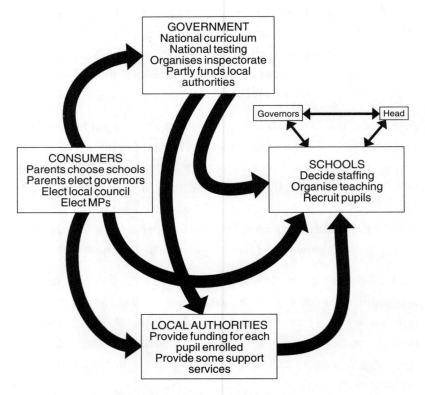

FIGURE 2.1: *How schooling is run.*

POLICY AND EDUCATIONAL INEQUALITY

The best education in terms of access to higher education is still generally obtained by those from the higher social classes. The relative difference in the rates of university entrance between the top and the bottom classes has remained remarkably constant. The overall level of educational achievement is closely related to the occupational class of the child's family. As table 2.1 shows, working-class people have few educational qualifications and a majority of unskilled and semi-skilled workers have none. The introduction of GCSE, however, has meant that a higher number of working-class children gain some qualifications at school.

| | Class | | | | | | |
	I	II	IIIa	IIIb	IV	V	All
Degree	32	17	17	6	4	3	10
Higher education	19	15	18	10	7	5	11
GCE A level	15	13	12	8	6	4	9
GCSE, grades A–C	19	24	25	21	19	15	21
GCSE, grades D–G	4	9	7	12	12	10	10
Foreign	4	4	4	3	2	2	3
No qualifications	7	19	18	40	50	60	35
	100	100	100	100	100	100	100

Source: CSO (1994) *Social Trends*, 24, HMSO, table 3.22.

TABLE 2.1: *Persons aged 25–59, not in full-time education (in Great Britain, 1990–91): highest qualification held, percentages by socio-economic group of father*

ACTIVITY 3

One of the aims of comprehensive education was to reduce the inequalities in educational achievement between the different social groups. How far has this been successful?

Table 2.1 presents data for 1990–91 of the qualifications obtained by adults and provides an answer to that question.

Study the table and answer the following questions:

1. The population represented in the table has been divided into six groups. Which two groups have the most similar educational qualifications?

2. Fill in the following table:

	Class I	Class V
Degree		
No qualifications		

3. Look at the table you have just completed. Write down the main single point that you conclude from it.

4. There are different possible explanations for the conclusion you have just reached. The moderate left for example would offer different explanations from those of the new right. Write down three different possible explanations for your conclusion.

5. Which of these explanations do you prefer, personally?

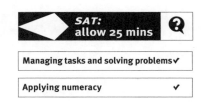

SAT:
allow 25 mins

Managing tasks and solving problems ✔

Applying numeracy ✔

Commentary...

Classes II and IIIa are most similar. Look, for example, at the proportion getting degrees. In both of II and IIIa, the proportion achieving a degree is 17 per cent (similarly with other qualifications).

	Class I	Class V
Degree	32	3
No qualifications	7	60

This table demonstrates that there is a high difference in educational achievement between Class I and Class V. Here are three different explanations sometimes offered for this difference.

- Class V children are genetically inferior to the other groups and, on average, have lower intelligence. Hence they are unable to profit from equal educational opportunities.

- Class V children are held back because they do not have a fair chance in life. Class V go to schools in areas which often cannot attract the best teachers. The schools may be run-down and serve an area with high unemployment and poor housing. Class I children often go to fee-paying public schools which are better resourced.

- Class V children are not encouraged at home, or by the culture of the areas they live in, to take education seriously.

You may have come up with different explanations. That is not surprising, since this is a highly contentious issue.

There has been constantly rising educational attainment as measured by the examination passes throughout the twentieth century. According to government statistics, this continued after the abolition of selective schooling and its replacement by comprehensives. Class inequalities, however, have not significantly declined. There are several reasons for this.

- Home background and what is sometimes called 'cultural capital' (the support for learning in the home and the knowledge and capabilities of parents) remains a major influence on educational achievement.

- Comprehensive schooling often involves differences in the education given to different pupils with systems of banding and streaming in which working-class children may sometimes be placed in lower streams than middle-class children of the same ability.

- The differences which exist between comprehensive schools which reflect social differences in their catchment areas, are substantial.

- Sometimes businesses subsidise private school fees for the children of senior managers and board members.

- The government's 'assisted-places scheme' for children going to fee-paying schools mainly benefits middle-class children.

Health services

Another major area of welfare provision is the health services. From the early twentieth century, the health of the workforce has been a concern of business. Health provision developed piecemeal throughout the first half of the century. This culminated in the creation of the National Health Service (NHS). This was the first major reform of the Labour government elected in 1945. It provided a universal and free system of health care covering hospital medicine and general practice. For business and the economy, it meant that a great deal of previously untreated illness was now given medical attention helping to produce a healthier workforce.

CHANGES SINCE 1979

Since the election of the Conservative government in 1979, it has been policy to subject the public sector to competition with private business where possible. Competition has been created by the use of **compulsory competitive tendering** (CCT) and **'contracting out'**. Hospitals have to allow business to bid for contracts to carry services such as catering, cleaning and laundry.

The government also attempted to introduce business methods into the running of the NHS. In 1983, the government set up an NHS management enquiry carried out by Griffiths, a senior executive of the grocery retailer, Sainsbury's. The Griffiths Report sought to restrict the power of doctors in the NHS by:

- bringing in general managers from business

- increasing the powers of management and reducing those of doctors

- introducing devolved financial control procedures so that managers at all levels had financial control over their operations.

However, the main recent reform of the NHS was undertaken on the basis of proposals published in *Working for Patients* in 1989. The proposals were in line with new-right ideas on how to modify the operation of the public sector so that it operated with some of the characteristics of a free market. The NHS was to be run using a **provider market**. A feature of this particular 'quasi market' is that the consumers are not the people, i.e. the patients, who actually receive the service, but health authorities and GPs who act on their behalf.

Many hospitals have gained 'trust' status and operate in part as independent businesses. District health authorities (DHAs) and **fundholding GPs** purchase services from the hospital which offers the best value for money. Fundholding GPs have their own budgets and can seek to manage them to make a surplus rather like an independent business. Services can also be purchased from private hospitals.

The changes made in the health services since 1988 represent a major shift in policy. Central control is retained but the NHS now contains a mass of separate units each with a degree of independence. These units can adjust their activities to market pressures.

ACTIVITY 4

SAT:
allow 10 mins

Managing tasks and solving problems ✔

What type of market operator in the National Health Service? Is it a free market or a quasi market? Explain briefly how it works.

Write up to 100 words.

Summarise your findings in the box below.

Commentary...

The National Health Service operates a quasi market rather than a real free market where the forces of supply and demand are unrestricted. Hospitals, for example, are not at liberty to abandon treating patients and move into a completely new area of business.

On the demand side:

- ◉ patients choose GPs
- ◉ GPs choose hospitals for patients

- district health authorities (DHAs) contract with hospitals to supply medical services of a given quality at a specified price.

On the supply side:

- trust hospitals choose which services they wish to supply and set a price for their services

- hospitals supply medical services to DHAs and GPs

- GPs supply services to patients on their list.

The future of the NHS?

There is currently a debate taking place on whether the provider market will lead to the destruction of the NHS as some on the new right would wish. Current policies are certainly designed to stimulate private provision and this is already taking place. Critics claim that private acute hospitals undermine the NHS because they provide a way of avoiding queues for services and offer better amenities to those that can afford to pay.

Whether or not the expansion of the private health business continues, the result is likely to be a two-tier system in which the private sector looks after those able to pay and the NHS deal with the remainder. This is similar to the pattern which is developing in public housing and, to a lesser extent, in secondary education.

The NHS has a special status in British political debate. Because of its political importance, even its opponents are wary of being seen to threaten its existence directly. Opponents of the NHS are attempting to replace the idea of collective and publicly financed provision of health care with an approach based on personal responsibility, private insurance and payment. The Patients' Charter, with its emphasis on individual rights to certain standards of treatment, emphasises the idea of the patient as a consumer.

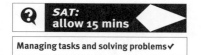

SAT:
allow 15 mins

Managing tasks and solving problems ✔

ACTIVITY 5

Describe three ways in which business methods and ideas are being used in the NHS?

Write up to 50 words.

Commentary...

Here are some of the points you could make. You may have been able to think of others.

- GPs can become 'fundholders' and operate like independent businesses.

- The NHS now has professional managers.

- There is competition between trust hospitals.

- Hospitals have to bid to DHAs for contracts to provide medical care.

Housing

Housing plays an important role in the workings of business and the economy:

- It provides shelter for members of the workforce. If it is inadequate, people's health and their capacity to work can be damaged. Poor housing can also affect the health of the next generation of workers.

- Housing also plays a key role in the mobility of the labour force. If workers are to respond to changes in the geographical demand for labour then they must be able to obtain housing in order to move to areas where there are available jobs.

PUBLIC SECTOR HOUSING

Subsidised local authority housing (council homes) was first built under the Housing and Town Planning Act (1919). In the 1930s, the practice of building council homes in massive estates was established and flats became popular in cities. In the inter-war period, 28 per cent of all new house building was of council homes.

During the Second World War, over 3.5 million dwellings were damaged and 475,000 destroyed. At the end of the war an extensive housing programme was undertaken and over 800,000 council houses were completed between 1945 and 1951. Relatively high levels of council building continued. Between 1951 and 1976, the percentage of households living in unfit or substandard houses, suffering overcrowding or sharing accommodation fell from 69 per cent to 15 per cent. Housing standards improved – at least as measured by possession of an inside toilet and a bathroom. However, during the 1960s, many high-rise flats were built; these were not suitable for many families because they lacked gardens and secure outside play space for children.

POLICY CHANGES IN THE 1980S

Housing policy has shifted very substantially in the 1980s. The council housing sector has reduced in size and owner occupation greatly increased. The Housing Act (1980) introduced a number of changes:

- incentives for council-house sales

- an increase in council-house rents

- improved statutory rights for tenants.

Council house building was cut, with only 21,000 started in 1981. Private rents increased. Between 1981 and 1993, 1.5 million council houses were sold, often at subsidised prices. The proportion of council dwellings in Great Britain fell from a peak of 31 per cent of the housing stock in 1976 to 21 per cent in 1992. Housing Associations now have an important role in providing housing for rent. Housing associations are non-profit making bodies which build housing with the aid of a government subsidy.

The boom in house prices in the 1980s encouraged council house sales since the purchase of housing appeared to provide the chance of an untaxed capital gain. The subsequent reduction in many house values led to serious problems. Many house buyers found themselves with 'negative equity' in that their houses were worth less than their mortgage debt. This made it very difficult for them to move since they could not pay off their mortgage debt.

In the period 1990–95, around 300,000 people who had purchased council houses had them re-possessed because they failed to keep up with the mortgage payments.

This problem was exacerbated by job losses in the recession in the early 1990s.

THE IMPORTANCE OF HOUSING TO BUSINESS

The kind of housing people occupy is of interest to many areas of business since it has an important effect on consumption patterns. For example, renters are unlikely to spend much on house improvements. The housing of workers is also of importance. Labour mobility is restricted if housing stock is of the wrong sort and in the wrong place.

ACTIVITY 6

Form into groups of four and complete the following task.

Explain how each of the three types of housing tenure can form a barrier to labour mobility by making it difficult for people to move to take up a new job:

- Council housing
- Owner occupation (with a mortgage)
- Private renting

Write up to 60 words.

EXERCISE:
allow 15 mins

Working with and relating to others ✔

Communicating ✔

Managing tasks and solving problems ✔

Commentary...

Moving house is always a big step and often a major expense.

Council housing – it is often hard to transfer within a local authority and very difficult to transfer between them.

Owner occupation (with a mortgage) – you may be held up by 'housing chains'. Many owners now suffer from negative equity and cannot afford to sell their houses.

Private renting – this housing is often easy to obtain, but the quality may be poor. Better quality rented accommodation can be very expensive.

Crime and its impact

Crime is becoming increasingly important for business. In one sense, it is a business growth area. The private security industry now employs more people than the police. New business opportunities are opening up with the privatisation of parts of the system of law and order. The market for crime prevention devices relating to households and motor vehicles is large and growing.

Businesses are also targets for a range of criminal activities. Many of the offences committed against business are undertaken by employees. Technological developments have created new criminal opportunities. Various forms of electronic or computer-based fraud and theft are becoming more common.

The experience of crime and the fear of crime are having a major effect on communities and on people's behaviour. Some of this is of direct concern to business, e.g. when people are afraid to leave their homes after dark to go shopping or use recreational facilities because they are fearful of being a victim of crime.

ACTIVITY 7

List four ways in which crimes impose additional costs on households.

Commentary...

These are some ideas, but there are plenty of others.

Cost of replacing stolen property or repairing criminal damages

Expenditure on precautions against crime

Increased household insurance premiums

Restrictions on going out due to fear of crime

CRIME AND BUSINESS

Criminal activity is affected by the general pattern of economic, technological and social change. For example, the mass consumption of valuable, durable and portable consumer goods has been important in creating the motive and the opportunity for crime. The development of technology gives new opportunities for crime as the growth of fraud involving computer records shows.

Work Many employees steal from their employers. Office workers, for example, normally have access to the use of telephones and to items of stationery. They may also fiddle expenses paid by their employers. Many manual workers in manufacturing have access to equipment and finished products or components which may be stolen.

Corporate crime The ordinary operations of business are covered by a range of laws covering employment conditions and business practices. The extent to which these laws are violated may be very substantial. Surveys have shown that only a small percentage of violations of factory legislation lead to prosecution and that where this does take place, the penalties are normally light.

The Guinness case demonstrated a number of features of the UK financial system and the role of crime within it. In 1987, Guinness arranged for up to £100 million of company funds to be used by third parties to purchase Guinness shares in order to increase their market price. This operation resulted in an increase in the Guinness share price from 280p to 353p. The aim was to strengthen Guinness's position in the battle to take over Distillers. What went on was only revealed as a result of a tip-off from the US Securities and Exchange Commission. Many individuals and organisations benefited financially. Court cases resulted in the chairman of Guinness initially being jailed for his part in the affair.

Retailing Crime imposes considerable costs on many businesses. Retail firms are the most affected because they are often vulnerable to property crimes committed by both employees and from shoplifting. In total, staff steal almost as much as shoplifters. Theft by staff is referred to euphemistically as 'stock shrinkage'. A survey of 54,000 shops by the British Retail Consortium in 1994 estimated the total cost of crime at £2 billion in a single year compared to annual sales of £140 billion. In a year:

- a small shopkeeper can expect to be burgled at least once

- thefts by shop staff will cost £554 million

- losses due to customer crime will amount to £516 million

- burglary, arson, robbery and criminal damage will cost £600 million

- around 12,000 violent incidents occur annually in shops, about half when shoplifters are confronted.

ACTIVITY 8

Outline the kinds of workplace offences you think could be committed by the following categories of employees given the opportunities they may have:

- retail counter staff

- manufacturing shopfloor workers

- middle management

- board members.

Write up to 40 words.

Commentary...

Crime at work is not uncommon though you should avoid the cynical belief that 'everyone's at it' – there are still plenty of honest people about. You may have come up with some different answers depending on your knowledge and experience.

- retail counter staff – small-scale theft of stock

- manufacturing shopfloor workers – theft of components, raw materials, finished articles

- middle management – fiddled expenses, removal of stationary, private use of telephones

- board members – insider trading (using inside knowledge to make share deals).

Social policy reform

Since the early 1980s, major changes have been made in social policies and in the ways in which they have been delivered. It is useful to end this session by highlighting these. Many of the changes have involved either exposing areas of public provision to market forces or introducing management methods used in business. The combination of these has produced radical changes in the nature of public services and the jobs of those who work in them. The following general developments have taken place.

Privatisation Steps have been taken to encourage private provision in a number of areas such as prisons and health care. The biggest move towards privatisation in social services has been the massive programme of council-house sales.

Spending cuts Attempts have been made to reduce public expenditure, generally through the use of cash limits. In some areas, such as pensions, attempts to stimulate the private sector of business have been introduced along with spending cuts.

The introduction of markets Public sector services have been required to operate in quasi markets. This policy has been most highly developed in the areas of education and health where schools and hospitals now have to operate as competing units with their revenues depending on their success in attracting 'customers'.

Reducing professional power Policies have been designed to reduce the influence of the professionals who provide services. The influence of teachers over what is taught has been cut. Doctors have less control over hospitals than they had previously.

Central control Central controls have been increased to impose a pattern of service desired by the government. In schools, the National Curriculum now lays down in great detail what children should be taught. In housing, the government imposed new policies on local authorities forcing them to sell off council houses.

Customer orientation There has been an attempt to shift the view of users of state services from that of clients (of professional experts) to customers (of a service industry). There has been an emphasis on giving the customers more information. The publication of hospital and school 'league tables' is part of this policy.

ACTIVITY 9

Summarise the main changes which have taken place in education and health policies since 1980.

Identify how in each of the areas these changes have made use of ideas derived from business.

Assess the impact of these changes on consumer choice.

Write about 300 words.

Use a separate sheet of paper to record your answer. Summarise your findings in the box below.

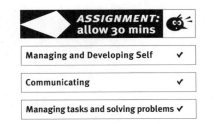

ASSIGNMENT:
allow 30 mins

Managing and Developing Self	✔
Communicating	✔
Managing tasks and solving problems	✔

summary

▶ State welfare policies have a significant influence on living standards, expenditure and business opportunities.

▶ The organisational framework used for the delivery of social services has been reformed to make it conform more closely to the kinds of organisation used in business.

▶ State welfare provision affects the operation of business in numerous ways through its impact on living standards, social attitudes and through the range of purchases it makes from business.

▶ Social security policies are not always successful in relieving poverty. However, social policies do redistribute income and alter patterns of consumption.

▶ The present education system does not provide equal opportunities for everyone.

▶ Housing policies and housing problems may limit the mobility of labour with adverse consequences for business.

▶ Crime is having an increasingly big impact on business both because of the costs it imposes and because of the new business opportunities it creates.

Technology and society

Objectives

After participating in this session, you should be able to:

- ▶ explain the significance of the role played by technology in producing social and economic change

- ▶ describe different interpretations of the impact of technological change on work and business organisations

- ▶ summarise the main debates on environmental issues, their relationship to technology and their significance for business

- ▶ describe the impact of new and emerging technologies on business opportunities and structure

- ▶ explain different views on the future shape of business and society brought about by developing technology.

In working through this session, you will practise the following BTEC common skills:

Managing and Developing Self	✔
Working with and Relating to others	✔
Communicating	✔
Managing Tasks and Solving Problems	✔
Applying Numeracy	
Applying Technology	✔
Applying Design and Creativity	

Technological change

This session examines:

- the impact of technology on the economy

- the effects of information technology on different kinds of work

- the role of technology in the home

- environmental issues and concerns about economic growth and their links with technology

- new technologies

- the nature of future society as technology develops.

The session focuses on technology and its influence on society in general and business in particular. Technological change is both a product of society and an important influence on other areas of social life. Technology has an effect on:

- the level of business productivity

- the living standards achieved in modern societies

- home life

- retailing and shopping patterns

- leisure and recreational activities

- cultural activity

- political participation.

> **!?!** **Technology** consists of tools and equipment used to perform specific tasks. It supplements or replaces human energy, dexterity, thought and memory. Technology is central to many business activities. It can be used to reduce costs and to increase efficiency and profit. Technology is the basis of new techniques or methods for performing tasks. New techniques advance through invention. Innovation is the application of these new techniques to production.

It is useful to look more closely at how people view technology. We all carry images of technology; these images are based in part on how we encounter technology in everyday life, both at work and in the home. The image of technology is also partly formed by what is taken to be the most influential advanced technology of the moment. For much of the twentieth century, technology was most associated with machinery of various kinds, normally that used for the production of goods. However, if we were living in the nineteenth century, our image of technology would be associated with the railways. At that time, they represented a major leap in the ability to transport large numbers of people and goods, very rapidly over long distances. They were viewed as a revolutionary force changing the whole face of society.

Today, we tend to take a similar view of **information technology (IT)**. IT – and the computer and the micro-electronics on which it is based – is having a major impact on all areas of life. Unlike the Victorian railways which were visually spectacular and offered a picture of movement, energy and power, the microprocessor works largely unseen, but it creates a range of new capabilities which are transforming modern society.

ACTIVITY 1

In a typical working day from rising to going to bed, what examples of modern information or computer technology would you normally encounter? How essential are they to your pattern of life?

Write up to 60 words.

SAT:
allow 10 mins

Managing tasks and solving problems ✓

Commentary...

There is an enormous range of possible answers here! Your answer could include:

clothes washed in an automatic washing machine

video recorder

car radio (RDS)

automatic bus ticket punch

computer

e-mail

TV with teletext

electronic calculator.

Many household tasks could not be done so easily without computerised equipment. Information technology has transformed many working environments.

TECHNOLOGICAL REVOLUTIONS

It is tempting to believe that technology is the major force shaping modern society. It can seem as if it has more influence over our lives than any other social or political factor and that if we want to understand the true nature of our society and economy we need above all to examine its technology. Those who hold this view are said to believe in **'technological determinism'**.

\?! **Technological determinism** is the view that history and social development are dominated by technology. It is sometimes expressed by describing history as consisting of a series of technological revolutions.

Three technological revolutions have been identified.

The first technological revolution involved the development and utilisation of steam power in the first half of the nineteenth century. This technology owed something to scientific research, though mainly it resulted from inspired mechanical invention and experimentation. Steam power enabled:

- the use of powered machinery

- the establishment of mechanised factory production

- quicker and more reliable transportation on land and sea.

This led to huge increases in productivity, the rapid growth of towns and cities and to national and international economic expansion.

The second technological revolution took place in the early years of the twentieth century through the growth of scientific knowledge, i.e. knowledge gained through systematic study, experimentation and the development of theoretical understanding. It brought about two major developments. One, based on the utilisation of electricity, led to:

- improved communications by telegraph and telephone

- developments in lighting which transformed homes and workplaces

- new power sources for production.

At around the same time, developments in chemistry produced a range of completely new materials such as petrochemical products and plastics. These resulted in new products and processes which were previously beyond the realms of possibility.

The third technological revolution, based on IT and micro-electronics, is taking place now. It involves equipment combining processing power with electronic communications.

- Computers can be used to streamline production processes through computer-controlled machines and robotics.

- Decision making can be improved by the use of expert systems.

- Domestic life may be transformed by the widespread use of computers in the home.

- Politics is likely to develop in new ways as a result of the technology.

- The new technology permits the emergence of a complex integrated system of communication covering the whole world.

The process of **globalisation** is a central characteristic of modern society which is largely produced by this third technological revolution. This involves a world-wide communications system based on the **information superhighway** linking people and businesses everywhere to massive computerised sources of information of all kinds.

The following key technological advances occurred in one of the three technological revolutions. Write each advance against the appropriate revolution in the box.

robotics

electricity

factory production

the wheel

the telephone

computers in the factory and office

mechanical inventions, like steam engines

plastics

telegraph

computers in the home

steam power

expert systems

mechanised production

automation

Revolution	Key Technological Advances
First	
Second	
Third	

Technology and business

There are a variety of ways in which technology affects business. It plays a part in the process of economic growth through which economies expand. It is also a factor in how work is organised both on the shop floor and in the office.

GROWTH AND TECHNOLOGY

The process of economic change is continuous in a market economy. **Economic growth** involves an increase in total output over a specified period, usually a year. Growth comes from existing businesses expanding their output and from the establishment and expansion of new businesses. At the same time, other businesses will be contracting and some will close down. Growth in the economy occurs when the elements of expansion outweigh the elements of contraction.

Improved technology is one means by which businesses are able to expand. Where costs of production are reduced, businesses can generally cut prices and increase sales. Across the economy as a whole, this contributes to increased output with the same total use of labour and capital resources.

For individual businesses, the contribution to increased productivity made by technological improvements can be erratic. In some periods, the production methods of particular businesses or industries are revolutionised, while in others they remain stable for long periods. The impact of technology on the size of a business's workforce mainly depends on the demand for their products. If consumers buy more when prices fall, the business may take on more workers. However, if sales remain constant, the business will hold its current level of output but with fewer workers.

Technology destroys some jobs and creates others. Over the past two centuries, since the beginnings of modern industry, major changes have taken place in the **occupational structure**. Since the eighteenth century, the proportion of the British workforce engaged in agriculture has fallen from 80 per cent to 5 per cent. In that time, millions of new jobs have been created in other industries.

RECALL:
allow 5 mins

Explain the following terms in your own words:

- **technology**

- **growth**

- **invention**

- **innovation**

Changing patterns of business

In a market economy, businesses are subject to a number of forms of change. Technology is one factor which leads to change. Other changes involve competition, concentration, instability and uneven development.

- **Competition** – businesses are under continuous pressure to pursue profits by cutting costs and expanding sales.

- **Concentration** – the process of competition leads to take-overs, mergers and bankruptcies. This creates a concentration of ownership as businesses tend to become larger and larger on a national and international basis, e.g. multinational companies.

- **Instability** – periods of boom and slump are a regular feature. In slumps, inefficient businesses go out of business, or are taken over.

- **Uneven development** – in a market economy, growth is unplanned and uneven. Some industries remain relatively archaic. Others are at the forefront of advance. Across the economy, the level of technology can vary from businesses relying on automation at one extreme, to those that rely on crafts at the other, where working methods may have changed little since feudal times. For example, jobbing builders or sheep farmers use working methods which have hardly changed for centuries.

LEVELS OF TECHNOLOGY

Technological change has led to the replacement of human labour by machines. The general advance of technology has brought:

- new sources of energy, such as electricity, gas, oil and nuclear power
- new forms of machinery and plant
- new products.

There has been a transformation in the way that goods are manufactured.

Craft production This is based on the use of hand tools powered by the user. Until the development of the factory system, this was the principal means by which goods were manufactured. While some crafts are still practised in their traditional form, a great many of the skills employed by craftworkers are now carried out by machines.

Fordism (mass production) The term Fordism has been used to describe the mode of assembly line production invented in the Ford Motor Company just before the First World War. The manufacturing process is broken down into separate tasks, each performed repeatedly by a single worker. Its characteristics are:

- large-scale mass production
- moving assembly lines
- specialized machinery
- high wages
- lost-cost products.

Throughout the twentieth century, Fordist methods of production have been pre-eminent in industry. They were the basis of the post-war 'long boom'. The combination of high wages and economic growth resulted in increased expenditure on a wide range of consumer goods. Millions of new jobs were created in businesses making washing machines, vacuum cleaners, fridges, cars, televisions and other household goods.

Post Fordism According to many commentators, we are now in the process of transition to a post-Fordist system of production. Post-Fordist methods may involve process production, automation and flexible specialisation.

- **Process production** – involving using machines to operate a continuous process as in a chemical plant. This is not a new system but it is likely to become more widely used because of developments in technology which make this possible.

- **Automation** – involving the automatic production of goods with little or no human intervention once the system is set in motion. A widespread example is the use of robots to replace workers on an assembly line. These are programmed to give the movements and actions needed which were previously undertaken by a human operator.

- **Flexible specialisation** – which is a move away from the uniform products of the mass production era. It is the most novel of the changes currently taking place. It involves the production of differentiated or 'customised' products in shorter runs. For example, you may be able to specify a range of features for your new car including colour, anti-lock brakes, sunroof, central locking and airbags. This contrasts with the mass production of the Model T Ford car of which Henry Ford is supposed to have said: 'You can have any colour so long as it's black.'

Flexible specialisation rests heavily on the use of computers to supply information about precise consumer requirements and to control frequent changes in the production process. It has the following characteristics:

- a flexible labour force with a range of skills

- rapid adjustment to changing product specifications

- production for 'niche' (i.e. small and specialised) markets

- computer control of production

- a system ensuring that the necessary components are available when required through 'just-in-time' (JIT) delivery of required parts from subcontractors.

The different levels of technology and their associated characteristics are shown in table 3.1

	Low	Medium	High
Production system	Small-scale manufacture	Fordism	Post-Fordism
Product	Crafted goods mass product	Homogeneous product	Differentiated
Equipment	Hand tools	Machine power	Linked machine powered tools Computer controlled plant Robots
Worker	Craftsperson	Semi-skilled operative	Technician Flexible worker
Organisation	Craft workshop	Assembly line	Automated plant Continuous process Just-in-time (JIT) production

TABLE 3.1: *Levels of technology*

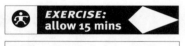

**EXERCISE:
allow 15 mins**

Working with and relating to others ✔

Managing tasks and solving problems ✔

ACTIVITY 2

Form into groups of four and complete the following task.

Provide an example of each of the levels of technology that are used in an organisation in which you are studying or working.

Commentary...

While we cannot anticipate your answer, it is likely that you will have been able to find examples of more than one of the levels of technology since even in the most high-tech organisations, some people are likely to be engaged in work using very low-tech methods.

Business and information technology

The kind of technology we use to do our jobs has an influence on what the job is like and how we feel about it. Craft workers who use hand tools to fashion objects from raw or partly worked materials may employ a great deal of skill and feel considerable pride in their work. Semi-skilled car assembly workers who perform endlessly repetitive tasks with highly sophisticated mechanical tools on an assembly line may employ far less skill and quite possibly may have less pride in their work.

Theories of technological determinism are often found in discussions of the changing nature of work. The suggestion is made that the organisation of work of necessity takes a particular form as a result of the use of a particular technology.

However, in reality, the nature of work is not 'determined' by the nature of the technology available. Technology may impose constraints but it is management which chooses how work will be organised. This choice is made on the basis of a range of factors including:

- education and training facilities available

- existing profit margins and funds available for investment

- the extent of competition

- the economic environment

- current wage levels.

MANUFACTURING

There has been a long-term decline in the numbers employed in manufacturing. Among manual workers, the effect of the introduction of mechanical sources of power was to reduce the number of heavy labouring jobs.

Fordism reduced the role of skilled craftworkers and largely replaced them with semi-skilled workers on an assembly line. However, skilled toolsetters and maintenance workers were still required to set up the production line and to keep it running.

Post-Fordist methods of production tend to replace tool-setting with forms of automatic control. Some semi-skilled manual workers are being replaced by robots. More workers are needed to monitor the process of production rather than physically participate in it.

Computer networks are very useful for controlling all kinds of stock inventories and they can play a major part in **'just-in-time' (JIT)** methods of production. JIT was developed in Japan for a range of manufacturing processes involving the assembly of parts that are shipped in from outside suppliers.

In many businesses, there is a move towards greater **labour flexibility** with workers being required to undertake a range of tasks rather than the repetition of a single small element in the production process. More workplaces have adopted forms of group or team production.

It is easy to overestimate the impact of information technology on manufacturing jobs. While some workers fit the stereotype of the white-coated technician controlling a complex automated process, others are still doing dirty, dangerous or repetitive jobs. Even in the most modern enterprises, floors have to be swept, toilets cleaned, repairs and maintenance undertaken. In addition, because of the unevenness of economic development, many workplaces in declining industries are still organised on traditional lines.

SERVICES

The service sector is often seen as being at the forefront of the developing post-Fordist economy. It is certainly true that the introduction of information technology has had an important impact on the operation of the service sector as the following examples show.

Retailing For many products, the shop may eventually become obsolete. Purchases from home using mail-order catalogues or telephone ordering is now widely used. 'Direct sales', for example, are now a major sales route for personal computers. 'Teleshopping' is likely to become increasingly important as a means of buying goods. Computer communications can also allow the contents of catalogues to be displayed on screen along with details of availability and methods of payment.

In retailing, bar codes and laser-scanning are now widely used. At the check-out, a laser beam reads the price from the code. It provides information for controlling stock levels and can be the basis for automatically making out restocking orders. It can also be used for repricing goods without having to relabel each item. The information can also be used to analyse sales patterns throughout the different parts of the store.

Leisure In the leisure and entertainment industries, computer networks are a means of providing instant information on the availability of services and of making bookings. Their use is widespread in travel agents, hotels and theatres.

Information services such as library catalogues, encyclopaedias and newspaper cuttings libraries can all make information rapidly available on the basis of 'keyword' searches. Many college library catalogues are now computerised and this allows students to find relevant material much more easily than in the past.

Personal finance Automatic teller machines (ATMs) have been around for two decades but now they can be used for a range of other functions thus reducing the need for counter services. Electronic banking is already in use in the UK and will become much more widespread in the future. Money itself is now often used in the form of credit card sales and direct electronic payment systems. These moves towards what has been called a 'cashless society' can be seen as a banking revolution. Certainly, the banking system is undergoing a major transformation and it is likely that still more bank staff will lose their jobs.

Education In education, the use of IT has developed slowly both because of the lack of funds to purchase equipment and due to the associated lack of suitable software. Teachers may also have resisted its use because of a lack of adequate training. In the UK, it is only widely used in well-resourced parts of higher education. While a policy was developed in the 1970s to have microcomputers in every school, the level of provision in many is rudimentary compared to what is available in, say, the financial services sector. IT has, however, had an effect on the curriculum and computer studies is a growth area in both schools and post-school education.

OFFICE WORK

Offices can use IT for processing, storing and retrieving information. The effects of using a computer to control the business is substantial.

**BUSINESS AND INFORMATION
TECHNOLOGY**

Much routine clerical work and record keeping has disappeared resulting in the employment of fewer typists and filing clerks. In the most advanced and best financed sectors, such as foreign exchange and share dealing, staff work with computers connected up to a massive electronic global dealing system giving instant access to information on the latest market prices throughout the world.

However, the application of technological advances to office work has developed unevenly. Many offices are still undercapitalised. Productivity is low and traditional office methods are employed. The wider use of IT in many areas of office work has sometimes been set back by the purchase of inappropriate systems and by failures in planning, training and supervision. Sometimes even large-scale computer systems have had to be abandoned, as the Stock Exchange discovered when it unsuccessfully attempted to computerise the documentation of share dealings in the early 1990s with its Taurus system.

The organisational change brought about by computerisation can cause power struggles as different groups strive to strengthen or hold their position. Managers can lose status if they are left with fewer subordinates. In middle-range jobs, the effects of IT can be dramatic. Jobs involving processing information (e.g. the routine recording of accounts) can disappear altogether. This can remove the need for the supervisory posts immediately above them in the hierarchy.

New technology can be used to give management greater control over the workforce. However, sometimes workers can become more autonomous. Where managers are not familiar with IT, workers may be able to exercise greater control over the pace and scheduling of work.

Computers also affect management structure. The trend towards 'flatter' organisations with fewer managerial layers can be facilitated by the use of computers which replace some decision-making functions. The creation of a **management information system (MIS)** can lead to IT or management information departments staffed by experts with new skills and a new language. This can create problems for managers who are not 'computer literate'.

ACTIVITY 3

What problems can the introduction of management information systems cause managers who are not computer literate?

SAT: allow 10 mins

Managing tasks and solving problems ✔

Commentary...

- Those in more traditional management roles may find it hard to communicate with IT experts.

- Decisions on installing computer systems and on the use of equipment can leave management at the mercy of computer specialists.

- Occupations such as systems analysts and programmers may exert considerable influence, since those with access to key information can control decision making.

New health and safety problems have also arisen. The continual use of computer screens may be hazardous. Constant keyboard work can lead to repetitive strain injury (RSI).

FORMS OF EMPLOYMENT

Important changes are taking place in the employment structure. In 1994, 15 per cent of men were self-employed. This has doubled in 25 years. This is mainly due to the recession and the growth of marginal forms of self-employment such as mini-cab driving and various forms of odd-jobbing.

Another feature of the modern workforce is the increase in part-time employment. In 1993, 31 per cent of the workforce consisted of part-time workers and the figure is rising. The figure for women is 45 per cent. Almost all the increase in employment in the 1990s has been in this sector of the workforce. Part-timers are much less likely to receive sickness benefit, paid holidays or occupational pensions. They are likely to be used as pools of temporary labour to be taken on and laid-off as demand dictates.

There has been a big increase in home working with up to a million people working in this way. The majority are women, many from ethnic minorities. Most of them are doing poorly paid assembly work, textile production and manufacturing rather than the high-tech activities commonly found in depictions of the 'electronic cottage'. IT, however, does enable people to work in their homes and there have been some moves in this direction.

The emphasis which business now puts on greater flexibility will lead to further changes in work. Many employees will need to be self-reliant, resourceful and prepared to change. They may be faced with a career made up of a series of projects rather than jobs. This will come about as businesses rely more on contract work, out-sourcing and consultants. Employees will need to be willing to reskill and retrain periodically.

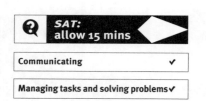

SAT:
allow 15 mins

| Communicating | ✔ |
| Managing tasks and solving problems | ✔ |

ACTIVITY 4

Conventional employment, where people go to work from 9 a.m. to 5 p.m. in an office or factory five or six days a week for the rest of their lives, may be declining but there are other ways of working which are increasing. The list below suggests some possible ways in which jobs may change in future.

○ **Working from home** – employees remain in contact with their employers and customers by telephone, teleconferencing and the like.

○ **Hot-desking** – salesmen and others work from their cars, and are allowed into the office only after hours. They may use an empty desk if they can find one, but have no place of their own.

- **Short-term contracts** – employment is no longer for life, but is for a limited period of say 2–3 years.

- **Part-time working** – the worker may take on employment for a limited time each week.

- **Multiple employers** – when working part-time, the employee or consultant may work for several employers at the same time.

- **Competition from the 'black economy'** – many jobs will be affected to some degree by the presence of untaxed activities by individuals running their own (unofficial) businesses.

Write down what kind of job you would like to have in the future.

Write down the ways in which this job might be affected in future referring to the points above where you think they are relevant. Your answer should relate specifically to your chosen job and the expected circumstances.

Commentary...

Most professional and skilled technical jobs will be affected to some extent by the trends mentioned above. It is a matter of judgement which will be affected most. But if you think that your job will be unaffected by any of them, then you may be in for a surprise.

Technology and the environment

> **\?/** **Environmentalism** is the name given to the political
> viewpoint which puts the protection of the environment at the
> centre of its concerns.

As technological advances have been pushed forward by high-tech businesses, a range of new environmental concerns have become the subject of political controversy. Environmentalism and the **green movement** began to make an impact in the UK in the 1970s and 1980s. Environmentalism is now an important area of international concern. In 1992, an 'Earth Summit' was held which committed all members of the UN to consume fewer natural resources and to protect the environment.

The political issues raised by the green movement have important implications for government, business and society. While the Green Party does not currently seem to be able to advance from its peak period of electoral success in 1989, an increased awareness of environmental issues is now apparent in political debate. The major parties have shown more concern with environmental issues though this has not led to a fundamental shift in priorities.

Some green issues have entered the conventional political arena. The consumption of lead-free petrol, for example, is now encouraged by a reduced rate of tax. Environmental issues have also played a part in some of the policy debates about transport, farming and energy policies.

Public perception of environmental issues in the UK has been influenced by a range of pressure groups. Some of these are long established, such as the National Trust and others are more recent and more radical, such as Greenpeace and Friends of the Earth. These groups have managed to force some new issues on the political agenda such as whaling and 'global warming'.

Green issues have also been forced on the agenda of business. The increased prominence of environmental questions provides both threats and opportunities for business.

Threats Threats to business arise from consumer resistance to products and processes which may be viewed as environmentally damaging. For example, nuclear power and nuclear power generating installations have been viewed critically and British Nuclear Fuels has chosen to attempt to improve the public image of the industry by substantial expenditure on public relations.

Opportunities Some businesses have found that environmental concerns present them with new opportunities. Many companies have benefited from associating their activities with a concern for environmental issues. The Body Shop, for example, has traded on its image of environmental concern as the basis of its marketing appeal. Environmental concerns have also affected the share market. Schemes for share buying based on what has been called 'ethical investment' frequently employ environmental criteria in selecting shares for purchase. The businesses involved benefit by improved access to capital for purposes of expansion.

SAT:
allow 5 mins

Managing tasks and solving problems ✔

ACTIVITY 5

Outline three issues the green movement has forced onto the political agenda.

Write down the item you think is you think is most important.

Give reasons for your choice.

Write up to 60 words.

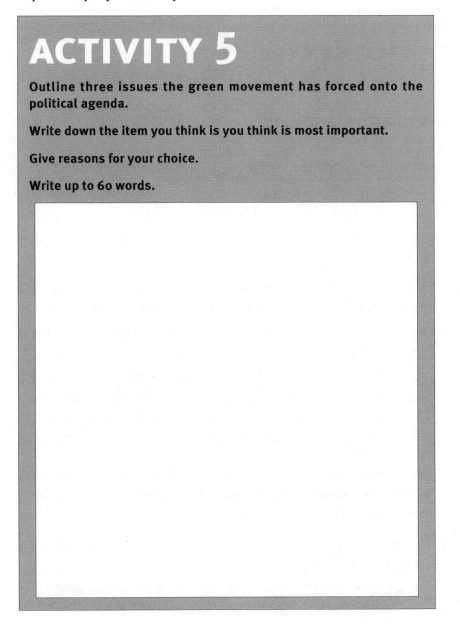

Commentary...

Here are some issues that the green movement has raised. You may have found issues that are not on this list.

- open-cast mining
- nuclear power
- battery farming
- global warming
- lead in petrol
- over-use of cars

There are many different reasons why people are concerned about green issues. Your reasons could be personal, or to do with economic or social costs, or the impact on health, or cruelty.

ALTERNATIVE TECHNOLOGY

Environmental concerns are often linked with issues related to the technologies developed and used in business. Environmental issues generally focus on technology having a destructive impact on some kind of natural process. For example, the dumping of waste at sea can affect the marine ecology and lead to the death of plants and creatures which live in it.

Environmentalists argue that the use of the most advanced technologies is not always appropriate since they are often the most damaging to the environment. A distinction is sometimes made between **'alternative'** or **'soft technology'** and **'hard technology'**. Soft (or alternative) technology is less sophisticated and operates in a more environmentally friendly way. Hard technology involves attempts to achieve production goals regardless of the environmental costs. The advocates of the use of soft or alternative technology propose a different way of organising society generally. Overall, soft technology implies a system of production based on the 'small is beautiful' principle and an economy characterised by stability rather than the pursuit of growth. The key differences are summarised in table 3.2.

	Soft technology	Hard technology
Energy use	Low input	High input
Pollution	Low	High
Resource use	Renewable/recycling	'One way' use
Production system	Craft production	Mass production
Division of labour	Low specialisation	High specialisation
Mode of regulation	By need	By profit
Economic process	Steady-state	Unrestricted growth

TABLE 3.2: *The characteristics of soft and hard technology*

While a wholesale shift to a society based on soft technology is not a possibility at present, soft or alternative technologies can be and are being applied across a range of products in modern industrialised society. They are having an important influence in a number of areas.

Energy A number of schemes for alternative sources of energy generation are being developed and piloted in the UK:

- Wind power is being used for electricity generation on a number of wind farms.

- Experiments have been carried out in an attempt to use wave energy from the sea to produce electricity.

- Other schemes using the energy of the tides for hydro-electric purposes have involved plans for tidal barrages in which the sea water at high tide is dammed behind a barrage. After high tide, the dammed up water is allowed to drain out through turbines used to power generators.

- Many small-scale schemes have been established to generate electricity by burning methane from the decomposition of organic waste.

Food The technology of modern agribusiness with its emphasis on intensive farming is criticised. Alternatives based on organic farming are becoming important in food retailing. These methods avoid chemical fertilisers and intensive stock rearing methods. Farm animals are kept outside and untethered rather than in intensive rearing sheds. Schemes to label foods in a way that indicates the processes used to produce them have been developed.

Shelter Some aspects of housing design are becoming more environmentally friendly. Modern housing is better insulated to prevent waste of energy. Experiments with buildings designed to allow the sun to contribute to heating and providing power for the building have been undertaken. In 1995 in Newcastle, a building was

**TECHNOLOGY AND THE
ENVIRONMENT**

constructed using large numbers of solar cells to generate electricity. On a smaller scale, solar panels are used to heat water in some new houses.

Transport Environmentalists stress the role of public transport as being more energy efficient and causing less air pollution, than the use of private cars. There is also support for increasing the use of bikes as form of local transport through the provision of cycle lanes.

Medicine There has been a great deal of criticism of high-tech medicine and various alternative therapies have become quite popular. These include acupuncture, aromatherapy and reflexology along with more well-established therapies such as homeopathy. These new therapies cover both physical and mental health and there are some signs of official recognition for some of them. Certainly, the medical profession now takes them more seriously than in the past.

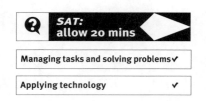

**❓ SAT:
allow 20 mins**

Managing tasks and solving problems ✔

Applying technology   ✔

ACTIVITY 6

Imagine that the organisation in which you work/study (or the part of it that you work in) is to be reorganised on the basis of the principles of soft technology. Taking each of the characteristics on the left of table 3.2 briefly outline the changes that might need to be made.

Write up to 100 words.

Summarise your findings in the box below.

Commentary...

The table below shows what might be suggested for a typical FE/HE college.

	Soft technology	Suggestions
Energy use	Low input	Improve insulation
Pollution	Low	Can't think of any!
Resource use	Renewable/recycling	Re-cycle all paper, plastic, cans and glass. Refill computer printer cartridges.
Production system	Craft production	Employ more teachers and give more personal contact
Division of labour	Low specialisation	More team teaching to learn new skills
Mode of regulation	By need	Provide more adequate grants for students
Economic process	Steady-state	Cut down on grandiose building plans

LIMITS TO GROWTH

A major part of the environmentalist case involves opposition to the unrestricted pursuit of economic growth. Concern about possible **limits to growth** became a public issue in the 1970s. The criticism of growth took a number of forms.

Resource depletion   Many environmentalists focus on the over-exploitation of the environment and the problems which will result when various essential raw materials and other natural resources run out. It has been suggested that there is a limit to the extent to which growth can be sustained. The new-right view is that the market mechanism can solve all problems of resource availability. When shortages arise, the resulting increase in prices will lead businesses to increase investment to extract the resource and/or develop alternatives.

Environmental damage   There has been an increasing concern about the environmental damage caused by various production processes employed by businesses. The most extreme versions of this suggest that the ability of the planet to sustain human life is being damaged by pollutants which result from modern systems of production and consumption. The excessive use of fossil fuels, for example, is causing an increase in atmospheric levels of carbon dioxide which may be causing the temperature of the atmosphere to rise ('global warming') which will result in uncontrollable climatic changes. The widespread use of aerosol sprays may be damaging the ozone layer in the upper

TECHNOLOGY AND THE
ENVIRONMENT

atmosphere resulting in increased risks of skin cancer as the filtering effect of the ozone is reduced.

Social limits Another critique of the pursuit of economic growth rests on the idea that increases in consumer satisfaction resulting from the more widespread consumption of a range of luxury goods cannot be sustained. There are certain **positional goods** such as country cottages with an unspoiled view, where there are limits to the numbers that can be 'consumed' without the benefits of ownership declining. This occurs because as building increases, cottages soon begin to dominate the landscape and ruin the view for all cottage owners. Motor cars are another example of a positional good. As more people own cars, there is less personal mobility because of increased congestion. The result is that, beyond a certain point, increased expenditure on these products does not produce greater consumer satisfaction.

THE ENVIRONMENT AND POLITICAL CONTROVERSY

Specific environmental issues have become a source of social and political controversy. These issues arise at both a local and a national level. Business has also been drawn into the debate.

Conservation Conservation has become an important issue in national and local politics. One major focus of conservationist sentiment concerns the appearance of the environment. This can involve both the landscape and the cityscape (the appearance of towns). Some conservation issues concern distinctive features of the ecology of the environment including the desire to retain designated 'sites of special scientific interest'. These often contain habitats supporting rare plants or animals. Conservation issues are sometimes linked to the growth of the 'heritage industry' and a general interest in the past. The government has responded by setting up the Department of National Heritage.

There are important implications for business. The greater concern with conservation means that businesses can find themselves embroiled in public controversies if they expand existing production sites or establish new ones. This particularly affects developers building new housing, establishing new sites for industry or demolishing old buildings.

Air pollution A major concern about air pollution has centred on power station emissions which are believed to be responsible for 'acid rain'. This is rain that falls through air containing sulphur products and thus becomes acidic. It damages trees and other vegetation. A costly government programme to reduce this is at present in place. Another issue has been lead emissions from motor vehicles, which have been linked to brain damage, especially in children. Increasing problems with air quality in cities was highlighted in the spring of 1995 by the large number of hospital admissions of asthmatic patients during a spell of hot and still weather.

Water pollution Both rivers and the seas around the coast have been polluted by industrial waste and sewage. The issue of sewage polluting the beaches at holiday resorts and making the sea unsafe for bathing has been taken up by the EU which sets standards for water quality. Many British seaside resorts have fallen short of these standards, affecting tourism and the businesses which depend on it.

Recycling The issue of recycling has arisen, in part, through concern about the depletion of non-renewable resources. It is also linked to worries about the over-packaging of consumer goods. There are now numerous local schemes for recycling a range of materials such as:

- glass
- paper
- aluminium
- metals
- fabrics.

The recycling business itself is expanding and provides an important source of raw materials. Some major food retailers now make a point of reducing unnecessary packaging.

Energy use Since the dramatic oil price rises of the early 1970s, some attempts have been to reduce energy consumption and restrict the wastage of energy. Government grants for home insulation along with improved insulation standards for new buildings have had some impact. Businesses have become more energy conscious and some now produce energy audits detailing their usage of energy.

**TECHNOLOGY AND THE
ENVIRONMENT**

SAT:
allow 15 mins

Managing tasks and solving problems ✔

ACTIVITY 7

In the last 10 years, comment on whether or not the following have been made more 'environmentally friendly'?

○ Cars

○ Aircraft

○ Aerosol sprays

○ Electricity generation

○ Farming

Write up to 100 words.

Summarise your findings in the box below.

Commentary...

These are matters of debate and you may have different views.

○ Cars – yes, lead-free petrol, catalytic converters to reduce exhaust emissions

○ Aircraft – yes, quieter engines

○ Aerosol sprays – maybe, some are now 'ozone friendly'

○ Electricity generation – debatable, nuclear power reduces fossil fuel emissions but it raises other possible environmental problems over the storage of nuclear waste

○ Farming – debatable, there has been a small movement towards organic farming but high-tech and intensive agriculture is still going strong.

New technologies

There is no doubt that technology will continue to develop. New processes and new products will continue to appear though it is usually difficult to make anything more than educated guesses about the precise form these might take. Governments find it hard to plan and shape the advance of technology. For much of the post-war period, the main impetus of state support for technology has been in aerospace, weapons and nuclear power. These industries employ around three quarters of all trained scientific workers in Britain. However, in terms of producing profitable products for normal use, they have not been particularly successful. Indeed, in the view of many critics, the development of science and technology has been pushed in socially damaging directions by these industries.

In Britain and the USA, though not in Japan, some of the advances made in electronics have resulted from the intensive research effort made in the defence industries. While there have been some remarkable technological achievements, it is debatable whether this was an effective policy for scientific and technological advance. A common criticism of British science policy has been that technological innovations have often failed to be supported up to the point where they became commercially viable. An example is the hovercraft, which was initially invented in Britain but developed fully elsewhere. British industry has long had a relatively poor record of expenditure on research and development (R&D) compared to other leading industrial nations. British businesses on average spend twice as much on shareholders' dividends as they do on R&D.

During the 1970s and 1980s, the Department of Trade and Industry supported advanced technology projects. It provided money for developing IT through the Alvey Programme. This provided support for research into chip technology at a state-owned company, Inmos, to develop the transputer. In many countries, technological development continues to be subsidised by R&D contracts awarded by a ministry for industry. However, in accordance with the new-right view that the market is best left to make these decisions, the Department of Trade and Industry has been reducing its R&D grants.

The main focus of future policy will be on the Technology Foresight Programme which was announced in the 1993 White Paper on science. This is designed to identify technologies likely to be important in the future. Fifteen steering groups with representatives from business and universities have been set up to deal with areas such as finance, chemicals, transport and leisure, and learning. The idea is to identify future markets and relate them to anticipated advances in science.

COMMUNICATIONS AND MICROPROCESSORS

Products designed to improve communications have come into widespread use in the last decade. They are based on microprocessors (the 'chip'). Chips have become more powerful and more widely available at low cost.

Electrical communication in the form of the telephone has been around for much of this century. As originally developed, the phone carries electrical analogue signals representing speech. It has become a major form of personal and business communication.

Modern technology has found new uses for the digitally based phone system. These are now used for transferring information after conversion into a 'binary' form for transmission using pulse code modulation. By this means, any information, including pictures, can be sent. The following are ways in which phone lines can be used to transmit information.

- The **fax machine** has become a standard form of business communication allowing the rapid transmission of documents.

- Computer files can be sent along phone lines using a **modem**.

- **Teleconferencing** facilities, whereby several people on different phone lines can talk together, are now easily accessible.

- **Video telephones**, where the speakers can see one another, are now becoming available.

Combining document transfer with teleconferencing using video phones provides a means of doing business with people on remote sites without having to travel to them. This could reduce the amount of business travel and the sales costs of many firms, especially those involved in importing or exporting.

'Comms' (communications) now allows personal computers to be linked to a central computer via the telephone lines. Numerous sources of official and commercial information can be 'accessed' in this way. For example, library catalogues, Stock Market prices and the complete 'Yellow Pages' are available on computer. There is also a flourishing informal and unofficial information network made up of 'bulletin boards' which allow users to communicate electronically with others.

E-mail (electronic mail) is the transmission of documents from computer to computer. This uses a network of linked computers to allow messages to be sent and received. Small networks can link up a single workgroup within an organisation. Large networks like the Internet can link up a series of separate communication systems, such as CompuServe, and allow millions of people all over the world to communicate cheaply.

Satellites now play a major role in electronic communications for TV transmission and telephone calls. The first communications satellite was put up in 1962. Now there is a world-wide system.

Fibre optics is a technology which converts digital electrical signals to light and vice versa. It allows large amounts of information to be sent down a single fibre. Fibre optic cables provide the means to offer a range of services to households including health advice and education as well as entertainment.

In 1984, the Cable and Broadcasting Act created a regulatory framework for the cable industry. Two thirds of investment in the cable industry in the UK has been undertaken by American-owned companies. These are expected to invest about £6 billion by the end of the century. When the 129 franchises already granted are completed, cable services will be available to about 14.5 million households in the country.

The cable networks are likely to become the main routeways for the **information superhighway**. It opens up a range of new opportunities:

- Cable provides access to up to about 40 TV channels.

- It can be used as a link into the phone system.

- It has the capacity to be interactive with two-way flow between the user and broadcaster for teleshopping, for interactive education, for obtaining customised information (e.g. about local services) and for gauging public opinion on particular issues.

Nano technology is a form of engineering involving the manufacture of miniaturised devices made with accuracies below a micrometre. It is a spin-off from the silicon chip industry. The technology has developed to the point where tiny motors less than a millimetre across can be made. Research is under way to develop micro robots that can be placed in the human body to perform surgery. The technology is also important in the manufacture of miniaturised sensors monitoring physical or chemical changes. These are applicable to a wide range of industrial process.

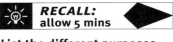

RECALL:
allow 5 mins

List the different purposes for which the telephone network can be used by businesses.

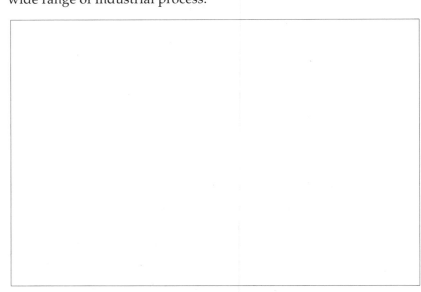

SAT:
allow 15 mins

| Managing tasks and solving problems | ✔ |
| Applying technology | ✔ |

ACTIVITY 8

What types of business might decline or emerge and grow as this superhighway develops? Give reasons for your answers.

Write up to 150 words.

Summarise your findings in the box below.

Commentary...

Trying to anticipate the future is always very difficult but all businesses have to think about it.

The businesses which might decline are those which now provide information in a non-electronic form, such as magazine and newspaper publishers, colleges and universities. At best, in order to prosper they may need to make heavy use of these new forms of communication.

Businesses which have to display their products to consumers might also find that customers prefer to do this at home. This could affect all kinds of shops which personally 'serve' customers.

Those likely to emerge and grow are any businesses involved in collecting and communicating trade information (such as advertisers, brokers, estate agents, holiday operators and travel agents), those involved with communications between people (such as phone companies) and firms dealing in entertainment (such as computer games, live and recorded entertainment of all kinds, music, films, plays and television).

BIOTECHNOLOGY

This is sometimes called **genetic engineering**. It involves the manipulation of genetic material. Some commentators have suggested that biotechnology will be the foundation for major technological changes and whole new areas of business in the coming decades. Because of the dangers posed by new organisms which might be produced in this way, the Department of the Environment has already issued regulations requiring the licensing of experiments involving genetically modified organisms (GMOs).

In agriculture, current work in biotechnology has led to the development of new strains of plants with desired characteristics. Genetic engineering means that new strains can be developed much more quickly than by the older methods based on cross fertilisation. It also holds out the possibility of entirely new species with a defined set of characteristics being developed. Genetic engineering is also applicable to stock rearing and should accelerate the improvement of farm animals.

Another major area of application for genetic engineering is medicine. It facilitates the development of new drugs. More controversially, it permits **'gene therapy'** in which the genes responsible for various hereditary diseases could be altered to prevent them occurring. Animals can be produced and bred which contain some human genes in order to produce substances required for certain therapies.

The most ambitious current project in biotechnology is the **human genome project**. This is designed to map the entire human genetic system providing information on all human genes and genetic diseases. Over the next decade, genetics researchers will produce a mass of information on the 100,000 or so genes written into human chromosomes. It could provide knowledge of the susceptibility to particular diseases of people with particular genes. This might allow those involved to ensure that they avoid transmitting these conditions. Critics however, point out the dangers. Foetuses might be genetically tested, with those that fail being aborted. Those with 'bad genes' might be discriminated against in areas such as jobs, health insurance or the right to have children.

Future scenarios

The operating environment of business is influenced by economic, political, social, cultural and technological changes. It is, of course, impossible to make accurate predictions about the future, but this does not make all speculation about the future futile. **'Futurology'**, predicting future developments, is an important part of business and government planning. A coherent depiction of the future is often called a 'scenario'. There are two main methods which can be used to produce scenarios:

- the future can be seen as the consequence of existing trends

- the future can be identified by combining the views of experts on likely changes in the economic, political, social, cultural and technological structure.

Though there will always be disagreement, we can outline a limited number of possible futures which cover most of the predicted outcomes.

One school of thought views the future optimistically. It suggests that the problems of the present will be solved in the future. Economic growth will continue and living standards will continue to improve.

Another set of views sees the future in pessimistic terms. The problems of the present will be magnified, eventually leading to social breakdown.

Optimistic scenarios

Steady progress Social stability and moderation will prevail in politics. Governments will employ effective forms of economic management to ensure the maintenance of the conditions for growth. Technical solutions will be found to overcome shortages of raw materials and fuels. The stability of the international economic system will increase as the developing countries gradually move toward economic maturity.

Many undesirable features of present society will gradually disappear. Business will move away from an exclusive focus on profits, to a recognition of wider responsibilities to its 'stakeholders'. Working conditions will improve as technology takes over the more unpleasant jobs. Greater productivity will allow hours of work to be reduced and holidays to be increased. Poverty will disappear and remaining inequalities will be generally accepted. Over the long-term, economic and social progress will continue.

The information society This view emphasises the pace and extent of the changes taking place. It sees these as driven forward by developments in science and technology. This is producing a 'new industrial revolution'. These changes are seen as producing a qualitatively new kind of society. The application of IT will lead to production based on automation. In consequence, the economic and social system will be transformed.

The service sector of the economy will dominate production and the industrial sector will continue to decline. Attractive workplace conditions will become the norm. Working hours will be drastically reduced and leisure will become the main business of life. This will be a society based on the possession of knowledge. Those in jobs requiring higher education will constitute a new **'technocratic' elite**. Technocracy is the term used to describe government by technical experts. Class conflicts arising from the scarcity of goods will disappear. Possession of knowledge rather than property will become the basis of status and authority. Political conflict will mainly involve technical disagreements about the best means to reach agreed ends.

Pessimistic scenarios

Bureaucratic socialism There is a right-wing view which sees the future as involving a progressive erosion of support for the values of self-help and private property. This will result from continuing increases in state intervention in industry and the provision of social services. The influence of the trade union movement is viewed as potentially threatening. Continued economic decline will sap national confidence. The future will involve a form of bureaucratic socialism which will stifle initiative and bring a reduction in political freedom.

Technocratic oppression A radical-left scenario envisages an oppressive future whereby the masses are lulled into passive acceptance of their inferior position. Increases in the standard of living will result in more leisure and greater consumption. Many people will withdraw from any concern with the wider society, into a 'privatized' life based on high consumption. Improvements in communications technology will give the elite greater power to manipulate opinion and prevent opposition from arising. They will rule over a demoralised mass unable to organise effective opposition to the existing order.

Intensified exploitation This radical-left viewpoint identifies the major trend as the intensification of class conflict. The concentration of the ownership and control of productive assets will continue. Industry will increasingly come under the control of foreign multinational companies. International competition will intensify. Economic inequalities will persist. The economy will become more and more unstable with high levels of inflation and unemployment. Social services will be cut back further. Economic decline will lead to a fall in living standards. As a result, there will be growing working-class opposition to the system and a mass political movement supporting a radical ideology will emerge. Economic collapse may eventually result in a major political change bringing to power either a left-wing government or a dictatorship of the right.

Ecological breakdown This viewpoint sees social breakdown as likely to result from the consequences of the pursuit of economic growth. It rests on the belief that economic growth can no longer be relied on to bring about improved living standards. Reserves of raw materials, such as oil, are rapidly being exhausted, while the demand for them continues to grow. Nuclear energy, increasingly used as a substitute, is both inefficient and dangerous. The consumer goods on which the modern economy is based are becoming more and more wasteful, because of 'built-in obsolescence' and over-elaborate packaging. Industrial processes create ever-increasing pollution and environmental damage. This will result either in social breakdown or in the victory of the green movement leading to radical social and economic reorganisation. The new approach would produce fewer and simpler goods using a non-polluting 'alternative' or soft technology. Renewable energy resources, such as solar power, would be employed. The trend towards larger and larger units would be reversed and organisations and human settlements would be reduced in size.

ACTIVITY 9

SAT:
allow 20 mins ❓

Managing tasks and solving problems ✔

Applying technology ✔

Select two different scenarios of the future: one which you would like to see, and one which you would not. Which of the two is more likely to occur, the one you want or the other?

Give reasons for your selection.

Write up to 120 words.

Summarise your findings in the box below.

Commentary...

Many different futures are possible and while it is not possible to prove that one or the other will come about, thinking systematically about them is an important exercise in planning for the future.

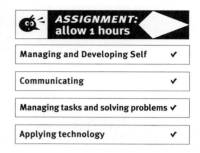

Managing and Developing Self ✔

Communicating ✔

Managing tasks and solving problems ✔

Applying technology ✔

ACTIVITY 10

Produce a report on the impact of technological development on your organisation over the next ten years with the focus on:

(a)   required workforce skills

(b)   markets for services/products

(c)   the way production is organised.

Write up to 1,000 words.

Use a separate sheet of paper to record your answer. Summarise your findings in the box below.

summary

- Technology plays a significant role in generating social and economic change.

- There are different views of the effects of technological change on work and on how businesses are organised and managed.

- Technology is transforming domestic life and the role and functions of the home, with important implications for business.

- Environmental issues are often related to the development and utilisation of technology by business.

- Modern business has to be sensitive to a range of environmental issues and problems.

- New and emerging technologies, especially the development of IT, is of major significance for business, its future structure and the opportunities open to it.

- A variety of different possible futures can be outlined and whichever emerges will have a major influence on the shape of business in the coming decades.

The political process

Objectives

After participating in this session, you should be able to:

▶ describe the main political ideologies in the UK and outline their importance for business

▶ identify the different factors influencing political behaviour

▶ describe the role of business in public policy making

▶ explain the role of business methods in the implementation of public policy.

In working through this session, you will practise the following BTEC common skills:

Managing and Developing Self	✔
Working with and Relating to others	
Communicating	✔
Managing Tasks and Solving Problems	✔
Applying Numeracy	✔
Applying Technology	
Applying Design and Creativity	

Government and business

This session examines the political context in which business operates. The focus is on how the political system works and the part played in it by business.

One way to make sense of politics is to view it as a 'system'. All systems have 'inputs', 'processing' and 'outputs'. Politics viewed as a system can be illustrated as:

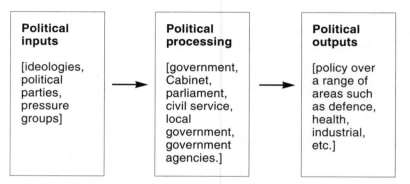

Political inputs	Political processing	Political outputs
[ideologies, political parties, pressure groups]	[government, Cabinet, parliament, civil service, local government, government agencies.]	[policy over a range of areas such as defence, health, industrial, etc.]

This session deals with the first two boxes, political inputs and political processing, i.e. the factors which influence how the government acts (political inputs) and the way it goes about formulating policies and putting them into practice (political processing). The third box, political outputs, concerns the actual policies that the government carries out. This is not dealt with in this session but it is examined in the following parts of this book:

- Section 1 Sessions 2 and 4 deal with economic policies.

- Section 1 Session 3 includes material on government policy towards financial institutions.

- Section 1 Session 5 covers industrial policy.

- Section 2 Session 2 deals with government policies on the welfare state.

- Section 3 Session 2 covers policies directed towards business activities, labour and industrial relations and the environment.

- Section 3 Session 3 deals with various controls on business operations by agencies established by the government.

Business operates in an economic and social environment which is strongly influenced by the operation of government. Almost all government policies have some impact on business and some polices are specifically directed towards it.

- Since business is affected by government action, an understanding of the role of government is useful because it helps to explain how governments make policy, the kinds of policies they make and the pressures that influence them in doing this.

- An understanding of political ideologies is important for business since it allows an appreciation of the general direction taken by policy and its likely impact.

- Business needs to be aware of the ways in which business interests and problems are viewed across the political spectrum in order to play a meaningful role in the debates about policies that affect it.

This session starts by examining some of the key 'political inputs' including political ideologies, parties, elections, and the role of business pressure groups. It then goes on to focus on 'political processing' by examining the operations of government and the organisations which implement public policies.

Political ideologies

Ideologies are important in politics.

> **\?!** **Ideologies** are sets of ideas about:
> - how society should be run
> - who should exercise political control
> - the principles on which political leaders should govern
> - the kinds of policies they should pursue.

Ideologies provide the general ideas on which debate about politics and policies takes place. They are also often associated with political parties which promote or sustain a particular ideology. Ideologies in industrial society often make reference to the role of business and the workings of the economy. For example, the Labour Party promotes an ideology which broadly supports reforms in the interests of 'labour', i.e. the working people. The Conservative Party has often been associated with maintaining the interests of those in senior positions in business, management and the professions. It also emphasises the importance of business profitability.

Laissez-faire (literally translated as 'leave alone') is the term given to the ideology which asserts that the economy should be based on free markets and the private ownership of industry. This ideology was originally formulated in the late eighteenth century as modern forms of business began to develop at the time of the industrial revolution. The belief in free markets was adopted by many factory owners and by many professionals whose position depended on the prosperity of business. *Laissez-faire* was the most influential ideology in Britain throughout the nineteenth century and, in a modified form, up to the 1940s.

In the period from around 1940 to the early 1970s, *laissez-faire* ideas were less influential and political debate was based on a broad middle of the road **'consensus'** or agreement between the main political parties in the UK. In this period, there was no longer a marked ideological division in Britain. There was considerable agreement on major policy objectives and on the rules of the political game.

This consensus covered the views of moderate socialists who dominated the leadership of the Labour Party and moderate members of the Conservative Party. Both major parties were united in their support for Keynesian economic policies. Keynesian policies worked on the assumption that the government could keep unemployment to a minimum and ensure prosperity by careful economic management.

During this period of consensus, government policies sought to produce:

- full employment

- adequate living standards for all

- a range of social services making up a 'welfare state'

- economic growth and prosperity through a measure of economic planning.

This ideological consensus broke down in the 1970s when the **'long boom'** ended. The long boom is the name given to the sustained period of economic expansion and full employment which lasted from the end of the Second World War in 1945 until the early 1970s. Since the mid-1970s ideas based more on the principles of the new right have gradually become widely accepted.

The changes which helped to destroy the post-war political consensus in the 1970s included:

- the failure of Keynesian policies to maintain full employment

- increased inflation followed massive oil price rises

- the growing cost of the welfare state

- the re-emergence of widespread poverty

- the breakdown of the stability of the international economic system

- the revival of free market ideas on the right and of radical socialist ideas on the left.

A wide range of political ideologies are found in Britain. These different ideologies have different views on a wide range of issues though for most of them, the role that should be played by business, is a key concern.

The 'new right'

The 'new right' is the name given to a set of economic and political ideas which gained in influence from the 1970s. In the UK, the labels 'Thatcherism' and 'neo-liberalism' have a similar meaning. The term **neo-liberalism** means a modern version of liberalism (meaning nineteenth century *laissez-faire* ideas). The ideas of the new right involved a sharp break with the consensus which had prevailed in the immediate post-war period.

The new right sees the private sector of business as wealth-creating and the public sector of public services and nationalised industries as unproductive. State social and economic intervention is distrusted. Individuals and businesses should be left to pursue their own self interests. The new-right doctrines stress:

- the pursuit of economic prosperity through free markets

- support for inequality as an incentive

- opposition to state social and economic intervention

- freeing individuals and businesses from state controls

- the need to balance the public budget

- the central importance of the elimination of inflation rather than the reduction of unemployment

- the belief that inflation results from excessive growth of the money supply partly fuelled by government borrowing

- the need to cut trade union power.

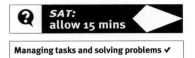

SAT:
allow 15 mins

Managing tasks and solving problems ✔

ACTIVITY 1

List what do you see as the three main implications for business of the ideas of the new right.

Write up to 30 words.

Commentary...

A wide selection of answers is possible here; three of the most significant points are:

- lowering taxes – to let people choose how their money should be spent

- weakening trade unions – to increase efficiency and reduce business costs

- reducing controls on businesses – to encourage enterprise.

TORYISM

Toryism is a very old ideology which fosters support for established institutions and emphasises order, tradition and continuity as desirable features of society. The Tory ideology is one of the two main strands of opinion found in the Conservative Party; the other is the neo-liberalism of the new right.

Toryism has a long pedigree and it has proved adaptable to the new political circumstances which have developed in the twentieth century with the rise of democracy and the welfare state. The basic principles of Toryism emphasise of the following concepts.

- **Tradition** – long-established institutions, such as monarchy and the family, have stood the test of time so they should be retained.

- **Hierarchy** – society has a 'natural order' in which some are more fitted by birth or education to exercise leadership and authority.

- **Authority** – people should respect and defer to those in authority. However, those in positions of authority should also accept an obligation to treat their subordinates properly to maintain this respect. In business, this might involve a 'paternalistic' concern for the welfare of employees by their employers.

- **Property** – property ownership should be encouraged as it gives individuals a stake in society and a sense of belonging.

- **Religion** – is important as the basis of morality which is the foundation of an orderly society.

- **Family** – is seen as the bedrock of society with its internal structure based on a clear division of roles and responsibilities. It is seen as model of how society as a whole should operate with fatherly leadership and with the other members loyally performing their respective duties.

- **Duty** – Toryism stresses that all members of society have responsibilities. Those of high status have a paternalist obligation to look after the weaker members of society. Those in subordinate positions should show respect for their social superiors.

THE CENTRE

Those in the political centre are sometimes termed 'moderates'. They occupy the centre ground between the right and the left. They support a middle way between capitalism and socialism. They accept the market, but think that the state has a wide role to play. The approach is based on the view that carefully planned state action can be used to solve a wide range of economic and social problems. Many of these problems, such as unemployment, or low wages, may be thrown up by the workings of business. However, those in the centre are not anti-business; they merely wish to make sure that any undesirable side-effects of the competitive market economy are dealt with by government action.

Key elements in the moderate or centre perspective are:

- backing for a wide array of social services to meet social needs

- support for the basic features of capitalism, such as the profit motive and private ownership

- support for the ideas of Keynes and Beveridge

- support for progressive taxation

- a desire to abolish poverty

- the use of state economic management to reduce unemployment

- support for equality of opportunity.

Representatives of this approach are mainly found in the Labour Party. In particular, the centre has generally dominated its leadership.

RECALL:
allow 10 mins

What views does the centre hold on:

- **the proper extent of regulation of business by government?**

- **the economic role of government?**

- **social inequality?**

- **the welfare state?**

THE RADICAL LEFT

The ideas of the radical left are linked to the Marxist analysis of capitalism. Capitalism is pictured as a society based on the exploitation of the working class by a capitalist class. The radical left is in a minority within the Labour Party but sometimes its ideas do influence policy. This may occur during periods of disillusionment with the performance of Labour governments.

Members of the radical left believe that capitalism, which is based on free markets and the private ownership of business should be replaced by socialism based on a collective approach to the economy and common ownership of business. They are likely to hold many of the following views:

- capitalism is based on inequality and exploitation

- society is dominated by a wealthy capitalist class who control private business

- the working class makes up the majority of members of society

- the interests of capitalists and workers are opposed

- class conflict is a central feature of a capitalist society

- capitalism is inherently unstable and wasteful

- redistributive and egalitarian policies should be enacted to eliminate poverty and exploitation.

FEMINISM

Feminism is an ideology which has grown in importance in British politics since the 1970s. Feminism does not fit into the left–right spectrum into which the ideologies discussed so far can be placed. Feminism can be divided into two main variants: one reformist and one radical.

Reformist feminism This is a centrist viewpoint. It makes a number of assumptions about the position of women in society and claims that:

- discrimination is the main problem faced by women

- discrimination is based on prejudice

- **sexism** (discrimination on the basis of sex) is mainly the result of an illiberal attitude on the part of men

- education and legislation against discrimination are the best way to improve the position of women.

This is a moderate viewpoint that seeks reforms in the belief that these will improve the position of women. Many businesses support this approach.

Radical feminism This sees the attitudes and behaviour of men as the main problem facing women. Radical feminist are likely to hold the following views:

- 'patriarchy' (the exercise of authority by men, in the interests of men) is the dominant issue

- 'sexism' (prejudice and discrimination against women) are an in-built part of major social institutions

- the unequal treatment of women has deep roots in the culture

- the situation can only be rectified by an active policy of anti-sexism

- 'gender' (the different ways in which men and women are viewed and treated) is seen as the main form of social inequality.

Anti-feminism The existence of a feminist movement has led to a backlash and sometimes an anti-feminist case is put forward. This view is held by some with Tory views and some on the new right. It has a number of components:

- it emphasises the biological superiority of men

- it claims that sex inequalities have a biological justification

- it adopts a traditional family-centred view of women's role.

NATIONALISM

Nationalism plays an important part in British politics particularly in the smaller nations which form part of the UK. It generally rests on the idea that:

- a nation is a cultural unit with its own traditions and values

- the nation should govern itself as a nation state

- the boundaries of the nation should form the borders of a state

- the interests of the members of a nation can only be protected by self-government.

Nationalism is also an element in the debate in Britain over membership of the EU. The Conservative government has been split over how far Britain should cede power to the EU and the 'Euro-sceptics' have tried to present themselves as protecting 'British' interests against 'Brussels' (i.e. the European Commission).

RACISM

This view assumes the cultural or biological superiority of some racial group (see Section 2, Session 1). It suggests that people of different cultures do not like to mix. It also argues for repatriation (return to their country of origin), either forced or assisted, for migrants and their families, especially if they are black. It also holds that minorities should embrace all features of the British 'way of life'.

Reformist institutions such as the Commission for Racial Equality are viewed derisively as part of the 'race relations industry' and as having an interest in stirring up political conflict and/or as being 'anti-white'.

ENVIRONMENTALISM

Like feminism, environmentalism (see Session 3 of this section) does not fit easily into the left–right spectrum. Environmentalism or 'green' ideology has become increasingly important in Britain and other western nations over the last decade or so. It owes a lot to criticisms of the activities of business where these can be seen as pursuing profits at the expense of the environment.

The Green Party first participated in elections in Britain in 1974 but achieved little success until the Euro-elections of 1989 when it obtained 15 per cent of the vote. However, this level of support has not been sustained. There are a variety of green positions across the political spectrum.

'Light green' environmental reformism lies in the centre ground of politics. It seeks a less exploitative use of resources and sustainable growth.

'Dark greens' seek an entirely 'green' society based on the full implementation of green principles. This society has been described as an **'ecotopia'** where people live in complete harmony with the natural world.

'Red-greens' on the radical left advocate an environmentally sound socialist society. They see environmental problems as caused by the pursuit of profit by private business without regard for the environmental consequences.

Environmentalism has also been taken up by the established political parties. Toryism has a green element since Tories have always had a concern with land, the countryside and rural values. They emphasise the duty of stewardship of the legacy of the past which must be preserved for future generations. Other political parties also claim a concern for the environment. Some Liberals have long proclaimed green credentials. The Labour Party also offers some support for green issues. However, its belief in economic growth and rising living standards may conflict with the principles of environmentalism.

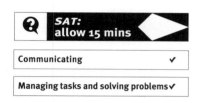

SAT: allow 15 mins	
Communicating	✓
Managing tasks and solving problems	✓

ACTIVITY 2

The ideology of the new right implies that businesses should be free from state control. Therefore we would expect a new-right government to reduce the amount of rules, regulations, and legislation that constrains business activities.

Briefly describe two ways in which you would expect governments to behave towards business if they represented (a) the radical left, (b) environmentalist ideology, and (c) feminist ideology.

Write up to 75 words.

Commentary...

These are the points we came up with. Your answers could differ substantially since each of these ideologies has many other relevant implications for business.

(a) Radical left – Workers might be given more influence at the workplace. Taxation of wealth and high incomes would increase.

(b) Environmentalism – Businesses would have to use non-polluting methods of production. They would also have to make sure their products were environmentally safe.

(c) Feminism – Facilities for female employees would need to be improved, e.g. a crèche might be provided for working mothers. Job opportunities for women would need to be improved.

Pressure groups

> **⸮** **Pressure groups** are organisations, such as the RSPCA or the Institute of Directors (IoD), which seek to influence governments, but do not wish to take over the formal power of government themselves, in contrast to political parties.

A range of different groups, organisations and interests continuously attempt to exercise an influence over governments. Policies and proposals are also examined in the media and perceptions of 'public opinion' also play a part in influencing government. For this reason, some pressure groups try to influence the government by winning the support of public opinion for their policies.

Business makes up one of the central activities in our society. As a result, business activity creates a range of interests, concerns and causes which a wide variety of pressure groups have been established to pursue.

There a number of ways in which pressure groups can be classified.

Interest groups seek to advance the material interests of their members. The Automobile Association, for example seeks advantages for motorists.

Cause groups promote the shared beliefs of their members. The group called Keep Sunday Special (KSS) seeks to promote the cause that Sunday should be a day set apart with few commercial or retailing facilities opening.

Insider groups are accepted by the government as legitimate partners in the process of making or implementing policy and provided with opportunities to do this. Many groups representing business interests, such as the Confederation of British Industry (CBI), the Institute of Directors (IoD), or the Engineering Employers Federation (EEF) have insider-group status.

Outsider groups are not accepted as legitimate partners in the process of making or implementing policy. They have to attempt to impose their views on the government. Greenpeace is an example of an outsider group which undertakes campaigns to influence public opinion and the government.

In seeking to influence governments, pressure groups may operate in a number of different ways, including:

- direct consultation with government

- contacts in parliament

- influencing public opinion

- influencing political parties

- professional lobbyists and PR firms.

Direct links between pressure groups and government take many forms:

- key insider groups, such as the National Farmers Union, will normally be consulted on policy

- insider groups may help to administer policy

- representative of business may be on government-appointed advisory or consultative bodies.

ACTIVITY 3

SAT:
allow 15 mins

Managing tasks and solving problems ✓

Answer the following questions.

1. Name four pressure groups which attempt to influence government policy towards business.

2. Identify whether they are interest or cause groups.

3. Do they have insider or outsider status?

4. How do they pursue their interests?

Write up to 60 words.

Commentary...

Here are four examples.

Name of business pressure group	CBI	Consumers association	National Union of Mineworkers	Keep Sunday Special
Interest or cause group?	Both?	Interest	Interest	Cause
Insider or outsider status?	Insider	Possible insider	Outsider	Outsider
How they pursue their interests	Lobbying Meeting ministers	Lobbying Campaigning Influencing public opinion	Strikes Bargaining Campaigning	Lobbying Seeking public support

The commentary suggests there are three major interests which relate to the operation of business and which attempt to influence governments and government policy:

- employers

- labour

- consumers.

EMPLOYERS

Employers in industry and finance have a common interest in prosperity and profitability. However, there may be some conflict between the political demands of small business, national firms and multinational enterprises. The City of London tends to favour the free market and monetarist policies of the new right. Manufacturing industry, in contrast, may welcome government intervention involving financial support and low interest rates.

Industrial interests are represented by trade associations in particular industries, such as the Engineering Employers Federation (EEF), and by 'peak organisations', such as the CBI. These usually have direct access to government and representation on various government agencies.

The interests of the City are exercised informally through the Bank of England which represents City views to the Treasury. The City also exerts influence through the financial markets. City disapproval of government policies can lead to uncontrolled selling of sterling or government securities and result in a financial crisis and problems for the government. The need to retain business confidence can force Labour governments to pursue policies favoured by this section of business.

ACTIVITY 4

Briefly outline three ways in which the interests of business are represented to the government.

Commentary...

Among your three you might have some of the following:

- through peak organisations such as the CBI
- through lobbying and PR
- through links with the governing party (if it is the Conservatives)
- through donations.

LABOUR

The central place of business and the importance of work and wages mean that groups representing the interests of labour are likely to play a major part in attempts to influence government policies. The influence of labour is mainly based on the collective strength of employees acting, threatening to act, or believed to be likely to act, together. This strength is normally channelled through trade unions. Trade unions may attempt to exercise their influence over employers or over the government.

In the past, Labour government policies have been influenced by Labour Party links with unions. Unions have normally avoided open conflict with governments though sometimes public campaigns have been used to oppose some government economic policies. From the Second World War and throughout the long boom, the unions gradually secured insider-group status. This led to direct contact with governments and representation on numerous state bodies. On occasions governments have pursued **'corporatist'** policies. These involve the representatives of labour and employers working together with the government to formulate and implement economic policy. Various government schemes to regulate business through controlling prices and incomes used this corporatist approach in the 1960s and 1970s.

According to the new right, trade unions have no legitimate role in politics and during the period of Conservative government from 1979, they lost their insider-group status. The unions have also been weakened by:

- falling membership

- high levels of unemployment

- legislation placing legal restrictions on them

- the decline of industries which were centres of union strength

- the failure of Labour to secure election since 1979

- the defeat of militant unionism (e.g. the failure of the mineworkers' strike in 1984–85).

Labour is still a powerful interest but the long period of Conservative rule after 1979 has left it weaker than it was.

CONSUMERS

According to proponents of the market, the protection of consumers results from competition between producers for their custom. However, consumers faced with giant corporations may have rather less power than this suggests.

Consumers are not easy to organise. Consumer groups lack resources and rarely have insider-group status. Consumer groups began to have an influence after establishment of the Consumers' Association in 1957. This now has a staff of around 400. It publishes *Which?* and other journals comparing products on quality, performance and value.

There are now a wide range of consumer groups. Some are very specific such as the Campaign for Real Ale, which was set up by consumers themselves. Others are organized on behalf of groups such as the aged or the homeless. Lacking insider-group status, these cause groups sometimes use direct action to publicise their views.

The state also plays a part in promoting consumer interests:

- In 1975, the government set up the National Consumer Council (NCC) to represent the interests of consumers to government.

- Town planning authorities are required to undertake public participation exercises to discover residents' views.

- Community Health Councils for the NHS were established in 1974 to represent the interests of patients.

- The 'regulators' of former nationalised industries such as gas and water have to take consumers' interests into account when setting the regulations under which the industries are to operate.

- Consumers are given rights through the use of 'charters' laying down standards of service.

- Provider markets are used to give 'consumers' a say in the running of health and education services (see Section 2, Session 2).

RECALL:
allow 5 mins

List three different ways in which governments have established means by which consumers can influence businesses.

Government and the state

The state has been defined as the organisation which possesses a monopoly of the legitimate (i.e. accepted) use of force within its boundaries. This sounds very complicated but in fact the idea is quite simple. What makes the state a special kind of organisation is the general acceptance of its right to use coercive power to enforce laws. These laws, of course, have to be made in the accepted way. In Britain, this means that legislation has to be approved by parliament.

THE GROWTH OF THE STATE

In the mid-nineteenth century, the state did little more than involve itself in the maintenance of order and the protection of property. It was widely believed that business would prosper only in the absence of state interference. Policy was guided by an ideology emphasising *laissez-faire* and self-help.

In the twentieth century, there has been an expansion of state responsibilities leading to a massive growth in public spending and in the size of the **public sector** (i.e. the organisations run or set up by the government such as local authorities or nationalised industries). After the Second World War, governments also accepted a duty to manage the economy. There was also an extension of public enterprise and social services.

A number of economic factors have been linked to the growth of the state in the twentieth century.

- Economic growth produced a need for state expenditure on the economic infrastructure to keep down business costs.

- Rising tax revenues from economic growth have permitted an increase in public spending without higher tax rates.

- The inter-war depression increased demands for state intervention to deal with economic problems.

Political and social factors have also encouraged state intervention.

- Population growth led to a need for increased spending on the social infrastructure of schools, hospitals, etc.

- Both world wars led to a massive increase in state economic and social intervention not all of which was abolished when the wars ended.

- The long lead times and high capital requirements of some projects such as aircraft production and nuclear power led to state support for investment.

- Competition between political parties to attract electoral support has served to push up public spending.

- The rise of the labour movement sometimes led opponents to attempt to head off support for Labour by bringing in social reforms of their own.

- Pressure for increased spending has sometimes come from public officials committed to the extension of their services.

- The improvement of living standards generally has led to increased expectations concerning the quality and level of state provision.

Some of the main factors involved in the growth of the state in the twentieth century are illustrated in figure 4.1.

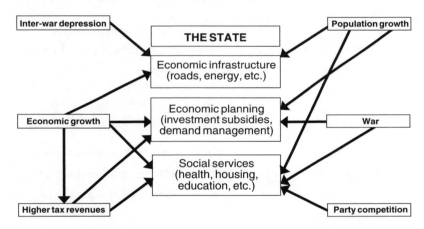

FIGURE 4.1: *Factors involved in the growth of the state.*

ALTERNATIVE VIEWS ON THE ROLE OF THE STATE

Different political ideologies take very different views on what they see as the proper role of the state. They disagree about:

- the extent to which the state should intervene in the affairs of individuals and businesses

- the purposes of this intervention

- the means by which it should be undertaken.

The centre Those in the centre believe that the state has responsibility to promote economic and social welfare. They see Britain as a welfare state with a mixed economy. They believe that the private sector of business requires state management to operate efficiently. They see state officials as guided by an ethos of public service.

The radical left Those on the radical left believe that the main function of the state is the maintenance of the capitalist system. They view it as being used to promote the interests of the middle and upper classes. A great deal of state intervention, even in the apparently benevolent area of social provision is viewed in this light. Health services and state pensions may be seen largely as a means to make working-class people accept the present system. They emphasise the class bias of senior state officials due to their upper-class social background.

The new right Supporters of the new right see the growth of state power as the 'road to serfdom'. State expenditure is viewed as inefficient. It tends to 'crowd out' private business. It creates a 'dependency culture' which destroys individual responsibility and it leads to inefficient and 'overloaded' government. They think there are inherent tendencies for the state to expand.

- Civil servants running public sector organisations will seek to maximise their own powers and budgets.

- Political parties bid for votes by promising more public spending.

- Pressures for increased expenditure come from professionals who provided services, such as lecturers and social workers, and from groups and businesses dependent on the state for benefits and subsidies.

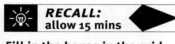

RECALL:
allow 15 mins

Fill in the boxes in the grid on interpretations of the role of state intervention.

	Radical left	Centre	New right
Motives of top civil servants			
Effect on business efficiency			
Sources of pressure for state spending			
Impact on individuals			

PARLIAMENT

The main role of parliament is to debate policy and to approve new laws. The House of Commons is made up of the MPs elected at the previous general election plus any subsequent by-election winners. The leader of the party with the most MPs is normally appointed Prime Minister.

The Prime Minister chooses the members of the **government**. The government is the term used to describe all ministers who exercise power by holding posts in the various ministries which make and administer policy. Members of the government are elected MPs or, sometimes, members of the House of Lords.

The Prime Minister and the **Cabinet** are at the centre of government policy making. The Cabinet is made up of the senior ministers in the major government departments such as the Treasury (economic policy), the Foreign Office, the Home Office, the Department of Trade and Industry (DTI) and the Department of Health. It is chaired by the Prime Minister. The Cabinet's power comes from its ability to depend on the votes of the majority of MPs. The Cabinet generally has around 20 members and usually meets weekly.

Government ministers must explain and defend government policy in parliament. Ministers are open to parliamentary questions, to scrutiny by MPs in debates, and to examination by all-party Select Committees. These committees specialise in particular areas such as economic or defence policy.

If a government loses a 'vote of confidence' in the House of Commons, it is expected to resign. However, a government with a majority can normally get its legislative proposals approved because it is able to rely on the support of the MPs of its party. Where the government lacks an overall majority, as occurred from 1974 to 1979, ordinary MPs may have more influence over the government.

It is the job of the government to make policy. Governments do not normally make policy in isolation. As we have seen, pressure groups play a part. Very often, policy is made by **'policy communities'**. Policy communities comprise the civil servants, pressure groups and political parties within which policy is discussed and often determined. Pressure groups may have close working relationships with elected representatives and with appointed officials. They may be included in the actual development of policy.

Policy communities can evolve into what has been termed 'clientelism'. This can occur when business interests are allowed to exercise a controlling influence over policy. Examples might be the relationship between the Ministry of Agriculture with the National Farmers Union or between the Department of Transport and road building and car manufacturing interests.

POWER AND THE STATE

Opinions differ on how the political system in the UK operates. In particular, there is disagreement about how much say ordinary people actually have despite the existence of free speech and the right to vote. The two main views are the 'pluralist' and the radical left (or Marxist) perspectives.

Pluralist perspective In the pluralist view, political power is widely distributed and democracy is a reality. Civil and political rights, such as freedom of speech, association and movement, and the right to vote are available to all. Free speech and a free press ensure an informed public. Elections and political parties ensure that the government reflects the views of the public. Major interests, such as labour, employers and consumers, have their say, along with numerous interest and cause groups and no one interest can dominate.

The state is the guardian of the national interest against powerful sectional forces. It performs the following functions:

- it acts as a 'referee' between conflicting groups

- it regulates the power of major interests

- it responds to the expressed wishes of the people.

Radical left perspective In the radical left (Marxist) perspective, political power is seen as concentrated in the hands of a dominant capitalist class which owns and controls industry and finance. It is ownership and control of these key areas of business which are seen as the basis of real power and influence. This class exercises power through the 'establishment'. This consists of those with class, educational and family links occupying the higher reaches of manufacturing industry, the financial institutions of the City and the state (top civil services, judges, etc). This establishment exercises considerable power regardless of which party controls the government.

The state is the guardian of the interests of the capitalist class and its allies. The power of this class is reinforced by:

- control of the mass media allowing its ideas to dominate society

- attempts made by all governments to secure business confidence to advance its interests

- the enaction of minor reforms to defuse opposition to the existing order

- the use of the full coercive power of the state against organised opposition where necessary.

RECALL: allow 15 mins

Pluralism and Marxism compared: read through the previous material and check your understanding by filling in the grid.

	Pluralism	Marxism
How much power do ordinary people have?		
Are people well informed on political issues?		
Who benefits from the activities of government?		
What groups exercise most power?		
Is the state neutral?		

Implementing state policies

The state implements many of its policies through direct control of the **'public sector'.** There are major differences between the public sector and the private sector. The **private sector** comprises organisations, such as privately owned businesses and voluntary bodies like charities. They are set up by people acting in their capacity as private individuals. Parliament may regulate how they operate through company law and health and safety regulations, but they choose their own objectives and methods of carrying them out.

Private sector organisations such as businesses can do anything which is not against the law. In contrast, public sector organisations are subject to the *ultra vires* principle under which they can only do what they are expressly allowed to do by law.

The private sector is normally subject to the discipline of the market while the public sector generally is not. This gives private business a simple criterion of success which the public sector lacks – profit. It is not always easy to measure precisely what public sector organisations produce. For some services (such as defence) there is no easily visible product. For others (such as health and education), considerable debate exists about the most appropriate measure of performance.

The state carries out its functions through different kinds of organisation. These are all established by laws laying down what they should do and how they should do it. There are three main types of public authority:

- central government departments

- local authorities

- state agencies and quangos.

CENTRAL GOVERNMENT DEPARTMENTS

Central government implements its policies through departments which deal with different areas of activity. Some departments (such as education and health) regulate public services. Others have different roles. For example, the Treasury controls overall policy on finance.

At the head of each major government department is a minister who is a member of the Cabinet. The job of the senior civil servant in the department is to advise the minister and to organise the implementation of policies. However, they also exercise some influence over policy since departments have their own traditions and favoured approaches to policy problems. Civil servants in the Treasury, have often promoted an approach to economic policy known as the 'Treasury view' which is based on keeping public expenditure down and balancing the government budget.

The way the British civil service has been organised since the late nineteenth century is in the form of a 'bureaucratic' structure. This kind of hierarchical structure is also found in many large business organisations. A bureaucracy has the following characteristics:

- hierarchical organisation

- rules which staff have to follow in doing their jobs

- specialisation and division of labour

- written records to ensure consistency

- prescribed conditions of service for staff

- recruitment and promotion based on qualifications and ability

- pensionable career.

Organisations with a bureaucratic form have undoubted advantages for governments since policy can be laid down at the top by a member of the government. Because of the hierarchical organisation and the written rules, the government can be sure that the policy is implemented as planned. However, bureaucracies can be rather inflexible and those working in them may find few opportunities to use their initiative. For these reasons, they have always had their critics. However, with the advance of new-right ideas the criticism became much more intense.

SAT:
allow 10 mins ❓

Managing tasks and solving problems ✔

ACTIVITY 5

Explain what you think are the new right's criticisms of the civil service.

Answer in 100 words.

Summarise your findings in the box below.

Commentary...

The new right does not accept that civil service bureaucracies efficiently administer the policies laid down by parliament. In the view of the new right, civil servants, like everyone else, are driven by self-interest.

The new-right view of the civil service bureaucracy claims that:

- each civil servant pursues his/her own self-interest

- top civil servants, while they do not have profits to maximise, seek to maximise their budgets

- to do this they would try to secure the widest possible role for their minister, i.e. expand the bureaucracy.

The Conservative government elected in 1979 broadly accepted these criticisms and believed that the civil service was inefficient and wasteful. It introduced a range of measures based on business principles to try and make it work more efficiently.

The Financial Management Initiative (FMI) was announced in a Government White Paper in 1982. It was designed to improve financial management. To be efficient, departments needed clear objectives and accurate output measures. It argued for a model of organisation based on that used in many businesses. It proposed:

- budget devolution, with each unit having control over how it chose to spend its money to do the required task

- the division of departments into separate cost centres with each cost centre having its own manager.

In 1982, Sir Robin Ibbs produced a report on the civil service entitled The Next Steps. This recommended:

- establishing separate agencies to carry out major government functions (later examples included the Child Support Agency)

- giving senior civil servants an entrepreneurial role where they were given a set of objectives and a budget and required to organise things themselves to get the job done.

The idea was to have a clear separation between policy making done by the minister and his advisors, and service delivery carried out by semi-independent agencies run on business lines.

Derek (now Lord) Rayner, of Marks and Spencer, was appointed head of an 'efficiency unit' to inject private business methods and promote efficiency. By 1986, £950 million of savings had been identified against scrutiny costs of only £5 million.

LOCAL AUTHORITIES

The powers of local authorities are laid down by parliament. Over the last century they have gradually become more and more under the control of central government as:

- government grants cover most of their income

- the amount of revenue from council tax is largely controlled by the government

- they have little discretion in the services they provide.

Local authorities are run by elected councillors. They provide services including education, public health, leisure and social welfare. Control over these is exercised by committees of councillors. They also have regulatory responsibilities in areas such as planning, consumer protection, and environmental health all of which have a major impact on business.

As elected bodies, local authorities have to respond to pressures from the electorate though these are weakened by low turnout in local elections. Increasingly local authorities are also under pressure from residents about the quality of services provided by local authorities.

Local government services affect businesses. Firms benefit from the provision of economic infrastructure, such as roads. Some local authorities also attempt to stimulate the local economy by encouraging firms to set up in their area. Local businesses are linked to the local authority in a number of ways:

- by paying the business rate to finance local government

- by dealing directly with the council as developers, contractors, competitors and suppliers (as a result of compulsory competitive tendering (CCT)

- through regulation of environmental, public health or planning issues by the council.

Local authorities also have to deal with a range of other local groups and interests:

- residents' and tenants' associations

- cause groups with a purely local concern

- local branches of national pressure groups

- voluntary organisations.

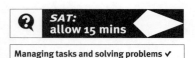

Managing tasks and solving problems ✔

ACTIVITY 6

Note down any ways in which your organisation (or local business) is affected by the activities of the local authority:

- **through being subject to regulation**

- **through doing work for the local authority**

- **through paying money to the local authority**

- **through using services provided by the local authority.**

Write up to 80 words.

Summarise your findings in the box below.

Commentary...

The following answer relates to a university:

- Being subject to regulation – the refectory has to meet public health standards.

- Working for the local authority – providing customised courses under contract.

- Paying money to the local authority – paying the business rate and purchasing other services such as car parking facilities.

- Using services provided by the local authority – having rubbish removed by the council.

Since the early 1980s, major reforms have been introduced to change the way that local government operates. New-right ideas have been influential in these reforms. They were based on the view that local authorities were inefficient and insufficiently accountable. It was further claimed that some major urban local authorities were controlled by the radical left. Services were also seen as too much under the influence control of professionals like teachers and social workers.

The reforms have involved the application of market principles and business methods in an attempt to increase efficiency and accountability. They involve:

- more competition and an emphasis on consumer preferences (e.g. parental choice of schools)

- more council financed private provision (e.g. a proportion of the community care budget must be used to purchase residential care from the private sector)

- privatisation (e.g. council house sales)

- compulsory competitive tendering for contracts for council services

- an increased role for the voluntary sector working in partnership with local government to deliver services. For example, 'meals on wheels' are organised by the Women's Royal Voluntary Service but with costs met by the council.

The new-right criticism of the lack of accountability of local authorities has been tackled by requiring the Audit Commission to publish information on their efficiency. The community charge (poll tax) was introduced in England in 1988. It was designed to bring home to electors the costs of voting for councillors who were in favour of high levels of local authority spending. In fact, it provoked widespread opposition and caused such deep unpopularity for the government that its abolition was announced in 1991.

The main aim of the various reforms of local authorities has been to move towards the model of an **'enabling council'** announced in the

1991 local government review. Here, the council would not provide services directly; it would simply be responsible for contracting private businesses to provide a specified range of provision.

STATE AGENCIES AND QUANGOS

The **public corporation** is a type of appointed state agency with a long history. Public corporations are the legal form generally used for nationalised industries. The BBC is also a public corporation. All public corporations have:

- a separate legal entity existence as a corporate body

- powers and duties, laid down by statute

- public ownership

- staff who are ordinary employees rather than civil servants.

Many public services or functions are delegated to state agencies created by statute outside central or local government control. In many cases, these organisations are now required to operate on the lines of a private business as semi-independent agencies.

Agencies were introduced by the government in the late 1980s in line with the *Next Steps* proposals. Around 100 agencies have been set up covering 340,000 civil servants, 64 per cent of the total.

In theory, managers are given freedom to manage and control agency budgets. However, in reality expenditure and staffing levels are controlled by the Treasury.

The Benefits Agency is the largest, employing about 65,000 staff. Other important agencies include the Child Support Agency, HM Prison Service and the Student Loans Company.

Quangos (quasi non-governmental organisations), sometimes also called 'non-departmental agencies' or '*ad hoc* authorities' are under the control of people appointed by ministers rather than elected by the public. They have been used for a variety of executive, advisory and consultative purposes.

Quangos have also been used for public services provided on a non-commercial basis, such as higher education corporations which run the new universities, and agencies regulating business activity, such as the Monopolies and Mergers Commission.

ACTIVITY 7

What are the arguments in favour of making use of quangos?

SAT:
allow 15 mins

Managing tasks and solving problems ✓

Commentary...

The traditional reason given for quangos is the need to insulate some services from party political interference. It is also claimed that a degree of autonomy encourages greater efficiency.

In the mid-1990s, many critics have seen the growth in numbers of these state agencies as a threat to democracy. They argue that important areas of state expenditure are now controlled by unelected and unaccountable political appointees. These have been said to make up a 'quangocracy'. They include grant-maintained schools, NHS trusts, Training and Enterprise Councils, and bodies which have been removed from local authority control, such as further-education corporations.

In 1993, quangos controlled £46.6 billion of public expenditure. There are over 5,500 quangos run by over 70,000 people appointed by ministers. A substantial number of these are people active in business. There has also been some controversy about the numbers who are claimed to have links with the Conservative Party. Formally, quangos are accountable through ministerial responsibility to parliament though in reality, this is largely a fiction. Only a third are subject to public audit by the National Audit Office or Audit Commission. Less than 10 per cent have to hold an annual public meeting.

These concerns have been considered by the Nolan Committee after increasing allegations of 'sleaze' in government during 1994. Initial recommendations were considered by Parliament in May 1995.

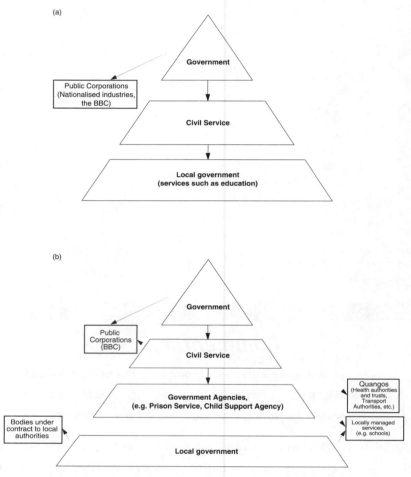

FIGURE 4.2: *Implementing public policy – who runs what? (a) Before and (b) after the reforms of the 1980s.*

The changes taking place in the organisations which implement policy involve a substantial shift away from the practices of the period before 1980.

- Market principles conflict with administrative controls based on conformity to legal rules rather than attempts to minimise costs.

- The formation of multiple cost centres undermines the centralised character of public administrative bodies where all decisions come from the politician heading the organisation.

- Public servants no longer have job security. They are put under new pressures by the introduction of performance-related pay and the ending of advancement based on seniority.

- The traditional local government and civil service ethos based on rules, precedents and the concept of 'public service' conflicts with the more entrepreneurial approach now required.

- The growing use of quangos expands the power of the governing party since ministers are able to appoint those who run these organisations.

- Democratic supervision of many public services is further reduced by their removal from immediate control by elected bodies.

ACTIVITY 8

ASSIGNMENT: allow 1 hour

Managing and Developing Self	✔
Communicating	✔
Managing tasks and solving problems	✔

1. **Identify, and describe using examples, the different business methods which are influenced the reorganisation of the provision of government services since 1980.**

Write 500 words.

2. **Prepare arguments for and against the view that business exercises excessive influence over policy making in British governments.**

Write 500 words.

Use a separate sheet of paper to record your answer. Summarise your findings in the box below.

summary

▶ The main political ideologies in the UK differ in how they depict business and its problem.

▶ People hold different political views and some of these are related to the different roles they perform in business.

▶ Pressure groups representing business, labour and consumers have an important role in the British political system.

▶ People prominent in business, along with organisations representing business, often have an important influence on the making of public policy.

▶ Business methods are now often used in implementing government policies.

Business Firms in Markets

The competitive environment

Objectives

After participating in this session, you should be able to:

▶ undertake a PEST analysis

▶ analyse the competitive environment in which a firm operates

▶ describe different competitive strategies

▶ explain how firms grow.

In working through this session, you will practise the following BTEC common skills:

Managing and Developing Self	✔
Working with and Relating to others	✔
Communicating	✔
Managing Tasks and Solving Problems	✔
Applying Numeracy	✔
Applying Technology	
Applying Design and Creativity	

The external environment

The first two sections of this workbook looked at the broad external environment in which business organisations operate. You will have discovered that it is extremely varied, complex and subject to continuous change. Moreover, these changes are difficult to predict. There are many economic models which try to predict what is going to happen in the economy in the near future. An indication of the difficulty of prediction is that they usually all have different predictions and often get things wrong. Part of the reason is that the models are based on assumptions about the way people behaved in the past and behaviour patterns are constantly changing. Equally they cannot handle 'shocks', for example totally unpredictable change such as the Gulf War, the unification of Germany and the collapse of communism.

An added problem for decision makers is that the pace of change is accelerating. Spyros Makridakis (Management in the 21st Century, *Long Range Planning,* 22 (2), 37–53, 1989) argues that before 1750 there were relatively few technological innovations and that these, by today's standards, were relatively simple, e.g. tools, the clock and mechanical calculators. The pace of innovation increased from about 1750 onwards in what is known as the industrial revolution. This period saw the introduction of engines, electricity, telecommunications, aeroplanes and mass-produced chemicals. The last 50 years have seen a new revolution, the information or computer revolution, which has produced similar results to the industrial revolution but in a quarter of the time. Makridakis compares the manufacture of a watch 200 years ago with today. The 250 parts needed would have been made separately and taken about one month to complete. Today digital watches can be made, automatically, in less than one minute. He envisages that in 50 years' time, giant computer-guided machines may construct new types of aeroplanes in less than two minutes. This may sound like science fiction but many of today's products and production processes would have been hard to believe at the beginning of this century.

What then is the modern manager to make of this uncertain environment? One thing is sure, that to wait for changes to happen and then react to them is to be always locked in the past. In business, as in sport, defending a lead and staying ahead of the competition is easier than trying to catch up. Successful managers will try to stay ahead by anticipating possible change and placing the organisation in a position to deal with new opportunities. This session puts forward a way of making sense of the broad external environment and also looks at how the more immediate or competitive environment can be analysed. This will give you a framework for analysing the impact of the broad external environment on the business organisation. From this analysis, you will then be able to identify appropriate competitive strategies.

PEST ANALYSIS

It is easy to produce a long list of external environmental changes which might affect any organisation. How can they be organised so that the picture becomes more manageable? One way is to undertake what is known as a PEST analysis. This stands for political, economic, social and technological analysis.

This model divides the business environment into four sectors into which the different environmental conditions, events and trends can be usefully sorted.

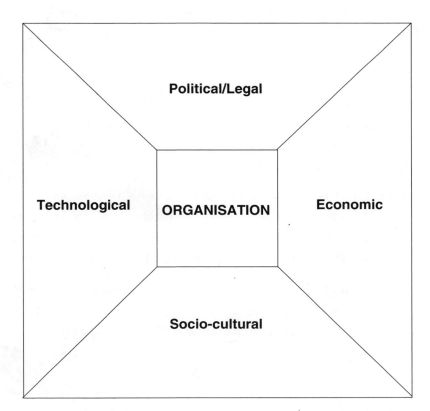

FIGURE 1.1: *The external environment.*

The first stage of the analysis is to scan the environment for those forces which may impact on the organisation using the PEST classification.

This analysis will help to raise awareness of the complexity of the external environment and at the same time impose some order on chaos. It can also stimulate discussion about future changes in the environment and how the organisation might respond.

You may be thinking that the external environment is a threatening environment and you would be correct. But as well as posing threats (e.g. competitors developing new products), it is also the source of opportunities (e.g. the identification of new markets). It is the identification of these opportunities and threats which is the purpose of the external environmental analysis.

PRIORITY IMPACT MATRIX

Having listed the possible environmental forces, the next stage in the analysis is to judge the probability that each event will occur. Nobody knows what the future holds. However, planning requires assumptions to be made about the future, a 'feel' for which can be gleaned from talking to people and reading papers and trade magazines. (There are also a number of more sophisticated techniques for assessing future trends from past events but these are beyond the scope of this text.)

The final stage is to say what the likely impact of these external forces will be on the organisation. This need not be a very detailed assessment in the first place, but may come later. A rating on a scale of low to high is sufficient to begin with.

You will then have a list of factors which have been assessed as to the probability of their occurrence and the impact each will have on the organisation. The next question is what to do with this information. How do you know which of the events you should be preparing for?

One way of assessing this is to organise your information into a grid, known as an **issues impact analysis grid**. On one side of the grid you can measure the impact of the event and on the other the likelihood of it occurring.

		Impact on the organisation		
		High	**Medium**	**Low**
Likelihood of occurence	**High**	Action	Action	Monitor effects
	Medium	Action	Contingency plan	Track
	Low	Contingency plan	Track	Track

Source: Peters, J., 1993, Business Policy in Action, *Management Decision*, 31 (6).

FIGURE 1.2: *Issues impact analysis grid.*

Those issues which fall in sectors in which there is a medium to high probability of occurrence require action. If there is a medium or low likelihood of occurrence matched with a medium or high impact, some kind of **contingency plan** is required. A contingency plan is a plan of action in case things do not turn out as expected. Any other combination requires either that you monitor the effects of an event or that you track the event in case it occurs.

For example, a horticultural firm growing lettuces is currently worried about the possible threat of EU legislation concerning the level of nitrates in the ground. If the legislation is passed, it will make it impossible for the firm to grow lettuces which will conform to EU legislation at certain times of the year. What should the firm do?

The probability of the legislation being passed is fairly high. As lettuces are the only crop this firm grows, the impact on the organisation is very high. Clearly this firm needs to start making very detailed action plans to deal with this eventuality. If lettuces had been a minor crop for this firm then the impact would have been less serious and it may have been sufficient to draw up a contingency plan or even just keep track of events.

EXERCISE:
allow 40 mins

Working with and relating to others ✓

Managing tasks and solving problems ✓

ACTIVITY 1

Divide into groups of four and complete the following task.

Read the article in Resource 2 at the back of the book. This provides a background against which you can try some of the ideas in this session.

Try to construct an impact matrix for a large brewer in the brewing industry. In each box, write in the factors which are going to impact on the brewer. If you think there is a high probability that some factor or event will occur enter it in the top row. If you think it will have a high impact put it in the first column.

For example, if you think that excess capacity is an urgent problem and will have a high impact, insert the statement in the box in the top row, and in the first column.

For events or influences that have moderate or lower probability of occurrence or strength of impact, then use the other boxes. You may of course have more than one event in each box.

Commentary...

		Impact on the organisation		
		High	**Medium**	**Low**
Likelihood of occurence	**High**	Excess brewing capacity Declining beer consumption	Declining demand for keg beers Increasing demand for cash ales Too many pubs Increase in home drinking Increased competition	Increase in cross-channel imports
		Action	Action	Monitor effects
	Medium	Continuing price wars	OFT action	
		Action	Contingency plan	Track
	Low		EU decision on competition laws 1957	
		Contingency plan	Track	Track

FIGURE 1.3: *Impact matrix for a large brewer.*

Does your grid look anything like this? As the article deals with current problems most of the events will be in the high likelihood of occurrence boxes. A couple – the possible Office of Fair Trading action and EU action – are medium to low possibilities. There may well be many other events not mentioned in the article which are more distant which would appear in the boxes in the bottom row. Assessing the impact on the organisation is difficult without a more detailed knowledge of the brewer. But you can see that the end result is very useful in prioritising issues and formulating plans.

One of the external factors that is of clear importance is competition. Although this is part of the external environment it differs from the other factors. It is not really an issue but a continuous process which firms are subject to on a daily basis. Competition refers to the rivalry between firms in selling their goods and services. This rivalry may take the form of firms attempting to reduce their costs so that they are able to compete with others by reducing their prices. Alternatively they may seek to differentiate their product in some way from others in order to stress the superior nature of their product. Products may be differentiated according to differences in design, quality, service, packaging or some other distinctive feature.

It is through an analysis of the process of competition that the impact of the other environmental issues can be analysed.

Our diagram of the external environment now looks like this:

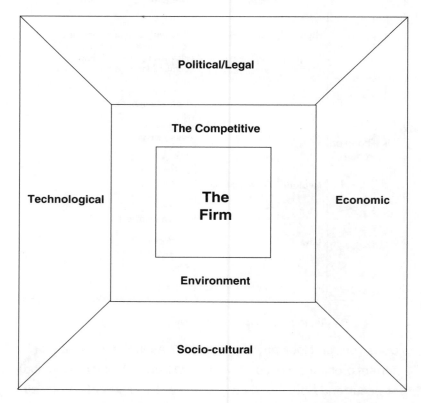

FIGURE 1.4: *The external environment and competition.*

For a business to succeed, it is essential to understand the industry and markets in which it competes. An industry refers to all those organisations supplying a particular product. A market, on the other hand, refers to all those firms who compete with each other. The difference is most easily demonstrated by looking at the car industry. The industry includes all producers of cars, but it also comprises a number of markets, e.g. luxury cars, fleet cars and sports cars. Rolls Royce and Robin Reliant might be in the same industry; they are not in the same market.

Industry analysis

One way of analysing competition in industries has been put forward by Michael Porter of Harvard University. He defined an industry as a group of firms producing products or services which are close substitutes for each other. This is very much like the definition of the market used above.

According to Porter, 'competition in an industry is rooted in its underlying economics, and competitive forces exist that go well beyond the established combatants of a particular industry'. Competitive rivalry takes place between the existing firms in an industry but the intensity of this rivalry is also affected by other players, namely suppliers, buyers, potential entrants and substitute products. The five main forces driving industry competition are summarised in figure 1.5. The combination of forces in an industry determine how profitable activity in that industry will be. The more intense is the rivalry then the lower the profitability. In industries where there is little rivalry, profit margins tend to be higher.

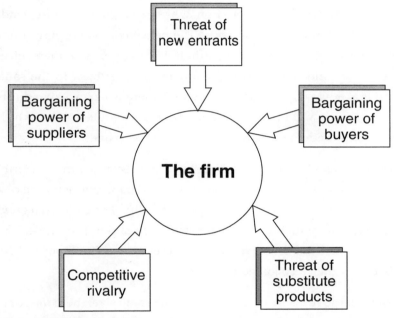

Source: adapted from Porter, M., 1980, *Competitive Strategy*, Free Press.

FIGURE 1.5: *The five competitive forces model.*

COMPETITION FROM EXISTING RIVALS

In most industries, the main source of competition comes from existing firms. Firms compete in a number of ways. In some markets there is fierce price competition. In others, firms compete through advertising and promotions, product design and new products, service or packaging. The degree of rivalry depends on a number of factors:

- the number and size of competitors

- the extent of product differentiation

- the rate of growth of sales

- the structure of costs

- excess capacity

- the height of exit barriers (explained later).

The number and size of competitors In terms of competitive rivalry, the more firms there are and the more alike they are in size, the more fierce tends to be the competition. In industries dominated by a single large firm, there tends to be little competition with the dominant firm able to set the price it likes. If an industry has a few large firms (known as **oligopoly**) then a number of possibilities arise. Firms may collude to 'fix' prices or they may closely follow each others (parallel pricing). In these cases competition, which may still be intense, tends to be through non-price methods. The petrol companies have often been accused of parallel pricing although they argue that their prices reflect costs and that all petrol companies are subject to the same costs. It is however an industry in which there is heavy expenditure on advertising and in which supermarket petrol retailers have little difficulty in undercutting the major petrol companies.

There may also be occasional price 'wars', especially if the few firms are of a similar size. The price war in the newspaper industry is a case in point. *The Times* reduced its price to 30p. *The Daily Telegraph* responded by reducing its price from 50p to 30p in June 1994. This was followed by a further reduction in the price of *The Times* and *The Independent* then also joined in the war.

Even if all the firms in an industry are the same size, there may well be many other differences. They may for example be following very different objectives. Some may be aiming to maximise profits while others may wish to maximise the growth in size of the organisation. This would lead them to very different competitive strategies. The former may wish to charge as high a price as possible while the latter may wish to reduce prices to maximise the volume of sales. Not only might objectives be different but the 'way they do business' may be different. This is especially true if we are looking at international competition.

The extent of product differentiation Product differentiation refers to the way in which suppliers attempt to distinguish their own product from those of competitors. These differences may be real in terms of product quality, design, styling, packaging and so on. They may also be imaginary and re-enforced by persuasive advertising claiming the product is better than competitor's products or it 'washes whiter than white'. Whether consumers really know, does not matter. The important point is that buyers should believe the product is different.

Advertising requires that the products are also differentiated by name. These are known as **brand names**. Some of these brand names have become so well known that the products are often known by the brand name, e.g. vacuum cleaners are often known as 'hoovers', sticky tape as 'Sellotape', white correction fluid as 'tippex'.

A feature of many consumer products is **brand proliferation** with many very similar brands. Brand proliferation is the marketing of many different brand names for what is essentially the same product; for example, personal computers and baked beans are sold under many different brand names.

In terms of competitive rivalry, the greater the degree of differentiation, the more able are firms to increase prices above their competitors. ICI, for example, has created a strong **brand loyalty** for its Dulux paint. Brand loyalty means the willingness of consumers to purchase and continue purchasing the brand of a particular supplier in preference to competitors' products. This enables the supplier to charge prices above their competitors without losing customers. As long as customers believe the paint to be better, they are prepared to pay the higher prices.

Where products are very similar as in commodity markets such as oil, most crops, precious metals or in currency markets, then there is less opportunity for branding. In these markets, customers' buying decisions are generally based on the price of the product.

The rate of growth of sales The rate of growth of sales can be affected by a number of factors. Sales in all industries tend to follow a similar pattern of growth called the **industry life cycle** as shown in figure 1.6.

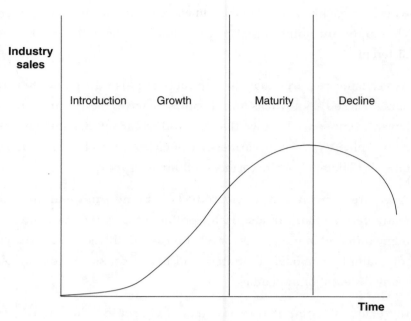

FIGURE 1.6: *The industry life cycle.*

In the introductory stage, growth is relatively slow as a few firms struggle to launch their products. As the products become accepted, the rate of growth accelerates. In this stage, competitive rivalry is relatively weak and good profits can be made. Eventually, the industry moves to the mature stage in which the market becomes saturated and demand is mainly to replace previous purchases. This is followed by decline when new superior products replace old products. In these latter stages, competitive rivalry is usually intense because merely maintaining market share no longer provides sales growth.

The time period associated with each stage will differ from industry to industry. Some industries, such as housing and clothing, may never decline but stay in the mature stage. For most, the life cycle is becoming shorter and shorter as the pace of technological change accelerates. A good example of this accelerating pace of change is in the music recording industry. Vinyl discs took off in the 1960s and were the main form of recording for many years. Vinyl was increasingly replaced by cassette tapes which, in turn, are now being supplemented by compact discs. The compact disc introduced in the 1980s took only six years to reach the mature stage in the USA and is probably approaching that in the UK.

The structure of costs In industries where the ratio of fixed costs to total costs is very high, firms need to maintain a high volume of sales in order to cover their costs. It costs much the same to fly an aeroplane full or half full. The additional cost to the airline of flying an extra passenger is virtually zero so that the income from selling the ticket can be used as a contribution to fixed costs. This explains why airlines offer heavily discounted tickets to try to fill their flights.

Excess capacity Excess capacity refers to the gap between a firm's potential output and actual output. This can result from long-term and short-term reductions in growth. It can also occur because of the 'lumpiness' of capital. In other words, the minimum size of additional investment may increase capacity at a faster rate than the market is growing. This is typical of many industries such as steel, petro-chemicals, hotels, airlines and theme-parks. Where this is the case, there tends to be greater competitive rivalry through increased price competition.

The demand for cars increased throughout the 1980s, resulting in a greater demand for tyres. Tyre manufacturers invested in new plant which came on stream around the end of the decade just when the demand for new cars had begun to decline. The demand for tyres also fell, leaving the tyre manufacturers operating at about 80 per cent of capacity.

The height of exit barriers If it is becoming difficult to survive in an industry then inevitably some firms will want to leave. Some may cease business completely but most want to use their resources to produce different and possibly new products. This is not always so easy because **exit barriers** exist. Some resources are both geographically and occupationally immobile. A shipyard cannot be moved although it may well be used for a different purpose. Aircraft can be moved but they have a limited number of uses. The same can also be said of people. Many, for a variety of reasons, are geographically immobile and we have already seen that the acquisition of new skills is a major challenge for the UK workforce. Where firms find it difficult to leave an industry, this can add to the intensification of competition.

SAT:
allow 20 mins

Managing tasks and solving problems ✔

ACTIVITY 2

The article 'Fresh ferment for the brewers' in Resource 2 at the back of the book tells you something of the structure of the brewing industry.

In not more than 150 words, describe the competitive pressure in the brewing industry.

Summarise your findings in the box below.

Commentary...

The brewing industry is dominated by a small number of brewers each with a wide portfolio of products. There is extensive product differentiation and this is supported by heavy advertising of leading brands. The major brewers have invested large amounts of capital in large plants in which they reap economies of scale. There is probably not much scope for further reductions in costs. There is considerable excess capacity in the industry in both brewing and public house ownership. This is exacerbated by the fact that some would like to leave the industry but are finding it difficult to do so. This situation intensifies the rivalry. Much investment is taking place in differentiating pubs to appeal to different customers.

THE THREAT OF NEW ENTRANTS

Another feature of a competitive market is the freedom of firms to enter markets. If firms are making good profits then this will be an attraction to new firms. This will increase supply and ultimately lower profits but only if firms can gain entry to the industry and this is not always possible. Entry may be frustrated in a number of ways:

- economies of scale
- the experience curve
- capital requirements
- product differentiation
- source of supply and access to distribution channels
- defensive reactions
- government and legal barriers.

ECONOMIES OF SCALE

Economies of scale refer to the reductions in unit costs that can be achieved as the scale of the firm's output is increased. In other words, the more you produce, the lower the average cost of production. They are often an important way of gaining a competitive advantage over existing rivals. They may also act as a significant barrier to new entrants if these scale economies cannot be matched. Economies of scale can occur in a number of areas.

Technical economies are associated with the production process itself.

- **Specialisation** – where output is relatively low, workers may have to undertake a number of different tasks. As the volume of output increases, there are greater opportunities for workers to specialise in one job. This increases proficiency in that job, and saves time in switching between jobs and in training.

- **Specialised machines** – as volume is increased, there are greater opportunities to use bigger and technically more efficient specialised machinery. In the car industry, a firm producing only a handful of cars per week such as Morgan sports cars would not be able afford to use the kind of specialist robots used by the mass car producers such as Ford.

○ **Indivisibilities** – some types of equipment have a high minimum size. An oil refinery, a blast furnace and a steel rolling mill, all need to be of a certain minimum size. This minimum may be a technical limit but it is more likely to be an economic limit, i.e. the market may not justify the cost of a smaller plant as these fixed costs must be met whatever the level of output. This problem is exacerbated when a number of different machines with different capacities are linked in the production process. In this case, a large volume of output would be necessary to employ the most efficient combination of machines.

○ **Increased dimensions** – cost savings may arise because of the physical dimensions of the project. Doubling the dimensions of oil tankers, buses, boilers and storage tanks, for example, does not double the costs of production.

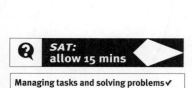

SAT:
allow 15 mins

Managing tasks and solving problems ✔

Applying numeracy   ✔

ACTIVITY 3

Imagine that you want to manufacture a product which involves three different stages of production. The machines in the three different stages have capacities of 30 units per hour, 40 units per hour and 50 units per hour, respectively. To maximise efficiency you want to make sure that all machines are run at full capacity.

Calculate the minimum output necessary to achieve a level of production at which all machines are working at full capacity, and calculate the numbers of machines required in each stage.

Explain in your own words why economies of scale might make it difficult for a manufacturer to break into an existing market.

Commentary...

If only one machine of each type were in use then the maximum output possible would be 30 units per hour. This would mean that the other two machines were being run with spare capacity, 10 units per hour in one case and 20 units per hour in the other. This might be typical of a small firm with a small output.

To find the output level which would ensure all machines were running at full capacity you would have to find the lowest common multiple of 30, 40 and 50, i.e. the lowest number into which each of these numbers divides.

That number is 600. So the level of production required to run all the machines at full capacity is 600 units per hour. You would need 20 of the 30 units per hour machines, 15 of the 40 units per hour machines and 12 of the 50 units per hour machines.

This is another technical economy of scale which is usually referred to as the **principle of multiples**. It also follows from this that production can only be increased efficiently in multiples of 600 units per hour. Try working out how many machines you would need to produce 900 units per hour to check this.

Your answer should have made reference to the reduction in unit costs that come from increases in the size of the organisation. Note that it is unit costs that are important, i.e. the cost of producing each unit of production. Total costs will, of course, be bigger but, in competing with other firms, it is the cost of each unit that is important. The difficulty then that new firms would face in trying to enter the market is having a sufficiently large share of the market to take advantage of any economies of scale. Unless a new firm is able to do this it will be at a serious cost disadvantage in competing with existing firms.

Economies of scale are found not simply in the production process.

- **Purchasing** – the larger the company, the greater the possibility of employing specialist buyers. There will also be increased opportunities to obtain discounts for bulk purchases of production and other materials.

- **Finance** – large firms find it easier to raise finance. Small firms are generally limited to borrowing from the banks whereas large firms have access to a wide variety of financial institutions. In addition, they can borrow money by issuing debentures or they may chose to issue new shares.

Large firms also find it cheaper to borrow money. This is because they offer greater security and because economies of scale also exist in lending money; it is cheaper per pound to lend £1 million than £1,000.

- **Marketing and distribution** – as with purchasing, the larger the firm, the greater the possibility of employing specialist sales staff. These staff may be better deployed possibly on a regional basis so saving wasted travelling time.

  Large firms may also develop their own distribution network. They may make significant savings by organising their deliveries more efficiently than a small business operating one or two lorries nationwide.

  Savings can also be made on promotional costs, such as leaflets and advertising printing. The most expensive advertising media is television which may only be affordable by large firms. It is, however, the most effective in terms of its impact and its reach, reducing the cost per person reached.

- **Managerial** – there are several cost savings associated with management. One is that larger firms can afford to hire specialist managerial staff and thus improve efficiency. As there tends to be some positive correlation between organisational size and managerial salaries, large organisations should be able to attract 'better' management. There are also economies in terms of the number of managers needed as the organisation grows. A doubling of turnover should not result in a doubling of management numbers. Some management functions can now be fulfilled by computers but, as in production, the volume of output must be sufficient to warrant the expenditure on the machines. This trend would further increase the managerial economies available to large firms.

- **Research and development (R&D)** – this is becoming increasingly sophisticated and costly. It may, as a consequence, be only financiable to any great extent in the largest firms. Large-scale research is likely to lead to reduced product development costs and production costs.

ACTIVITY 4

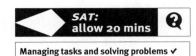
Review the text on economies of scale.

Make a list, with a brief explanation of each item, of the economies of scale you think would be possible in the operation of a chain of supermarkets.

Note which economies of scale you think would not apply in this case.

Commentary...

One of the major economies enjoyed by supermarket chains is their 'purchasing power'. This is so great that they are often able to dictate terms to their suppliers.

They are also in a position to achieve 'financial' economies in that they have access to a wide variety of sources and can borrow at relatively low rates of interest.

These chains usually have their own regional warehousing operations and fleet of lorries enabling them to enjoy economies of 'distribution'.

'Advertising' economies are also available in that they are able to afford high-cost but effective TV and press advertising. Although high-cost in relation to sales, it is relatively cheap.

Finally, they employ specialist 'managers' in all their divisions.

Economies which would probably not apply are the technical and R&D economies.

In addition to economies of scale, there are several other factors which can frustrate firms' attempts to move into new markets.

The experience curve The experience curve theory says that as a firm gains experience in production and distribution, it learns from that experience and, as a consequence, the costs of production will fall.

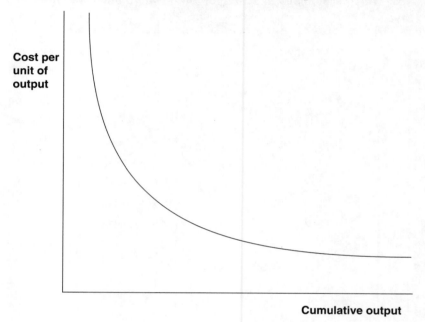

FIGURE 1.7: *The experience curve.*

One group of management consultants in America (the Boston Consulting Group) claimed that doubling production experience would produce a fall in costs of 30 per cent. This may be true for some industries but not for all. The cause of the decline in unit costs is a mixture of scale economies, the learning curve for labour (i.e. that as each worker becomes more experienced, his/her output per hour increases) and capital labour substitution. Therefore, the more capital intensive and complex the operation, the more likely it is that the experience effects will be greater. The effect is less in service industries and in fragmented markets.

The implication in those markets where experience curve effects are strong is that, if firms can grow faster than their competitors, they should have the lowest unit costs. It also follows that the firm with the largest market share should have the lowest unit costs. Firms who are not very far along the experience curve have difficulty competing on costs and should pursue some other competitive strategy.

Capital requirements To break into some markets, especially those where there are substantial economies of scale and where existing firms are well down the learning curve, may require massive capital outlays. This investment may be for capital equipment, research and development, advertising or on operating losses in establishing a foot in the market. This may be beyond all but the largest of existing firms who can use profits from other areas of business.

Product differentiation In industries where there is product differentiation, new entrants have to overcome brand loyalty. This may require heavy expenditure on advertising to gain brand recognition.

Brand proliferation also means that the potential market share of a new firm with a single new brand may be much lower than existing firms with a number of brands. The UK detergents market is dominated by two producers, Proctor and Gamble and Unilever, each producing a number of brands limiting the potential market share of a new competitor with a single brand.

Source of supply and access to distribution channels In order for new firms to enter an industry they must be able to access sources of supply and channels of distribution. If either of these are controlled by exiting firms then access may be denied. Distributors may also have strong preferences for existing brands as creating space for new products is both risky and costly.

Defensive reactions In assessing whether or not entry into a new market is wise, account must be taken of how existing firms will react to a new entrant. This depends very much on the structure of the industry and the extent of competitive rivalry. It can be gauged by looking at past behaviour when threatened by new entrants. Entry might be forestalled by price-cutting or increased expenditure on advertising. Firms may also invest in excess capacity to deter entry. The existence of excess capacity may be seen as a threat by potential entrants because existing firms would be in a position to increase output at any time and thereby reduce prices.

Government and legal barriers Entry into some industries may be subject to regulation. Banking, broadcasting, taxis, public houses, telecommunications, mining are some examples where entry is subject to regulation. Patents and copyrights also act as barriers in the information industry.

Government competition policy, discussed next, can also prevent firms' entry into new markets. The provision of subsidies and investment incentives may also influence entry.

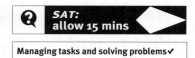

Managing tasks and solving problems ✓

ACTIVITY 5

You have entrepreneurial flair and decide that you will set up in business.

You are considering whether to set up in business as one of the following:

- **A brewery**

- **A hairdresser**

- **A pet food manufacturer**

Write a short paragraph on how you will be affected by barriers to entry in each of the businesses.

Commentary...

A brewery – The costs of setting up a small brewery are relatively small and many people have done just that in the last 15 years. However, the brewery will remain small. There are significant economies of scale in production which you will not be able to match but these can be more than offset because the advertising and transport cost of large brewers are enormous. So you may end up with a pint of beer which costs less to get to the market than the big brewers' pint. But where will you sell it? The big brewers control many of the outlets and this is the biggest obstacle to expansion. There is also much excess capacity in the brewing industry with some players keen to leave.

Very little capital is required to set up as a hairdresser. Premises can be rented. Assuming you have some talent for cutting hair then there is nothing much to stop you. But be warned, there are an awful lot of hairdressers.

The pet food market is dominated by Mars and Spillers in dog foods and Mars, Spiller and Quaker in cat foods. There are substantial economies of scale and these are essential to compete on price. Mars and Spillers continually invest in new technology to reduce costs. They also advertise heavily. Many large companies have withdrawn from this market.

THE AVAILABILITY OF SUBSTITUTES

The availability of substitutes is an important determinant of the price that can be charged and therefore the rate of return. The greater the number and the more alike the substitutes are, the more likely are customers to switch to a substitute if there is a price rise – in other words, the greater the price elasticity of demand for that product.

Price elasticity of demand refers to the responsiveness of demand to changes in price. Economists refer to the responsiveness of demand to changes in the price of another product as the cross elasticity of demand. For example, if the price of tea increases and this results in a rise in demand for coffee, the two are substitute products. They would have a positive **cross elasticity of demand**. The higher the measure of cross elasticity (i.e. if a relatively small increase in price brings about a relatively large increase in demand), the greater the substitutability. If the cross elasticity is negative then the goods are said to be **complementary goods**. As the price of one increases, the demand for the other falls. This is the case when goods are in **joint demand**, e.g. tennis rackets and tennis balls. If the price of rackets goes up, the demand for tennis balls falls.

Identifying substitute products is not always easy. In one sense, all goods are substitutes for each other in that they compete for a limited amount of income but this is not very useful to a firm trying to identify competitor products. In markets where there is not much branding (e.g. commodity markets or petrol), products tend to be close substitutes. In these cases, there is not much room for price differentials between competitors as customers will soon switch from one to the other, assuming switching costs are low.

Switching costs are the costs involved in switching from one supplier to another. They also affect the degree of substitutability and therefore the possibility of differential pricing. Gas and electricity are close substitutes for heating and cooking but switching from one fuel to the other involves expenditure on installing new appliances.

Time is another factor to consider when considering substitutes. In the example above, a small price difference between gas and electricity would not see customers changing their heating immediately. If the price difference remained then as customers came to change their appliances some would switch to the cheaper source of fuel.

In industries in which products are highly differentiated there may be no close substitutes. Here substitutability will be determined by the price-performance perception held by customers. In other words, customers will be prepared to pay a premium price for what they believe to be the better product. Once the price differential exceeds the perceived extra value, they will switch to a substitute product.

The threat posed by substitutes is not always easily identified. It is often a problem of identifying the market in which a firm competes. Clocks, for example, tell the time. The one in this office is a perfectly adequate clock for telling the time. It was cheap; it is reliable but it is not very attractive. On the other hand, the clock at home, is very attractive. It was very expensive but, oddly, it is not so reliable, but telling the time is less important than being an attractive ornament. Are these clocks operating in the same market?

The threat from substitutes will affect the profitability of the industry. Where there are close substitutes, profitability will tend to be low. Firms therefore need to identify substitutes and try to minimise the threat posed. They may reduce costs, try to differentiate or look for alternative uses for their own products.

ACTIVITY 6

SAT:
allow 10 mins

Managing tasks and solving problems ✔

Identify the main threat from substitutes in the following cases:

- a brewer of beer

- a public house

- a TV manufacturer

- frozen pea producer

- cinema

- tyre manufacturer

Commentary...

The obvious answers are other beer brewers, public houses, TV manufacturers, pea producers, cinemas and tyre manufacturers, but substitutes can also be similar products or activities. It is often a question of definition. For example, should public houses see themselves simply as places to drink or are they in the leisure and entertainment market?

Beer brewers' biggest threat has come from lager manufacturers but drinking habits change and alcohol-free drinks and wine are other threats.

Pubs face increasing threat from take-home sales from supermarkets and off licences. They also compete with other leisure activities.

TV manufacturer – other forms of entertainment

Frozen peas – tinned and packet peas but also other vegetables and foodstuffs

Cinema – other forms of entertainment and rented videos

Tyre manufacturers – no close substitutes other than other manufacturers' tyres.

THE POWER OF SUPPLIERS

Most of the above analysis has been concerned with the firm as a seller of goods or services but firms also operate as buyers. Firms may be buying raw materials, components, finance and labour. Firms are reliant on their suppliers in terms of availability, price and quality. Some buyers are very powerful and are able to dictate many of the terms on which they do business with their suppliers. In the food retailing industry, where a few large retail chains account for over 70 per cent of the market, some of them are able to charge suppliers for shelf-space for a new product.

Suppliers can also exert power, especially if they combine together. A good example is the oil producers who formed the Organisation of Petroleum Exporting Countries (OPEC) and were able to quadruple oil prices in the 1970s. Workers, who are rather more fragmented form unions to promote their interests and in some cases have proved to be very powerful.

Supplier power is likely to be strong when the following conditions exist.

- There are only a few suppliers and the supplying industry is more concentrated than the industry it is supplying. If the suppliers are numerous and less concentrated than the buyers then the buyers will be dominant. For example, the brewing industry is dominated by five large brewers who are in a very powerful position in relation to the thousands of pubs they supply.

- The industry is not an important customer of the supplier. If only a small proportion of sales go to the industry, the buyer will have little influence. The greater the proportion of the suppliers sales going to one customer then the greater the power of the buyer to exert influence.

- The input is important to the buyer. If, for example, it is a critical component in the production process of the buyer, this will give the supplier great influence.

- There are no close substitutes. Clearly, if buyers can find close substitutes, then suppliers have less power.

- The extent of product differentiation. This is similar to the last point. The more the supplier can differentiate the product and tie the buyer to the product because of some unique quality, the harder it will be to find a suitable substitute.

- Switching costs are high. If, for example, a soft drinks producer currently uses bottles in its production process and the supply terms change for the worse, converting to cans would involve setting up a completely new production process.

- There is the possibility of forward integration. If suppliers are in a position where they might enter the industry they are supplying because they are not obtaining the prices they require, this will increase their power. They do not have to enter; the threat of entry should be sufficient.

We tend to think of supplies as mainly raw materials and components but finance, labour, land and buildings are also important supplies. The same principles also apply.

THE POWER OF BUYERS

The analysis of buyer power is very similar to that of suppliers, as it is the same relationship but from the opposite perspective.

Buyer power is likely to be strong when the following conditions exist.

- The number of buyers is few and more concentrated than the industry they are buying from. This may be true when industry is buying from suppliers but in final goods markets, buyers are usually fragmented.

- Purchases are important to the seller.

- The purchase is not important to the buyer.

- There are close substitutes.

- There is little product differentiation.

- Switching costs are low.

- There is a real threat of backward integration, i.e. buyers entering their suppliers market.

You have already seen that supermarkets are a good example of a market in which there is considerable buyer power. Marks and Spencer are well known for being able to dictate terms to their suppliers. The lesson for any supplier is not to become too dependent on any one buyer.

COMPETITOR ANALYSIS

The analysis so far has two elements. The PEST analysis identifies the factors in the broad environment which impinge on the industry. The industry analysis shows how the structure of particular industries can affect competition and profitability. It also highlights opportunities for firms to influence an industry's structure in order to improve their competitive position and enhance their profitability. The next element in the analysis involves a much closer look at the firm's competitors.

In a fragmented industry, there are many different firms and there would not be much point in studying closely one of these firms (unless it was typical of many others) since any one firm would have little impact on the market. However, it is much more common to find that an industry is dominated by a few large producers. You can probably think of many examples such as the car industry, soft drinks, detergents, and the brewing industry. In each of these industries, dominant firms exercise a considerable influence on the market, and it is these we study when carrying out competitive analysis.

The analysis seeks to understand the competition and predict how they will react to environmental changes and to any changes your firm is likely to make. To carry out this analysis of competitor firms, the type of information that you need is as follows:

- The objectives of the other businesses – are they trying to increase their market share? Are they aiming at a particular level of profit? Are they achieving these goals?

- The methods they are using to achieve these objectives – are they launching new products? Are they moving into new areas? Are they opening new factories?

- The strengths and weaknesses of each of the competitors – this requires an analysis of each firms resources, financial, equipment, work force, product range, brand loyalty and management.

Understanding this information helps to determine the type of competitive strategy a firm should adopt.

ACTIVITY 7

SAT:
allow 1 hour

Communicating ✔

Managing tasks and solving problems ✔

Throughout this session we have been looking at the competitive environment in the brewing industry. With the background information in the article (Resource 2), you should now be in a position to analyse the industry using the 'five forces model'.

Write a short report (about 750 words) about each of the forces in relation to the brewing industry:

- threat of new entrants

- threat of substitute products

- bargaining power of supplier

- bargaining power of buyers

- competitive rivalry

Summarise your findings in the box below.

Commentary...

Your report should cover the following points.

Entrants There are few barriers to small-scale operators. Barriers to large-scale operation include substantial capital costs and economies of scale. The main barriers are in distribution and marketing. Many outlets are tied and the big brewers undertake considerable advertising.

Substitutes The main threat is from lager, but most lager is produced by the large brewers. Demand for cask ales is increasing which has helped some regional brewers but big brewers are busy developing their portfolios of these products. Alcohol-free and other drinks are also controlled by big brewers. There is a threat to pubs from home drinking and other leisure activities.

Power of suppliers This is real in relation to big brewers but ingredients are readily available.

Power of buyers Brewers control most of public houses. The ultimate buyer, the consumer, has no power at all other than not to drink. Supermarkets sell a large proportion of take-home sales. They are in a position to be able to bargain with the brewers.

Competitive rivalry There is very little price competition although excess capacity has squeezed margins. Brewers differentiate their products from others and brands are supported by massive expenditure on advertising. Competition also takes place through differentiating and refurbishing public houses.

Competitive strategies

Once we have analysed the total environment in which the organisation is operating, including the competitors, we are in a position to consider how a firm may gain a competitive advantage. According to Porter, this can be achieved through one of three generic strategies:

- producing a product at a lower cost than other competitors

- differentiating the product so that buyers are prepared to pay extra for what they perceive as a better product

● focus, or niche, strategy which aims to compete by being the lowest cost producer or by differentiation but in a narrow segment of the market.

These choices are illustrated in figure 1.8.

Source of competitive advantage

Competitive scope		Low cost	Differentiation
	Industry	Cost Leadership	Differentiation
	Segmented	Focused cost leadership	Focused differentiation

Source: Porter, M.E., 1985, *Competitive Advantage: Creating and Sustaining Superior Performance*, Free Press.

FIGURE 1.8: *Porter's generic strategies.*

Porter stresses that firms should pursue only one of these strategies otherwise it will become 'stuck in the middle'. Unless it chooses a clear strategy of either cost-leadership or differentiation, it will lose out to firms who are clear about their strategy.

COST LEADERSHIP

Cost leadership means becoming the overall lowest cost producer in the industry. The cost leader should exploit all sources of cost reduction. This may involve producing high volumes in order to reap cost advantages from scale economies. It also means looking to every part of the business (e.g. facilities, perks, overhead control and credit control) in order to reduce costs.

As a strategy, it is probably most effective in markets where there is not much scope for differentiation. Competition is then likely to be on price. There may well be differences in the products but not sufficient to charge a premium price for the difference. Being the least-cost producer allows the firm to compete on price or charge similar prices to others making above-average profits. These additional profits can then be re-invested in improving product quality.

Toyota (in the car industry) and Kwik Save (in the grocery business) are good examples of this strategy. They both pride themselves on being low-cost, efficient producers. Toyota's efficiency allows it to sell a range of cars at prices below that of its main competitors. Kwik

Save run 'no nonsense' stores (no bakeries, no crèches, no delicatessens) with low overheads. They therefore do not need the high margins and high sales volumes of their competitors. This allows them to sell a limited range of branded products at prices below those of their competitors, although neither of them have the lowest prices. A low-cost strategy does not necessarily mean charging the lowest prices.

They are also in a good position to counter other competitive threats. Being the lowest cost producer makes it difficult for competitors to sustain a price war. Low prices (or the threat of them) may also deter new entrants. It will be difficult for buyers to bargain down prices as cheaper alternatives will be difficult to find. Increased supply prices are not as threatening to the lowest cost producer as to other less efficient, higher cost producers. Price can also be used as a defence against substitutes which would either have to beat the price or offer some superior feature.

There are dangers in over-emphasising cost reduction. Firms may lose touch with consumer requirements.

- As consumers become more affluent they may well look for the 'frills' which may be missing in the low-cost operation.

- There is a limit to the cost reductions from scale economies and learning experience. As the industry matures, cost differences are harder to maintain.

- New technology can soon wipe out cost advantages held by firms using efficient manufacturing or distribution methods.

- Multi-product firms can cover their overheads on more profitable products, enabling them to reduce prices on some products.

Perhaps a low-cost strategy is the riskiest strategy because, in the end, there can only be one least-cost producer.

RECALL:
allow 10 mins

In your own words, describe
what is meant by a cost-
leadership strategy and say
in which circumstances it is
likely to be effective.

Write up to 50 words.

DIFFERENTIATION

This strategy is about developing products which are in some way
unique so that the seller can charge a premium price. This uniqueness
must be easily recognisable by the consumer and difficult to imitate.
Uniqueness can be achieved in many ways:

- superior technology

- product reliability

- delivery

- availability

- service

- design

- performance

- image

- durability.

You can probably think of many more. The main points to make are that:

- the buyer must perceive the uniqueness and that the
  uniqueness must be seen as having value – it is not sufficient to
  be unique

- the cost of creating the differentiation must be less than the price premium.

Once a firm has successfully differentiated its products and identified that product through a brand name, it has a monopoly of that brand. It is then in a strong position to protect itself against competition. It will have created brand loyalty which protects it from new entrants and substitute products, and weakens the bargaining power of buyers as there are no close substitutes. Customers will be less sensitive to price competition and more willing to accept any price increases that come about from increases in input prices.

As with cost-leadership strategies, there are also dangers.

- The costs of differentiation may exceed the price premium. Cost containment is still important.

- Some products can be easily imitated.

- Firms who differentiate across a number of market segments may lose out to firms who concentrate on a particular market segment.

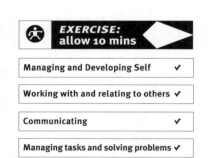

EXERCISE:
allow 10 mins

Managing and Developing Self	✔
Working with and relating to others	✔
Communicating	✔
Managing tasks and solving problems	✔

ACTIVITY 8

Divide into groups of four.

In list A are a number of products/organisations. In list B are a number of ways in which organisations may differentiate their products. Against each of the products/organisations indicate which factors are used to differentiate them from other competitor products. (As an example, the first one has been done for you.)

List A — Products

1. **Rolls-Royce cars — (a)(b)(c)(h)**

2. **Heinz Baked Beans**

3. **Carling Black Label**

4. **Dulux paint**

5. **Persil**

6. **McDonalds**

7. **Sainsbury's**

8. **IBM computers**

9. **Duracell batteries**

List B — Differentiating factors

(a) Superior technology

(b) Product reliability

(c) Quality

(d) Availability

(e) Service

(f) Design

(g) Performance

(h) Image

(i) Value for money

Commentary...

Rolls-Royce cars: (a) (b) (c) (h)

Heinz Baked Beans: (h)

Carling Black Label: (h)

Dulux paint: (c) (g)

Persil: (g) (h)

McDonalds: (e) (h)

Sainsbury's: (c) (i)

IBM computers: (a) (d) (g)

Duracell batteries: (i)

Your list may well differ from the suggested one. These are perceptions gained mostly from advertising, and your perceptions may well be different. A lot of these products sell on their image, however that is defined, created by heavy advertising. Duracell, for example, claims that its batteries last longer – therefore their differentiating feature has been listed as 'durability'. Without putting this to the test, it is difficult to justify the claim.

Focus

Focus strategies seek to achieve a competitive advantage from cost leadership or differentiation in a segment of the market rather than across the whole market. A market segment is a portion of a larger market. Up to now we have assumed that all customers in a market are alike but this is far from the truth. Market segmentation divides a market into a number of smaller sub-markets because not all buyers are alike. For example, the computer market can be divided into the business market and the home market. The home market could be further segmented into the serious computer user and those who only use computers for games. Having identified a segment, suppliers are more able to target the needs of a particular consumer. Banks, for example, well aware of the future earning potential of students, target that particular segment of the market with all sorts of special offers. The hope is, of course, that those students will stay with the bank for the rest of their lives.

There are many ways of segmenting a market:

- geographical area

- age

- lifestyle

- sex

- product use

- income

- socio-economic group

- occupation

- customer size

- usage rate.

ACTIVITY 9

From your knowledge of the UK car industry list nine possible market segments. To get you started, you might like to look back to the end of the section on the external environment.

SAT:
allow 10 mins

Managing tasks and solving problems ✔

Commentary...

Some of the segments you might have included are; family cars, fleet cars, sports, vintage, luxury, 'boy-racer', off-road, specialist, taxis, economic to run, small? This list is not exhaustive, but you should have the idea by now.

Having segmented the market, the firm can then focus its product(s) on the target market. The focused operator should be able to out-perform the broad operator because the requirements of the market have been analysed and the products designed specifically to meet that target need.

There are some dangers in this approach.

- The target segment for some reason changes, maybe tastes change or there are demographic changes.

- Your target is not sufficiently focused. In other words, it is itself made up of smaller segments which a competitor identifies and the focuser becomes 'out-focused'.

- Costs differences narrow to eliminate any cost differential.

These concepts – of cost leadership, differentiation and focus – are very helpful to managers thinking about strategy and ways of creating a competitive advantage. There are, however, problems in trying to classify firms into rigid compartments. In some industries, the strategies may be mutually exclusive while in others it is possible to pursue a combination of the approaches.

In the latter case, differentiation may allow for some premium pricing. Attention to costs may enable firms to boost margins to allow investment in 'frills' and, at the same time, deter price wars and entry by some firms into the market.

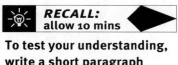

RECALL:
allow 10 mins

To test your understanding, write a short paragraph explaining the meaning of a focus strategy.

Strategic direction

Having analysed the external environment and selected a competitive strategy, you are then in a position to consider the future development of the business. There are three basic options: stability, retrenchment or growth.

STABILITY

This option assumes that the current performance is satisfactory. The aim is to retain market share. This does not mean do nothing; firms pursuing this strategy have to compete actively in order to maintain their position. The products and markets are likely to be the same but resources need to be aimed at increasing efficiency, reducing costs and increasing profits. The firm may grow but it will be because the whole market is growing rather than market share increasing.

RETRENCHMENT

Retrenchment occurs when a firm has to reduce the scale of its operations. This may mean liquidating part of the business if the operation is no longer profitable (possibly because of a declining market). Divestment (selling off part of the business) may occur if the business is considered peripheral to the firm's core activities. Finally, some businesses in dire straits may need to turnaround their operations. This may involve tightening up on costs and cutting back to basic operations. It may also include liquidation and/or divestment.

GROWTH

The options for growth are summarised in Ansoff's growth vector matrix shown in figure 1.9.

	Products	Present	New
Markets			
Present		Market penetration	Product development
New		Market development	Diversification

Source: Ansoff, H.I., 1987, *Corporate Strategy*, Rev. Edn.

FIGURE 1.9: *Ansoff's growth vector matrix.*

In this grid, four strategy alternatives are presented: market penetration, market development, product development and diversification.

Market penetration In this strategy, the firm operates with the existing products in the same markets. Growth comes from increasing market share. This involves taking customers away from competitors. The competitive strategies discussed above are relevant; improving product quality and/or reducing costs are the keys to winning more customers. This is probably easier in a growing market; in a mature, static market the leaders should have considerable scale and learning experience advantages. This is the least risk strategy as the firm is operating with familiar products in familiar markets.

Market development Here the firm operates with its existing products but seeks new markets. This is likely to occur where a firm has a successful product but growth in the current market is slowing. The most common development is to take the product into new geographical markets, although with minor modifications new segments may be opened and even new uses developed for the product. Doc Martens developed their market by turning boots and shoes for work into fashion items. Tobacco manufacturers who are seeing their traditional markets decline have been developing new markets overseas where regulations are less stringent and where there are greater opportunities for growth. Many other industries are seeking to 'go global' and their brands (perhaps with some modification to suit local tastes) are becoming internationally recognised. Coca Cola, McDonalds, The Body Shop, Levis, IBM, Nestlé are some examples. This is a higher risk strategy than market penetration as managers will be operating in unknown territory.

Product development This strategy involves the firm remaining in existing markets but developing new products. It would be typical of consumer goods markets where the life cycle of the products is relatively short and/or where brand loyalty is not very strong. This would be true of consumer electronic markets in which producers tend to bring out new models every year. The assessment of risk is difficult. Product development is very costly. Many new product ideas never reach the market and many of those that do, fail. Product development therefore tends to be modifications and improvements to existing products. This is still a costly business but the costs of not producing new models may be greater if sales are lost to new products from competitors.

Diversification The final, most complex and highest risk option is diversification in which the firm enters new markets with new products. This takes one of two forms:

- **Concentric diversification** – the firm expands into new but related activities. Many chemical companies, including ICI, have expanded into related products such as paint and pharmaceuticals, largely because of their research and development expertise. W H Smith has extended its retailing activities into areas other than stationery. Guinness purchased Distillers' range of Scotch whiskies which fitted closely to its existing product range. The hope is that the benefits of using existing skills and experience outweigh the risks.

- **Conglomerate diversification** – the firm expands into new unrelated activities. This may be a way of continuing growth when current markets have become saturated. It may also be a way of smoothing out the ups and downs of the business cycle or even seasonal variations in demand. Although it is probably the riskiest option, it can spread risk across a number of products and a number of markets. In most cases, conglomerates will be controlled by a holding company. The holding company will generally manage the overall finances of the organisation setting profit targets for the individual businesses. Lonrho is such a conglomerate, with interests ranging from mining to car distribution.

The trend in the 1960s and 1970s was to diversify so that risks could be spread but this trend has been reversed in the 1980s and 1990s. Many of the huge conglomerates proved difficult to manage in an increasingly turbulent world. The trend is now to divest themselves of their peripheral businesses and stick to what they know best, which is their core business.

INTEGRATION

Growth is often achieved through external growth strategies of merger, acquisition or joint ventures, collectively known as integration. Integration can take place either horizontally or vertically.

Horizontal integration refers to the combination of firms at the same stage in the production chain. Many of the large organisations of today are the result of numerous mergers and takeovers in the past. At the turn of the century, there were something in the order of 6,500 breweries. In 1992, according to the Brewers Society, there were 95. Some of the old breweries closed but most have been swallowed up by the five large brewers that remain.

In the car market, Ford have acquired Jaguar. Rover, previously known as Austin Rover and before that British Leyland, are now part of BMW. British Leyland was a combination of previously independent car producers such as Austin, Morris, Triumph, Wolsey, MG and Standard.

Horizontal integration increases the size of the organisation which should generate cost advantages. It will also eliminate competition and increase market share which may give the firm greater market power.

Vertical integration involves the combining of firms which are at different stages in the chain of production. This make take one of two forms:

- **Backward vertical integration** – a firm joins with a firm which is further back in the chain of production. In other words a firm takes over its sources of supply. Motor manufacturers may take over component suppliers; a chocolate manufacturer may take over a chocolate mould manufacturer or a cocoa plantation.

- **Forward vertical integration** – a firm seeks to control its outlets. Brewers own many of the public houses through which they sell their products. Most of the tyre distributors are owned by the six tyre producers who control approximately 85 per cent of world tyre production.

Many of the major oil companies are totally integrated in that they control everything in the chain of production: wells, drilling rigs, tankers, refineries and petrol stations.

Many of the benefits of vertical integration can be obtained without formal integration. Many firms today co-operate with others in joint ventures. Others, including Marks & Spencer and many Japanese companies, build close relationships with their suppliers. In this way, they can work together to develop new products and make sure that quality, availability and price are satisfactory to both parties.

RECALL:
allow 20 mins

Write a short paragraph which explains the following methods of growth:

Market development

Conglomerate diversification

Vertical integration

summary

This session has concentrated on making sense of the external environment. What is not included, because of the obvious difficulties, is any internal analysis of organisations. Analysing the environment and identifying opportunities and threats is only one element in charting a path for a firm. It says nothing about whether that firm is capable of following that path. That requires an analysis of the resources and capabilities of the firm.

> ▶ You now have a number of tools at your disposal: the PEST analysis, priority impact matrix, Porter's five forces analysis, competitor analysis.

> ▶ You should also understand something about the different strategies that firms may follow – cost leadership, differentiation and focus – and the direction they may take. This should enable you to make sense of a chaotic and sometimes turbulent external environment.

> ▶ You need to remember that the ideas in this session are tools to be used. Not all of them will apply in every situation. It is a case of selecting those that do and using and applying them to that case.

The legal regulation of business

Objectives

After participating in this session, you should be able to:

- ▶ outline different interpretations of the operation of legal controls on business

- ▶ explain the main features of the law and court system that are relevant to business

- ▶ specify the limits placed on business operations by the laws relating to employment

- ▶ describe the main features of the health and safety requirements imposed on businesses

- ▶ give an account of the legal framework of consumer rights

- ▶ describe the environmental and safety regulations governing business activity.

In working through this session, you will practise the following BTEC common skills:

Managing and Developing Self	✔
Working with and Relating to others	✔
Communicating	✔
Managing Tasks and Solving Problems	✔
Applying Numeracy	
Applying Technology	
Applying Design and Creativity	

The legal system

All forms of behaviour are governed by rules. Custom, convention and tradition are the main rules that govern behaviour in everyday life. However, some rules are made and enforced by the state. These rules make up the law.

Individuals and organisations, including businesses, operate within a legal framework. Laws exist to regulate behaviour and to resolve conflicts. The legal system is made up of laws along with the organisations and individuals involved in administering them, such as the legal profession, the courts and the police.

There are strong differences of opinion about the way in which the legal system works. There are three main viewpoints:

- **The centre** People in the centre see the law as a set of rules for resolving disputes and regulating behaviour, which works to the benefit of everyone as consumers, producers and citizens.

- **The radical left** People on the radical left see the legal system as means by which the interests of a wealthy and powerful minority are furthered at the expense of the majority of members of society and that where the law gives rights to ordinary people, they are often difficult to enforce.

- **The new right** People who hold new-right views believe that the law works to the benefit of everyone, but they also believe that its scope, particularly in relation to the operations of business, should be limited. They argue that there is far too much intervention in what should be the freely chosen behaviour of employers, employees and consumers.

It is usual to make a distinction between criminal and civil law.

Criminal law:

- Defines those actions which the state will punish

- Applies when offences are investigated by the police; proceedings are normally brought by the Crown Prosecution Service

- Requires proof to be 'beyond reasonable doubt'

- Means that the guilty are punished

Civil law:

- Lays down rules for the conduct of relations between persons or organisations

- Allows, where damage occurs, the person affected to seek compensation

- Applies when proceedings are normally brought by private parties

- Requires proof to be 'on the balance of probabilities'

- Means that successful actions normally end with an award of damages or an injunction (order) that the defendant behave in a prescribed fashion

The development of both the criminal and the civil law reflects wider economic, political and cultural changes in society. The emergence of Britain as a trading and commercial maritime power in the seventeenth and eighteenth centuries, and the growth of industrial capitalism in the nineteenth century, were associated with changes in law to regulate new patterns of economic behaviour. Industrialisation thus led to the expansion of new branches of law involving such issues as consumer rights and safety at work. Laws, and the legal system generally, are continuously being adapted to new economic and social circumstances.

SAT: allow 10 mins

Managing tasks and solving problems ✔

ACTIVITY 1

John Smith bought a bike from his neighbour. The bike fell apart when he got on it, damaging John Smith's left knee. John Smith wanted compensation. Should he go to the police or to a solicitor?

Write up to 40 words.

Commentary...

Damages are sought through the civil law, not the criminal law, and so John should go to a solicitor rather than the police. It would only be worth going to the police if the bike seller had broken the criminal law.

THE SOURCES OF LAW

Laws may be made in a number of ways.

- **Acts of Parliament**, or statutes, are the major source of law. These documents are normally drafted by lawyers in supposedly precise legal language and are often difficult for the layman to understand. Acts of Parliament can also give ministers the right to make detailed regulations on the basis of general principles laid down in an Act. These regulations are known as Statutory Instruments and they have the same force as statute law.

- **The common law** is another source of law. This consists of the set of rules of behaviour and procedure established over the centuries by the decisions of judges in particular court cases. The doctrine of **precedent** is important here. It involves deciding cases on the same principles as those governing decisions in past comparable cases. Senior judges also 'make' law in the sense that they interpret it in new ways. For example, corporate manslaughter became a crime as a result of the decision of a judge interpreting an Act of Parliament in a new way.

- In some cases, where the application of the law as it stands would lead to injustice, a branch of law known as **'equity'** may be employed. Equity has evolved along with the common law, on the basis of precedent and judicial decisions. It allows principles of justice and fairness to be applied where the strict letter of the law would lead to injustice. Statute law takes precedence over common law and equity where there is a clash.

- Certain laws of the European Communities are now binding in the UK under the European Communities Act (1972). **Community law** can be enforced in the European Court. In theory, where there is conflict with national laws, the Community laws take precedence.

The law is administered through the courts. Civil and criminal justice are administered through separate systems or jurisdictions. The courts in each system form a hierarchy with appeals from lower courts dealt with by higher courts. In both jurisdictions, the supreme court is the Judicial Committee of the House of Lords.

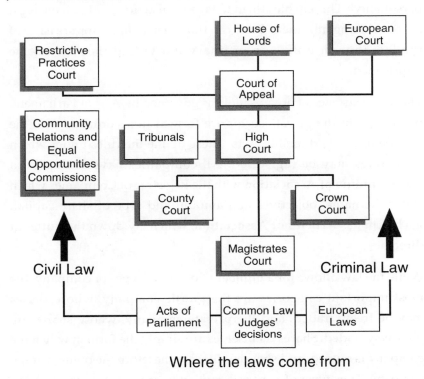

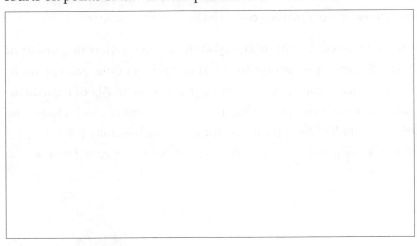

FIGURE 2.1: *Courts and related bodies, and types of law.*

Some courts, such as the Restrictive Practices Court have been specially set up to deal with business issues. In addition, there are tribunals which exist to resolve legal disputes. For example, disputes concerning dismissal or redundancy payments may be heard by an Industrial Tribunal. Tribunals generally operate informally and fairly cheaply. While they are not courts in the legal sense, appeal to the courts on points of law is often permitted.

RECALL:
allow 5 mins

List the different ways in which binding laws can be made.

BUSINESS ORGANISATIONS

To operate effectively, businesses have to be set up in a way that gives them legal recognition. Privately owned businesses, like people, have a legal existence. They are sometimes said to have a 'legal personality'. This enables them to take legal action, and to have legal action taken against them. They can thus be held liable for breaches of the law though unlike an ordinary individual they cannot be imprisoned.

The legal existence of organisations is governed by Acts of Parliament. Businesses in the private sector are formed in accordance with the Companies or Partnership Acts. These define the rules under which companies may be registered. All companies have to deposit a **Memorandum of Association** with the Registrar of Companies which states the name, objectives and amount and type of share capital. Each firm has **Articles of Association**, which lay down the duties of directors.

While the law allows for a number of different types of company, the most important categories are the **public company**, whose shares may be freely traded, and the **private company**, whose shares are not freely traded. Shares themselves are simply the form in which the company is owned, and shareholders are therefore the owners of the company. The owner of a share is entitled to participate in the running of the company through attendance and voting at the Annual Meeting. The shareholders elect the Board. They also receive the profits of the company through the dividends paid on their shares.

Many small businesses exist as **partnerships**. Partners not only jointly own the business but, unlike the shareholders of companies, they have a legal right to engage in its management.

A few businesses are organised as **producer co-operatives**. In co-operatives, the employees collectively own the company.

Private businesses may undertake any lawful action in pursuit of their objectives. In contrast, the legal status of a public enterprises or social service organisation usually derives from an Act of Parliament which sets out rules governing its structure and control. Under the principle of *ultra vires*, public sector organisations may not normally undertake any activity unless this is specifically approved by the law.

Business contracts and property rights

In order to carry out the purposes for which they exist, businesses have to make agreements with others which commit the two parties to an agreed course of behaviour. Agreements have to be made ensuring the supply of labour and materials. Customers have to agree to the terms on which an organization provides its goods or services. These agreements are covered by the law of 'contract'.

The **law of contract** has largely evolved as part of the common law rather than being created by Act of Parliament. It defines the conditions under which agreements requiring two parties to behave in a specified manner may be legally enforced as a valid contract. For a contract to be valid, the following conditions must normally apply:

- The parties must have the legal right to meet the terms and the agreement must be in a legally accepted form.

- The terms of the transaction have to be clear, agreed and intended to be legally binding.

- Each side must be providing something for the other.

If one party neglects to fulfil the terms of a contract, the other party may seek damages, or an injunction requiring enforcement, through the civil courts. Without the law of contract, many of the exchanges between businesses of modern economic life would be too risky to undertake.

Businesses and those who work in them, enter into a range of transactions with, or affecting, other businesses. Many of these involve buying and selling, with the aim of producing goods and services and making a profit. However, strict rules govern how people in working in business should deal with each other.

For example, **insider dealing** is a crime. It involves the use of confidential information relating to company affairs to buy or sell shares for profit. There have been some prosecutions, though these probably under-represent the number of offences. The Stock Exchange Insider Dealing Group has referred more than 250 cases to the Department of Trade and Industry (DTI) since 1980. Since 1984, the DTI has prosecuted 47 people and convictions were obtained in 18 cases.

Using bribery to facilitate transactions is also a crime. On average, only about a dozen people each year are imprisoned in the UK for corruption and bribery. However, evidence suggests that it may be more common.

**BUSINESS CONTRACTS AND
PROPERTY RIGHTS**

- Bribery is certainly a feature of the operation of multi-national businesses. Its use by British companies was well documented in the DTI investigation into Lonrho, published in 1976.

- In 1994, a Ministry of Defence official was jailed for four years after receiving £1.3 million in bribes from foreign arms companies between 1979 and 1984.

- Bribery in the public sector was most clearly illustrated in the Poulson case in the 1970s in which an architect secured housing contracts through bribing local councillors and council officers.

Even behaviour which causes investors to lose their money can create a legal liability. A group of 3,096 Lloyd's 'names' (investors) claimed compensation of £629 million for losses incurred from 1988 to 1990. They received damages of around £500 million as a result of a High Court ruling that they were victims of negligent underwriting. They had invested in four syndicates run by the Gooda Walker agency. The syndicates specialised in catastrophe insurance. They were hit by massive losses from the Piper Alpha oil rig explosion in 1988 and the Exxon Valdez oil spill in 1989. The judge held the underwriters at fault because the names' money was used for insurance which was 'unplanned and unjustified by any proper analysis of risk'.

Business activities have an impact on employees, on customers and on other members of the public. In addition, they can affect the appearance of the environment and its safety. All of these activities are subject to legal controls.

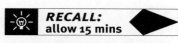

RECALL:
allow 15 mins

List the different legal forms which can be used for business organisations and try to give an example for each.

PLANNING CONTROLS

Businesses need premises from which to operate. However, they are not free to buy and sell land or construct or demolish buildings just as they wish. All these activities are now controlled by the law. The law provides for a system of planning controls. The system of statutory planning dates from the Town Planning Act (1947) which introduced the system of state regulation of development and land use by local planning authorities. The law was consolidated in the Town and Country Planning Act (1990) and the Planning (Consequential Provisions) Act (1990).

Planning is carried out by **planning authorities**. These can be:

- local planning authorities for counties and districts

- the joint planning committees for Greater London

- the National Parks

- enterprise zones set up under the Local Government, Planning and Land Act (1980)

- urban development areas established under the Local Government, Planning and Land Act (1980)

- 'housing action areas' under the Housing Act (1988).

The role of these authorities is generally to:

- draw up development plans, including structure and local plans containing proposals for future land use

- consider applications for development requiring planning permission

- enforce the terms of the Act using Enforcement Notices when the Act is breached

- give compensation where owners' rights are adversely affected.

The general principle of planning is that individuals and businesses have to obtain planning permission to undertake development. Development involves building, engineering or mining works which change the nature of buildings and land. Planning permission can be given by:

- a general development order

- a special development order

- designation of a simplified planning zone

- designation of an enterprise zone.

'Development orders' are covered by planning controls. 'Simplified planning zones' have specially streamlined procedures. In **enterprise zones**, any development not specifically ruled out is allowed. These are set up, usually for a period of ten years, in order to encourage development of derelict inner city areas. They are an example of the application of new-right principles since in enterprise zones the normal legal restrictions do not apply, and businesses have greater freedom to do what they want.

In some areas and for some buildings, special rules apply. The Planning (Listed Building and Conservation Areas) Act (1990) contains comprehensive provisions dealing with the preservation of the appearance of areas and the buildings in them. Listed buildings are those designated by the Secretary of State as being of 'special architectural or historic interest'. 'Conservation areas' are areas defined by the local planning authority as being of 'special architectural or historic interest'. In these areas, there are tighter controls on development and 'conservation area consent' is needed for the demolition of unlisted buildings.

Sometimes major public or private sector projects (such as building large factories, roads or airports) necessitate the acquisition of land. This is done through compulsory purchase. Compulsory purchase must be for a stated purpose authorised by an Act of Parliament such as the Town and Country Planning Act (1990). A Compulsory Purchase Order has to be issued under the Acquisition of Land Act (1981). Ownership is then acquired under the provisions of the Compulsory Purchase Act (1965) or by a Compulsory Purchase Order under the Compulsory Purchase (Vesting Declaration) Act (1981). Compensation is provided under the Land Compensation Act (1973). Where houses unfit for human habitation are involved, the Housing Act (1985) contains special provisions on the level of compensation due.

RECALL:
allow 10 mins

List the limits planning regulations place on the right of a business to set up where it wishes.

Intellectual Assets

The assets of a business are normally thought to be property or money. However, some of the assets may be in the form of ideas which are produced by, or held about, the business. Laws exist to protect these assets. Business success can depend on the successful utilisation of these ideas and legal means exist to protect them when the business has invested in their production. These assets include patents, copyrights, designs, trademarks and reputation.

Patents Many businesses are based on the production of a single product or the use of a single productive process which has been invented by the firm. Other firms can be prevented from using the process or making the product by taking out a 'patent'. Patents are held under the Patents Act (1977). They exist to encourage technological advance by giving the patent holder a monopoly over the commercial exploitation of an invention. The holder of a patent can sell it or license its use by others. Under the Patent Co-operation Treaty, a single application can cover several countries. There is also a European Patent system with a similar single application procedure.

In order for an invention to be patented it must:

- be new

- involve an inventive step

- have a commercial application.

The following types of invention cannot be patented:

- a scientific theory or mathematical method

- an artistic work

- a method for doing business

- a computer program

- something which would encourage anti-social, immoral or offensive behaviour.

To establish a patent, a specification has to be drafted, normally with the assistance of a patent agent and existing patents have to be examined to make sure that the invention really is new. A patent lasts for 20 years and there is an annual renewal fee. While patenting certainly provides protection for inventions, in view of the complexity of the procedure, many companies simply employ trade secrecy to protect their innovations.

Copyright The Copyright, Designs and Patents Act (1988) gives copyright protection for up to 25 years. Under earlier legislation, copyright lasted for the life of the author plus 50 years. There is legal cover for artistic work or written documents, though the ideas themselves are not protected. Many business documents will be covered. Copyright prevents others from benefitting from the mental effort of authors or artists. Copyright is obviously important in the publishing trade and for newspapers and journals but it also has some less obvious uses; the football league fixture list, for example, is copyrighted and the pools firms pay for its use.

Designs Under the Copyright, Designs and Patents Act (1988) design refers to features of the appearance of a manufactured article which are not necessitated by its function. Registration under the Act gives exclusive rights to the use of the design for five years. This can be renewed for further five-year periods up to a maximum of 25 years. Action can be taken where the design is copied even if the copy is not exact.

Trade marks Under the Trade Marks Act (1938) these can be used to identify a business or a product. Examples include names such as Microsoft, or designs such as logos, where a word is often presented in a special format or typeface such as the 'Esso' sign. Registration of a trade mark gives exclusive right to use it. Trade marks have to include the name of a company, a signature or some other distinctive mark but they cannot include a description of the product since other manufacturers would not then be able to so describe their products if they were similar. Effective marketing can mean that consumers refer to the article by its trade mark. Sometimes registered trade marks become almost synonymous with the articles themselves – typical examples are 'Hoover', 'Oxo' and 'Thermos'.

Business reputation Reputation is important in business and firms can take action to protect it. There is a tort (civil offence) of 'trade libel' or injurious falsehood. This occurs when false and derogatory assertions are made about a business. When these are published, the injured party can claim compensation without needing to prove damage. Action can also be taken against someone who falsely states that a particular business is no longer operating, if damage can be shown to have resulted. The distinction between trade libel and 'knocking copy' in advertising is a delicate one.

Computer records Businesses use computer records for a range of purposes such as mailing lists, personnel records, wages systems, and registers of suppliers and customers. They are now covered by the Data Protection Act (1984). This is based on the Convention for the Protection of Individuals with regard to Automatic Processing of Personal Data which was established by the Council of Europe in 1981. There is a Data Protection Tribunal to resolve disputes.

Under the Act, users holding information about living individuals must register with the Registrar of Data Protection. The subjects have the right to examine the Register, and apply to any user to view the data about them held on computer. This must be revealed within 40 days. The subjects have a right to correct inaccuracies and obtain compensation for loss suffered as a result of incorrect data.

The Registrar can obtain a warrant to enter and search premises and seize any documents or equipment, require rectification of incorrect data, and issue a de-registration notice preventing further processing of the data. Prosecutions in the Magistrates' Court can lead to fines of up to £2,000. In the Crown Court, the maximum fine is unlimited.

Exemptions are granted:

- where the data does not threaten the privacy of the subject
- where data are held for the purpose of tax collection
- where national security is involved
- where it would interfere with criminal justice.

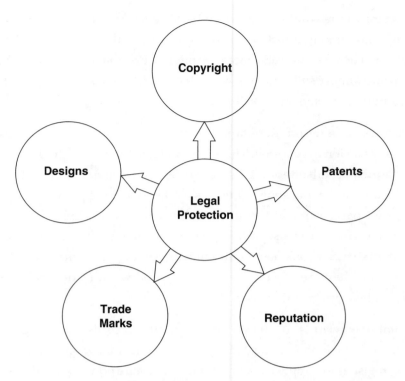

FIGURE 2.2: *Intellectual property protected by law.*

RECALL:
allow 5 mins

Briefly describe the meaning of 'intellectual property'.

What different forms of intellectual property can the law protect?

Employment law

Most businesses employ people and pay them a wage or a salary to do a job for the company. Some people take the view that the law should not intervene in this relationship between an employer and an employee. Many of those on the new right believe that any legal constraints in this area are a restriction of the freedom of both parties and also that they reduce economic efficiency. However, those in the centre and on the left believe that without some restrictions on the freedom of actions of employers, workers will lack protection against the superior bargaining power of employers. This will result in their being exploited, with low wages, excessive hours of work and poor working conditions.

In most modern industrial societies, the law regulates various features of employment including:

- the terms of the contract between the business and its employees

- the trade union rights of employees

- equal opportunities for women and minorities.

THE LABOUR CONTRACT

In the last 200 years, an extensive body of legislation has appeared which regulates various aspects of the relationship between employers and employees. All employees have a contract of employment though this may be oral or written, or consist of a combination of the two. Like all contracts, its validity depends on its conformity with the general legal rules governing contracts. The terms of an employment contract can be 'express' or 'implied'.

Express terms normally include:

- wages

- hours of work

- holidays

- the work to be done.

Other special terms may be included, such as the possession of a current driving licence, and a duty of exclusivity or of confidentiality. In general, express terms can only be changed by mutual agreement. However, many employers have used the device of terminating an existing contract and offering a new one with new terms.

Implied terms have developed over many years on the basis of common law decisions and precedents. They normally include stipulations that employees will:

- use reasonable care and skill in doing the job

- obey all reasonable and lawful orders

- give faithful service

and employers will:

- treat employees with respect

- pay wages promptly.

Under the Wages Act (1986) employers can pay by cash, cheque or direct credit, although some workers whose contracts formerly specified payment in cash may retain this right.

Collective agreements are made between a trade union and an employer. A collective agreement may deal with union recognition, disputes procedures, wages and hours, and other details. Sometimes, the terms may be designated as part of the individual employment contract.

Works rules are needed in order to meet the terms of the Advisory, Conciliation and Arbitration Service (ACAS) Code of Practice on Disciplinary Rules and Procedures, the law on unfair dismissal, and the Health and Safety at Work Act. These rules, in effect, form part of the contract of employment.

ABSENCE FROM WORK

The law recognises a number of circumstances in which workers have the right to be absent from work without losing their right to keep their jobs, including undertaking public duties, being sick, and having a baby.

Public duties Certain public duties are supported through businesses being obliged to give employees 'reasonable' time off to:

- serve as a magistrate, councillor, tribunal member, Health Boards member, school or college governor

- serve as a union official

- serve as a duly appointed safety representative

- seek another job or re-training when under notice of redundancy.

Sick pay There is no legal requirement for businesses to finance a sick pay scheme for their employees. However, businesses must provide statutory sick pay (SSP). This is governed by the Social Security Contributions and Benefits Act (1992). Employees who are sick receive a weekly payment from their employer. Employers obtain a refund of 80 per cent of the cost by deducting it from their payments of National Insurance contributions or income tax. In addition to this, small businesses receive a 100 per cent refund after six weeks.

Maternity rights In recent decades, more women have entered the workforce. Most women now work and seek to have a long working life. Awareness of the restrictions that society places on women has grown and there have been increased demands for improved rights for female employees. One area of concern has been the rights of mothers. There have been demands for workplace nurseries and crèches, and some employers have provided these although they are not obliged to do so by law. However, pregnant working women have gained some legal rights.

Initially, the Employment Protection (Consolidation) Act (1978) laid down the maternity rights of employed women. Employed pregnant women with two years' continuous service in their jobs have four main rights:

- not to be dismissed because of pregnancy

- to have reasonable paid time off work for ante-natal care

- to take maternity leave and to return to work afterwards

- to receive maternity pay and statutory maternity pay.

Under the 1993 Trade Union Reform and Employment Rights Act (implemented persuant to the EU Pregnancy Directive), maternity rights have been extended.

Since July 1994, all employees, irrespective of their length of service or whether they are full- or part-time workers, are entitled to a minimum of 14 weeks' paid leave. Employees with two years' service can extend this to 40 weeks although employers are not obliged to continue contractual benefits payments (pensions, assurance and health insurance) during this extension.

LOSS OF JOB

Businesses do not have a free hand in dismissing workers they no longer wish to employ. Many people now believe that workers have some claim to be able to stay in a job and that their job can only be taken away if legal safeguards are observed. The new right disagree; they see any legal control over the right of employers to 'hire and fire' as a restriction on individual freedom.

Laws cover unfair and wrongful dismissal, and redundancy. Where individuals have a legal claim under labour law, this is normally decided by an **Industrial Tribunal**. Industrial Tribunals were established by the Industrial Training Act (1964). The Industrial Tribunal Regulations (1985) specify the rules governing their operation. They cover most employment law issues although the most common cases involve claims of unfair dismissal. A tribunal has a legally qualified chairperson and a representative from each side of industry. As in other cases where tribunals are used, they are supposed to produce a speedy and cheap resolution of cases with an absence of legal formality.

Unfair dismissal This refers to dismissal where there is no fair reason nor a fair manner of dismissal. Workers have the right to claim damages at an Industrial Tribunal if they are dismissed unfairly. Where an employee is found to have been unfairly dismissed, they will be entitled to compensation and possibly reinstatement. This provision does not apply to members of the police or the armed forces although they do have recourse to race or sex discrimination legislation. Employers may dismiss workers for misconduct such as disobedience, negligence or incompetence.

This law is based on the principle that an employer must act reasonably when dismissing employees. Acting unreasonably might mean:

- not having the full facts

- acting where the situation did not warrant dismissal

- ignoring mitigating circumstances

- failing to make disciplinary rules clear.

Employees covered are those:

- employees working for 16 hours per week or more

- employed for eight hours per week or more for five years

- continuously employed for two years or more if they are under retirement age.

Wrongful dismissal This refers to dismissal which is in breach of contract. Employees who are wrongfully dismissed can take action under common law for wrongful dismissal though this seldom happens today.

Redundancy This occurs when an employer closes or plans to close the business, or no longer requires the particular work done by the employee. Workers who are made redundant are entitled to a redundancy payment related to their length of service as long as they have at least two years' continuous service with an employer. The redundancy payment depends on the employee's age, wages and time in the job at the time of redundancy.

Under the Wages Act (1986), employers have to pay the full cost of redundancies. In choosing workers to be made redundant, the employer should act fairly. Unfair selection for redundancy constitutes unfair dismissal.

List the different reasons for which employees can justifiably ask for time off work.

TRADE UNIONS

Since the repeal of the anti-combination Acts in 1824, there have been numerous Acts of Parliament and judicial decisions which have affected the legal status and rights of trade unions. Considerable political controversy has occurred over the circumstances in which strikes can lawfully take place and over the legality of various support actions such as picketing and sympathy strikes. Unions have immunity from civil actions for damages for breach of contract where these occur in furtherance of a legal trade dispute.

Disagreement still exists about the legal position of trade unions. The new right believes that their rights are excessive, particularly in relation to their immunity from actions for damages. The radical left suggest that even where the law appears to grant rights to unions, the judges frequently interpret the law in such a way as to work to their disadvantage.

A radical attempt to transform the legal status of trade unions was made in the Industrial Relations Act (1971). This was passed by a Conservative government which thought that trade unions were too powerful and were damaging the economy. This Act:

- established an Industrial Relations Court (NIRC)

- required unions to obtain approval for their rule book from a Registrar

- made collective bargains legally enforceable

- required strike ballots

- introduced 'cooling off periods'.

The labour movement opposed these changes and the TUC boycotted union registration and the NIRC, making the Act inoperable. Other provisions, such as cooling-off periods and ballots, had unintended effects. Disputes could sometimes be escalated by action under the legislation. The docks dispute over containerisation was intensified by the NIRC jailing the so-called 'Pentonville Five' shop stewards for refusing to stop picketing a blacked depot. The Trade Union and Labour Relations Act (1974) repealed the major provisions of the 1971 Act.

The Labour government of 1974–79 attempted to improve the rights of trade unions. This was done as part of a deal it made with the TUC known as the 'social contract' under which unions would be given improved legal rights in return for moderating demands for higher wages. The Employment Protection Act (1978) gave the following rights to all employees:

- not to be dismissed for taking any part in 'reasonable' trade union activity

- not to be dismissed, or subject to other action for refusing to join a 'non-independent' trade union (i.e. a 'company union' or staff association)

- not to be unreasonably banned from membership of a trade union which has a closed shop agreement with the employer or prospective employer.

When the Conservatives returned to power in 1979, policy towards trade unions became much more restrictive. New right principles viewed them as organisations which raised labour costs and reduced economic efficiency. Reforms to the law governing industrial relations in the Employment Acts (1980, 1982 and 1988) and the Trade Union Act (1984) established a range of new rights and obligations for employers and unions. Employers can now:

- restrain unlawful picketing

- restrain secondary industrial action

- decide whether or not to recognise unions

- take legal action and seek damages or injunctions against trade unions

- restrain industrial action concerned with issues other than disputes between workers and employers.

Union members were also given some clearly defined rights. They have the right to:

- regular ballots on the involvement of their union in political activities

- elect all members of the union executive by secret ballot

- restrain industrial action undertaken without a secret ballot

- protection against dismissal for non-union membership

- refuse to join a union with a closed shop agreement due to strongly held personal convictions

- inspect their union's financial records

- protection against union disciplinary action for going to work during a strike.

The provisions described above have weakened militant trade unionism though this has also been curbed by high levels of unemployment and by massive falls in trade union membership. However, the impact of these legal changes has not always been precisely what those introducing them have intended. For example, the provisions requiring greater and more evident union democracy may have increased the authority of some union leaderships.

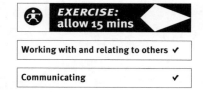

Working with and relating to others ✓

Communicating ✓

ACTIVITY 2

In a group of four discuss what part, if any, trade unions play at your workplace on issues concerned with:

- wages

- recruitment of staff

- health and safety.

Report your findings to the class.

Commentary...

Here is an answer for our university.

Wages – UNISON negotiates for many non-academic staff, and NATFHE for lecturers.

Recruitment – very little impact.

Health and safety – all the unions are represented on the Health and Safety Committee.

EQUALITY AND DISCRIMINATION

There now seems to be a broad consensus across much of the political spectrum that equal rights for women at the workplace are desirable. Many on the new right support this because they believe that it will improve economic efficiency by broadening the pool of talent from which employers can select. Opposition to women's rights comes mainly from two groups:

- some male trade unionists who feel that their jobs may be threatened

- some people who strongly support the traditional idea that 'a woman's place is in the home'.

The Equal Pay Act (1970), which came into force in 1975, puts a duty on businesses to treat men and women identically in the matter of wages, hours, sick pay and holidays, where they do 'work of a broadly similar nature' in the same firm, or any other firm owned by the same company. In addition, contracts of employment have to specify equal pay. This law also complies with Article 119 of the Treaty of Rome.

Businesses are forbidden to discriminate on the grounds of colour, nationality, religion, sex or marital status, under the Race Relations Act (1976) and the Sex Discrimination Act (1975). All cases under these Acts have to be brought by either the Equal Opportunities Commission (EOC), in cases of sex discrimination, or the Commission for Racial Equality (CRE) in cases of race discrimination. The Commissions may issue non-discrimination notices enforceable by a County Court injunction.

There are two types of discrimination that the law attempts to prevent.

Direct discrimination When this involves sex, it occurs if a woman is less favourably treated than a man would have been and this happens because she was a woman.

For race, this arises where a person treats another person less favourably because of their:

- colour

- race

- nationality

- ethnic origins

- national origins.

The definition of an ethnic group is that it must be seen as a community, with such characteristics as:

- a shared history

- its own cultural traditions

- a common geographical origin

- a common language.

In the past, there have been cases involved with the rights of a group to wear clothing associated with an ethnic characteristic such as religion. For example, Sikhs had to fight for the right to wear turbans in jobs where a uniform was required. In some bus companies, the simple solution was found of providing Sikhs with a turban in the colours of the uniform.

Indirect discrimination For race, this occurs when the extent to which different ethnic groups can meet a specified condition is not equal. For sex, this takes place when a condition applied equally to both sexes is one that the two sexes cannot equally comply with. For example, in the past there was a minimum height set for all police officers. The adversely affected women because their average height is less than that of men.

When someone believes that they have been discriminated against they take their complaint to the EOC or the CRE. Attempts at **conciliation** are then undertaken. Conciliation involves bringing the parties together to try to reach an agreement to avoid future discrimination. Only if this fails is a prosecution considered.

Very few cases of discrimination are upheld in a court of law. However, evidence suggests that discriminatory practices of both kinds are widespread. Experiments involving sending equally qualified job applicants of different sexes (for sex discrimination) or races (for race discrimination) have demonstrated this. In individual cases, however, it is extremely difficult to prove since some other factor can almost always be found to justify, say, an employer's preference for one applicant over another.

Recruitment of the workforce It is unlawful to discriminate on the grounds of sex or race in job advertisements, short-listing for interviews or in the job interview. The Guidance Notes produced by the Equal Opportunities Commission suggest that businesses should be careful how they use language and pictures in job advertisements so that they do not suggest that a certain type of person is the desired kind of employee.

Ex-offenders The Rehabilitation of Offenders Act (1974) is designed to encourage rehabilitation of ex-offenders by limiting or preventing the disclosure of 'spent convictions' where the sentence received was less than 30 months imprisonment. A rehabilitation period is specified, based on the seriousness of the offence.

Part-time workers A major division in the labour force is between those in full-time work and part-time workers. This division is also closely related to gender. Over the last ten years, the growth of part-time work has been a key feature of the British labour force. Over the 1980s as a whole, two-thirds of all new jobs went to women, and two-thirds of all these jobs were part-time. This is accelerating as a result of the government's promotion of 'flexibility' in the labour market. In practice, this means it is easier and cheaper to hire and fire part-time workers, who have fewer employment rights and little protection over wage rates. Businesses do not have to pay National Insurance contributions for people earning less than approximately £60 a week. Many employers now try to avoid employing full-timers and employ as many part-timers as they can. This could be seen as placing many women in a disadvantaged position in the workforce.

ACTIVITY 3

Does your organisation take any steps to prevent discrimination and ensure equal opportunities? If so, give an example of such policies.

Write up to 60 words.

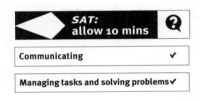

SAT:
allow 10 mins

| Communicating | ✔ |
| Managing tasks and solving problems | ✔ |

Commentary...

Here are the steps taken by one university. Following a case when staff were found to have acted in a discriminatory fashion, those involved in short-listing and job interviews are now given training to ensure that they are aware of ways to avoid discrimination on the grounds of race and sex.

Health and safety

The production of goods and services has the potential to cause danger and harm. There are disagreements about how far the state should intervene. Some people on the new right believe that a mass of detailed regulations are unnecessary so long as those affected have the right and opportunity to sue for damages. However, most people support a substantial degree of regulation. In Britain, the laws on health and safety have a wide scope. However, some people on the radical left argue that enforcement of them is not very strict. They suggest that many businesses are allowed to break the law, and that those that are prosecuted seldom receive a severe punishment.

HEALTH AND SAFETY LEGISLATION

The law is concerned with health and safety at work. An overall legislative framework for health and safety is provided by the Health and Safety at Work Act (1974). The Act was passed following the Robens Committee on Safety and Health at Work of 1972. The committee reported an annual toll of half a million injured and over 1,000 killed. Industrial injury and disease cost 23 million working days annually. On top of this, at least 1,000 people die each year from industrial diseases.

It is possible that the toll of death and disease from industry is actually much higher. The case of asbestos is a chilling example. In November 1994, the Health and Safety Executive (HSE) said that deaths from lung disease caused by asbestos will rise steadily each year and peak around 2020, with some 10,000 people a year dying from asbestos exposure which they suffered during the 1960s and 1970s. The increase in deaths reflects the amount of asbestos used in the past in factories, house building and insulation work.

The Health and Safety at Work Act (1974) covers all workers, including the self-employed, except domestic servants. It covers all places of work and it gives the government the right to make regulations concerning health and safety. A Health and Safety Commission exists to oversee the implementation of the Act and there is a Health and Safety Executive (HSE) to enforce the law.

The Act gives HSE inspectors and local authority safety inspectors considerable powers. They have rights to:

- enter premises

- inspect books and documents

- question people

- take measurements and photographs

- remove samples

- seize dangerous articles and substances.

Studies of the enforcement of health and safety laws have shown that there are a large number of violations committed by firms. Industrial accidents alone account for about 600 deaths and over 18,000 major injuries every year. Many other workers, and sometimes members of their families, are damaged by dangerous substances in the workplace. Despite the potential seriousness of the criminal violation of regulations, very few prosecutions take place.

For prosecutions in a Magistrates' Court, the maximum penalty is a £2,000 fine. In the Crown Court, it is an unlimited fine and/or up to two years' imprisonment. The attitude of firms, however, often seems to be that the benefits of breaking the law may well outweigh the likely costs. The average fine imposed is under £500. However, sometimes substantial fines are levied.

- In 1987, BP was fined £750,000 after three of its workers were killed.

- In 1993, the Channel Tunnel consortium was fined £200,000 after a worker was crushed to death.

- Manchester City Council was fined £25,000 after it fitted gas heaters in council properties incorrectly. This led to the death of a resident and serious risks to another 800 people. However, the fine will ultimately be paid by the local council tax payers, including those put at risk by the council.

While the penalties sound severe, there are only sufficient inspectors to ensure that each workplace is visited, on average, once every seven years. This contrasts with norms set by the International Labour Organisation which recommends two inspections per year.

Following a court decision in 1965, companies can be charged with manslaughter. A conviction requires proof that a director or someone in a position of control was grossly negligent concerning an evident risk of death or injury. Despite around 19,000 deaths in the workplace in the last 30 years there has not yet been a successful prosecution for corporate manslaughter.

Since the start of 1993, the implementation of the provisions of the Health and Safety at Work Act (1974) has been carried out using a new set of regulations. These implement six EU Directives under Article 118A of the Treaty of Rome. The regulations are being phased in and will be implemented in full by 1996. The health and safety duties of employers require them to:

- assess health and safety risks and record how they are to be dealt with

- carry out measures to deal with the risks – where there are five or more employees, there must be a written assessment of risk

- appoint competent safety advisers from within or outside the organisation

- establish procedures to deal with health and safety emergencies

- keep workers informed and give any necessary training.

Specific provisions require that

- structures must be soundly built with safe and unobstructed stairways

- the temperature of the working environment must be kept at 16°C or above after the first hour unless the work is strenuous

- ventilation must be adequate in rooms where people work

- lighting must be adequate

- there must be rest areas for non-smokers, nursing mothers and pregnant women

- furniture, furnishings and fittings must be clean and well looked after

- toilets must be clean and well maintained and ventilated with separate facilities for men and women

- washing facilities with hot and cold water, soap and drying facilities must be provided

- clean drinking water must be provided.

Organisations have a duty to protect the following groups of people:

Customers Businesses also have to make sure that they do not injure their customers or cause damage to their property. The Health and Safety at Work Act (1974) also specifies that articles designed and manufactured for use at work must be:

- safe while being used or maintained

- properly tested

- accompanied by documentation of safety factors with the information updated where necessary.

Visitors The Occupiers' Liability Act (1957) gives the occupier (not necessarily the owner) of business premises a duty of care to lawful visitors. Under this Act, the mental and physical capabilities of visitors need to be considered. For example, visiting children have a right to greater care to be taken on their behalf than adults.

Video display unit (VDU) users The widespread use of computers in offices has led to the development of new health problems. Concern has developed about eye strain and stress. There has also been a problem with repetitive strain injury (RSI) affecting the arms and hands of those doing continuous keyboard work, though the diagnosis of RSI is itself a matter of legal and medical controversy. Regulations under the Health and Safety Act (1974) require employers to:

- provide information and training for VDU users

- assess VDU equipment and reduce any known risks

- organise work so that users have breaks or a change of activity.

The operation of the law in the area of health and safety remains in dispute. The authorities claim that their main aim is to ensure voluntary compliance with the law, not to prosecute offenders. An alternative explanation from the radical left is that laws imposing obligations on employers are unlikely to be vigorously enforced. They also argue that various laws which appear to protect the rights of employees are ineffective because low penalties give employers an incentive to ignore or evade them. Businesses may treat the chance of

RECALL:
allow 10 mins

List the main health and safety requirements applying to offices and office workers.

prosecution as an acceptable risk to be paid for the benefits of violation. The new right, in contrast, suggest that employees are, if anything, over-protected by a mass of legislation which bears heavily on employers.

FIRE PRECAUTIONS

Legal requirements concerning fire safety at work are specified in the Fire Precautions Act (1971) and its associated regulations. When this Act was introduced, many businesses had to undertake spending on precautionary measures such as installing fire doors and improving fire escapes.

The inspection and issue of a fire certificate from the local fire authority is compulsory where:

- more than 20 people are employed

- more than ten persons are employed apart from on the ground floor.

In addition, since 1992, new regulations based on EU Directives are now in force. New workplaces are covered from 1993 and other workplaces from 1996. Under these regulations:

- an assessment of the fire risk must be made by employers with guidance from fire authorities

- emergency plans must be prepared and regularly updated

- well-maintained fire escapes are required

- fire detection systems and fire-fighting equipment must be in place

- those working in the building must be given training.

Consumer rights

Another important area of legal protection is consumer rights. Businesses need customers and most work hard to ensure that their customers continue to purchase their goods or services. Customers these days are sometimes referred to as one of the 'stakeholders' of a business. In the past, consumers received little protection from the law. The general approach was based on the idea of *caveat emptor*, literally 'let the buyer beware'. Some new right critics of modern consumer legislation would like to abolish the current wide-ranging provisions and return to this approach. However, there is also widespread support for consumer protection and many people now go to some lengths to make sure that their rights as consumers are properly enforced. For example, they might subscribe to *Which?*, the magazine of the Consumers' Association.

Consumer protection covers areas such as attempts by producers to limit their legal liability, false trade descriptions, and restrictions on the marketing of financial products, such as loans and insurance policies.

The Fair Trading Act (1973) set up the Office of Fair Trading (OFT) and provided for a Director General of Fair Trading (DGFT). The responsibilities of the DGFT are:

- to monitor business activities

- to collate information about unfair trade practices

- to recommend changes in the law where necessary.

The OFT has a wide range of regulatory functions relating to:

- monopolies and mergers

- restrictive trade practices

- advertising.

The DGFT can bring civil or criminal actions and seek promises from violators about future conformity with the law. The DGFT is also responsible for implementing the Estate Agents Act (1979).

Enforcement of laws relating to consumer protection is also carried out by the OFT along with Local Authority Public Health Departments. However, the latter rarely initiate prosecutions and have a limited capacity to monitor, seek out and record offences.

Consumers are protected by various laws concerning the goods they buy and the methods used to sell to them. The common law tradition assumes that it is the recipient who has to ensure that he or she is getting a fair deal when obtaining goods and services from the public or private sector. Under the common law, consumers injured by faults in goods caused by the negligence of the supplier may obtain damages. There are also a number of Acts covering food products which specify standards of quality. Laws also cover advertising, dangerous products and consumer credit.

THE SALE OF GOODS

Goods offered for sale have to conform to several legal requirements.

Description Where a description is applied to goods, they must conform to the description or the seller will be in breach of contract, and the buyer can insist on a refund.

Merchantable quality When consumers receive faulty goods they have a 'reasonable' time to reject them and claim a refund.

Fitness for purpose Goods bought for a specific purpose, which has been made known to the seller, must also be fit for the purpose for which they are intended.

Unsolicited goods Selling goods by sending them to a potential customer when they have not been requested was common in the 1960s and still sometimes takes place. Customers are told to pay or send the goods back. The Unsolicited Goods and Services Act (1971) makes this method of selling illegal and people do not have to pay for or return these goods at their own expense.

The legal rights of consumers of public services are dealt with separately. Recipients of National Insurance Benefits may appeal to a tribunal if they believe their entitlement to benefit is not being met. Quasi-legal remedies of this kind do not, however, exist for recipients of education and health care. However, Complaints Commissioners, or 'Ombudsmen', have been established to deal with complaints of maladministration in some areas not covered by tribunals, such as health and local government.

ADVERTISING

The Trade Descriptions Act (1968) and the Consumer Protection Act (1987) both cover false or misleading advertisements. These are unlawful regardless of whether or not there was any intention to mislead.

It is also an offence to apply a false trade description to goods, e.g. by passing off a used product as new. It is also a crime to make false statements about services or accommodation. These provisions have often been used against tour companies who have advertised non-existent holiday facilities.

There is also now a Directive on Misleading and Unfair Advertising from the EU which requires member states to provide for legal or administrative action to be taken against misleading advertising. The DGFT also has powers to obtain court orders to control advertisers, though they are very infrequently used.

The Department of Trade and Industry has encouraged the extensive use of self-regulation though Codes of Practice. For example, these cover restrictions on cigarette and tobacco advertising and on advertising aimed at children. The Advertising Standards Authority covers all advertising media including publications, cinema and poster adverts.

Control is exercised by a British Code of Advertising Practice and a British Code of Sales Promotion Practice. This is a form of self-regulation which is policed by the industry itself. The main sanction against firms is publicity. The effectiveness of the scheme is argued to rest on the possibility of statutory control if it proves ineffective.

CREDIT

Under the Consumer Credit Act (1974), the DGFT issues licenses to businesses involved with consumer credit. Credit given by unlicensed firms cannot be recovered without a court order. The OFT rules concerning credit require that:

- the agreement must be in writing with the consumer retaining a copy

- the annual percentage rate (APR) of a loan must be stated in writing

- if the agreement is not signed on the premises of the lender there is a 'cooling off' period of five days during which consumer can cancel the agreement

- seven days' notice of failure to meet the terms must be given before goods can be recovered

- property cannot be recovered without a court order if one-third of the purchase price has been paid.

DANGEROUS GOODS

Under the Consumer Protection Act (1987) firms have a general duty of safety and it is a criminal offence to offer goods for sale which are unsafe in terms of current safety standards. Local authority trading standards departments can prevent the sale of dangerous goods and can prosecute traders for being in breach of statutory duty to sell safe goods.

The Act consolidates existing safety regulations for goods such as electrical goods, toys, bikes and prams. It implements the European Product Liability Directive. The Act holds producers liable where death, injury or any loss or damage of over £275 is caused by a defect in a product unless the producer can show that current scientific and technical knowledge could not have revealed it. The Act introduces a broad notion of product liability since it does not specify that it has to be the buyer who suffers loss.

Exclusion or exemption clauses which attempt to restrict the rights of consumers are covered by the Unfair Contract Terms Act (1977). Unless they can be shown to be 'fair and reasonable', contractual terms which try to exclude the seller from liability resulting from negligence have no legal validity where goods cause:

- death or injury

- loss or damage.

Attempts to exclude or limit liability for breach of contract are also invalid unless they can be proved to be fair and reasonable.

ACTIVITY 4

Form a group of four and discuss what implications the law governing consumer rights have on the operation of your organisation/college. What checks are used to make sure that it is followed and to deal with problems with consumers? Report back to the class.

Summarise your findings in the box below.

Commentary...

Implications – These might include some (or none) of legal rights concerning the product and its fitness, trade descriptions and advertising and safety. In our university, we have to be careful we do not advertise courses that we cannot run.

Checks – You may have a department of consumer affairs to check these things and to deal with complaints.

THE DIFFICULTIES OF LEGAL REDRESS

It can be difficult for consumers to obtain legal redress following the purchase and/or consumption of dangerous products. Following years of use, many patients became addicted to supposedly safe tranquillisers and sleeping pills known as benzodiazepines such as

Valium, Librium and Mogadon. In March 1988, a massive legal claim was launched to sue the doctors who prescribed the drugs and the companies who had developed and sold them, for failing to warn of the danger of addiction. More than 13,000 people were granted legal aid and over 2,000 firms of solicitors and 40 barristers were involved. After six years and a number of preliminary hearings, the case collapsed when legal aid was withdrawn leaving a bill for legal work of £25–30 million. In Britain, no drugs company has yet been found liable for injuries caused by a product and no group action has even reached trial.

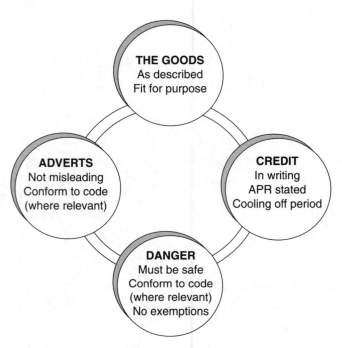

FIGURE 2.3: *Consumer rights.*

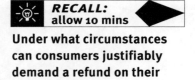

RECALL:
allow 10 mins

Under what circumstances can consumers justifiably demand a refund on their purchase?

Pollution and the environment

Business activities can cause pollution creating danger, nuisance or expense to the public. Pollution of various kinds is subject to a range of legal controls. Of course, businesses also benefit from this system of regulation since they are protected from what could be the adverse effects of the polluting activities of others. They are also protected from unfair competition from firms which might otherwise choose to use the cheapest methods of production regardless of the cost to the public in pollution. The scale of the regulatory operation is substantial. The agencies concerned with pollution employ 9,000 staff and in 1994 had a combined budget of £528 million.

THE LAW OF NUISANCE

The law of 'nuisance' deals with some environmental issues. Victims of nuisance can seek an injunction to prevent it continuing. Nuisance actions have been taken over noxious emissions, offensive smells and noise from business premises.

Private nuisance occurs when business activities 'unreasonably interfere' with activities taking place on neighbouring properties or land.

Public nuisance occurs when the public generally are affected. This is a crime. In addition, a civil action can be taken by someone who is particularly badly affected.

In addition to the common law of nuisance, statutory controls exist for the protection of the environment. Under the Health and Safety at Work Act (1974) businesses must not expose anyone to health and safety risks. Where people who are not employees might be affected, firms have a duty to give them information about this. Pollution controls and planning legislation set strict limits on business activities where these cause damage by air pollution, effluent, noise or waste disposal.

THE INSPECTORATE OF POLLUTION

In England and Wales, Her Majesty's Inspectorate of Pollution (HMIP) was formed in 1987 by merging the Industrial Air Pollution Inspectorate, the Hazardous Waste Inspectorate and the Radiochemical Inspectorate and adding a new Water Pollution Inspectorate. Its main purpose is to implement the Integrated

Pollution Control (IPC) provisions of the Environmental Protection Act (1990). Harmful industrial processes are 'scheduled' and require authorisation from HMIP. Firms must use the best available techniques to prevent or minimise pollution. Where applications for authorisation are made, these:

- have to provide comprehensive details about the process

- are normally open to public inspection

- may remain confidential where they involve commercially sensitive information.

ENVIRONMENTAL PROTECTION

Water The National Rivers Authority (NRA) was established following the privatisation of the water industry to maintain water quality and control the pollution of rivers, lakes, estuaries and coastal waters. It issues 'consents' for permitted discharges and keeps a register of them. The Water Resources Act (1991) allows statutory Water Quality Objectives (WQOs) for individual stretches of water. There are also rules covering farm waste. Bathing water standards are monitored in line with the EU water bathing directive. The dumping of sewage sludge at sea is being phased out by 1999. This is a matter of considerable controversy since many British beaches are badly polluted. Where this has an impact on the tourist trade, numerous local businesses are affected.

Air Local authorities have the main responsibility for clean air. They have streamlined powers to deal with smoke, dust and smells under the 1990 Act. In the past, smoke from domestic coal fires posed a considerable health threat due to smog. Under the Clean Air Acts (1956 and 1968), emissions of dark smoke are prohibited. New furnaces must, where possible, be capable of smokeless operation. The Clean Air Acts have produced major improvements in visibility and in the number of hours of winter sunshine especially in large cities. However, vehicle emissions are now causing renewed air pollution problems in many urban areas. In the countryside, straw and stubble burning has been controlled since 1992.

The Health and Safety at Work Act (1974) requires firms to use the best practicable means to prevent noxious atmosphere emissions. Violations can be met with an unlimited fine in a Crown Court or up to £20,000 in a Magistrates' Court. Dangerous atmospheric emissions from industrial processes are controlled by the Environmental

Protection Act (1990). Less damaging forms of air pollution have to be approved under local authority air pollution control (LAAPC).

Gases harming the ozone layer are also controlled. These include chlorofluorocarbons (CFCs) used in refrigerators, air-conditioning plants and in producing expanded polystyrene. EU legislation requires CFCs to be phased out within member states by mid-1997 with some exemptions for essential uses. In 1990, Britain agreed to phase out the use of CFCs and other substances by 2000.

Acid rain is mainly caused by emissions of sulphur dioxide and oxides of nitrogen from power stations and other fossil fuel burners. A phased reduction is taking place for oxides of nitrogen by 1998 and for sulphur dioxide by 2003. Electricity generation is being modified by the use of desulphurisation equipment and by switching from coal to gas.

Waste Waste disposal on land is regulated by the Control of Pollution Act (1974) and the Environmental Protection Act (1990) though this does not cover agriculture, mining and quarrying and radioactive waste, which are controlled by other legislation. From 1992, proper waste handling is also the duty of everyone who is involved in working with it.

Local authorities have a statutory duty to control waste. They have to:

- regulate the disposal of controlled wastes

- draw up waste disposal plans

- license waste disposal, treatment and storage

- license landfill sites.

Dangerous substances A number of dangerous substances are also covered by legislation. Pesticides are controlled by the Food and Environment Protection Act (1985). There is a Pesticides Safety Directorate and an Advisory Committee on Pesticides. Firms that work with radioactive waste have to register with the Nuclear Installations Inspectorate which is responsible for granting nuclear site licences.

Noise Local authorities have to monitor noise and investigate complaints. They can issue noise abatement notices where there is a noise nuisance and designate 'noise abatement zones' with specified limits to noise levels. There are specific controls over construction and demolition sites and the use of loudspeakers in public places. There are also controls over aircraft and motor vehicle noise. Compensation can be paid where there are reductions in property values caused by noise from facilities such as roads, railways and airports. Noise insulation may be provided for houses affected by new or improved roads or by construction work.

The present administrative framework for the enforcement of the laws on pollution is to be reorganised under a bill to come before parliament in the 1994–95 session. The Environment Agencies Bill will combine the NRA with HMIP and the local authority waste regulation authorities by January 1996. This is designed to reduce overlapping spheres of jurisdiction, impose uniform standards and create a single body to protect the environment.

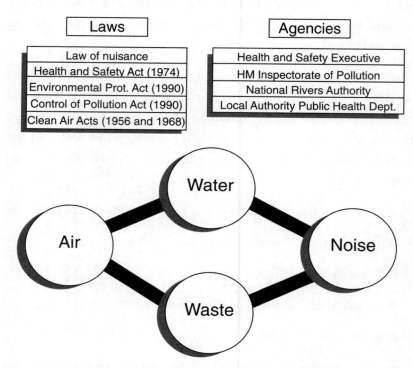

Laws
Law of nuisance
Health and Safety Act (1974)
Environmental Prot. Act (1990)
Control of Pollution Act (1990)
Clean Air Acts (1956 and 1968)

Agencies
Health and Safety Executive
HM Inspectorate of Pollution
National Rivers Authority
Local Authority Public Health Dept.

FIGURE 2.4: *Pollution laws and enforcement agencies.*

The effectiveness of the laws regulating health and safety, sex and race discrimination, equal pay, the sale of goods and environmental protection can be questioned. While the law as it stands appears to make clear demands on businesses, it has been claimed that by some on the radical left that, in practice, loopholes can often be found. The new-right view suggests otherwise, claiming that employees, consumers and the public are given too many protective rights which serve only to burden employers with extra work and provide jobs for a range of government bureaucrats and inspectors.

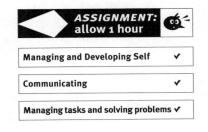

ACTIVITY 5

Write a report outlining the range of possible legal concerns which would need to be met if your organisation was to set up a new branch to produce and market a new set of products on a new site.

Use a separate sheet of paper to record your answer. Summarise your findings in the box below.

summary

▶ There are different ways of interpreting the impact of legal controls on business. In particular, the new-right views them as a largely unnecessary imposition and a cause of business ineffiency.

▶ The operations of the law and the court system are factors that businesses need to take into account.

▶ Limits are placed on business operations by the laws dealing with employment issues such as trade union rights and health and safety.

▶ There is a broad legal framework of consumer rights covering products and how they are marketed and advertised.

▶ Businesses are required to follow a range of environmental regulations covering products, production processes, emissions, noise and waste.

Regulatory agencies

Objectives

After participating in this session, you should be able to:

▶ explain the economic importance of the utilities to the UK economy

▶ describe the main agencies regulating utilities and competition policy

▶ explain the powers of the regulatory agencies, how they have been applied, and their impact on business

▶ describe the impact of the regulators on utilities, their competitors, and customers.

In working through this session, you will practise the following BTEC common skills:

Managing and Developing Self	✔
Working with and Relating to others	
Communicating	✔
Managing Tasks and Solving Problems	✔
Applying Numeracy	✔
Applying Technology	
Applying Design and Creativity	

Utility regulation

In Session 2 of this section, we examined the nature and extent of the law and its implications for business organisations generally. This session concentrates on two areas of regulation: utility regulation and competition policy.

A **public utility** is a firm supplying basic services such as energy, water, gas, electricity, and telephone services to the public.

Since privatisation, the utilities have been privately owned and subject to regulation which has been put in place to prevent them abusing their monopoly by exploiting their customers.

Company	Date privatised	Percentage sold	Cash Raised (£ billion)
British Telecom	June 1993	100%	14.0
British Gas	Dec 1986	97%	5.4
The 10 water companies	Dec 1989	100%	5.2
The 12 Electricity Boards	Dec 1990	100%	5.1
PowerGen	Feb 1991	60%	2.16
National Power	Feb 1991	60%	2.16
Scottish Power	June 1991	100%	3.15
Scottish Hydro	June 1991	100%	3.5

TABLE 3.1: *The public utilities*

Privatised industry is big business. British Telecom (the second largest UK company), British Gas (the sixth largest), the ten water companies, and the electricity industry serve millions of consumers, employ more than 500,000 people, have combined profits of over £5 billion and a combined stock market capitalisation of £65 billion. British Telecom, for instance, has more than 25 million subscribers; 18 million people receive gas bills; and the electricity industry has 22 million customers. These industries account for some 20 per cent of UK output.

The utilities are a very important element of the operating environment for many other businesses. They provide businesses with goods and services which are usually vital to their operations, e.g. energy and water. They buy enormous quantities of goods and services from business organisations and they also compete in some of the markets of other organisations. In short, they play an important role as:

- suppliers

- customers

- competitors.

Consequently, the business decisions made by the utilities can have a significant impact on other businesses, for example, electricity prices have an important influence on the cost competitiveness of big industrial users such as ICI and British Steel.

Utilities, after privatisation, retained immense monopoly power. Because of the absence of competition, the government retained some control over them. The utilities have a powerful market position which could be used to exploit consumers, competitors, or suppliers. The regulatory bodies were set up by the government to prevent exploitation taking place – showing that the government realised that decisions could not be left solely to managers in the utilities. The regulators are formally independent of government but with wide-ranging legal powers. The government intended that price regulation should be light, unbureaucratic and distant – in other words, it did not want the regulator interfering too often or too heavily in decisions. Regulation was supposed to be a temporary measure to stop the utilities exploiting the market until competition arrived to erode their monopoly power.

THE UTILITY REGULATORS – WHO ARE THEY?

Sector	Main Utilities	Regulator
Telecommunications	British Telecom	OFTEL
Gas	British Gas	OFGAS
Water	Water Boards	OFWAT
Electricity	National Power PowerGen National Grid Company* 12 Regional Electricity Companies (RECs)	OFFER

* Jointly owned by the Regional Electricity Companies

TABLE 3.2: *Regulation of public utilities*

THE POWERS OF THE REGULATORS

Regulators have the responsibility to promote competition – and to encourage firms to become more efficient and to share the benefits with customers. They are also required to protect the consumer through price controls, and safeguard service continuity and quality. Their terms of reference include a primary duty to ensure the delivery of a universal service and to meet 'all reasonable' customer demand.

At the same time, they must ensure that the utilities can finance their operations.

Regulatory agencies have been endowed with considerable statutory powers to intervene in a wide variety of business decisions, the most important being the prices customers pay. Regulators also have the discretion to play a significant role in other decisions concerning:

- investment
- profits
- efficiency
- quality of the product or service
- terms and conditions of sale
- policies towards competitors or potential competitors
- mergers.

Their main method of control is the price cap formula known as 'RPI–x'. RPI stands for the retail prices index which shows the amount by which retail prices have changed. The formula requires that each firm limits its price rises to x percentage points less than the rate of inflation. The regulator sets the value for x at a level based on the ability of the utility to cut its costs. So, for example, RPI–3 (x here equals 3 per cent) at a time of 10 per cent inflation allows prices to rise by 7 per cent. The value of x can be increased if the regulator reckons that the utility is earning too high a profit. Because the initial regulatory regimes established after privatisation were too generous to the utilities and too harsh on the consumer, the regulators raised x each time they reviewed it. British Telecom's x started at 3 per cent, rose to 4.5 per cent, then to 6.25 per cent, and subsequently to 7.5 per cent for four years after August 1993. An inflation rate below 7.5 per cent, as occurred in 1994, forced British Telecom to cut its prices. British Gas's has gone up from 2 per cent to 5 per cent.

This RPI–x formula is not applied to all utilities. In electricity, prices are capped in the naturally monopolistic sectors, transmission (the National Grid Company) and distribution (the RECs). The electricity generators, National Power and PowerGen, are regarded as competing so there is no need for such price control. Nonetheless, OFFER does have the power to influence their prices.

For the water boards, there is a k factor – the percentage above inflation by which a water company can raise its charges in any one year.

The boards can raise prices above inflation to finance the investment required to meet water quality and environmental standards laid down by the EU Drinking Water, Urban Wastewater, and Bathing Beaches Directives. The values for k vary from company to company because the Directives place big demands on regions with long coastlines and a high exposure to sewage, e.g. those like Wessex and Southern Water which have been dumping out to sea. For the ten years up to 2004, the k factor for the water boards, while still positive, has been reduced. The most badly affected was Southern Water whose factor was set at 0.5 per cent compared with the previous figure of 11.5 per cent (see table 3.3).

British Telecom	RPI – 7.5%
British Gas	RPI – 5%
Water Boards	RPI + 0.2% for Severn Trent to RPI + 3.5% for Southern Water
National Grid	RPI – 3%
RECs	RPI – 2%
National Power and PowerGen	Not subject to the price cap regime but, in 1994, to avoid a referral by OFFER to the MMC, both agreed not to increase prices above a certain level.

TABLE 3.3: *The price formula for the utilities in 1994*

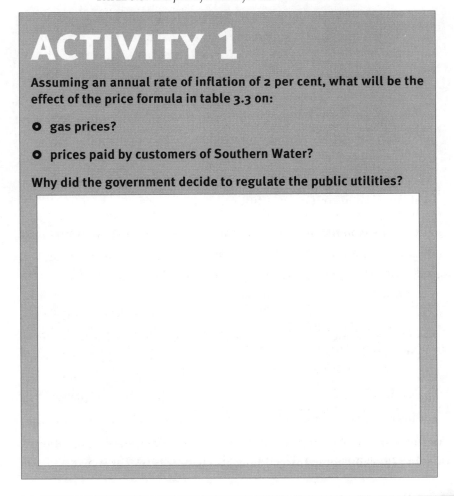

ACTIVITY 1

Assuming an annual rate of inflation of 2 per cent, what will be the effect of the price formula in table 3.3 on:

❍ gas prices?

❍ prices paid by customers of Southern Water?

Why did the government decide to regulate the public utilities?

SAT:
allow 10 mins ❓

Managing tasks and solving problems ✔

Applying numeracy   ✔

Commentary...

British Gas has to cut its prices by 2 per cent.

Southern Water can raise its prices by 5.5 per cent.

The government regulated the public utilities to prevent them exploiting their monopoly positions.

Privatisation was supposed to free firms from piecemeal, day-to-day interference by politicians and civil servants. The regulatory system which is evolving is a long way from the one that was intended – i.e. a stable, hands-off regulation of prices, subject only to five-yearly reviews. Regulation has not always gone smoothly. Numerous disputes have arisen between utilities and their regulators which have echoes of the pre-privatisation quarrels with Whitehall.

CONFLICT BETWEEN REGULATOR AND UTILITY

Because regulators have a lot of freedom to decide how to carry out their statutory responsibilities, there is a lack of any consistent or agreed procedure among them – everybody does it differently. It is little wonder that regulators have stamped their own interpretation on their duties, and hardly surprising, either, that there has been conflict between the utilities and their regulators. For example, OFWAT has been concerned about the increase in water prices, OFTEL about access to British Telecom's lines for Mercury, and OFGAS over the valuation of British Gas's pipeline network. Disputes between regulators and utilities can be referred to the Monopolies and Mergers Commission (MMC) but the ultimate power lies with the government. All of the regulators have used the threat of an inquiry as a stick to beat concessions out of the utilities.

The reliance on the individual regulator has been best exemplified in the relationship between British Gas and OFGAS. James McKinnon has been the most outspoken and most challenging of the first generation of regulators whereas other regulators, such as OFFER, have treated their utilities more gently, preferring negotiation rather than confrontation. Within months of taking over as director general of OFGAS, Mr McKinnon was threatening to take British Gas to court over its prices for domestic consumers. He referred the company to the MMC on two occasions (the first time, to find out why competition for industrial customers was growing so slowly, and the second time, to look at the profit British Gas was making from its charges to competitors for using its pipelines). He also forced it to keep down prices for industrial and business users, and accused it of restrictive practices. OFGAS's main stated concern has always been to ensure the best deal for the customer rather than the shareholder. To that end, it suggested splitting British Gas into 12 independent regional suppliers. This went down badly with the company. The Chairman said the proposed changes would cost nearly £3 billion in 10 years and increase the cost of gas to consumers. The government backed the company and not the regulator.

For many utilities, the regulatory system has created uncertainty within their industry particularly in the run-up to a price review, or to an MMC inquiry. Moreover, utilities claim that regulators have interfered unduly in managerial decisions and this has led to flawed investment choices.

SAT:
allow 15 mins

Managing tasks and solving problems ✔

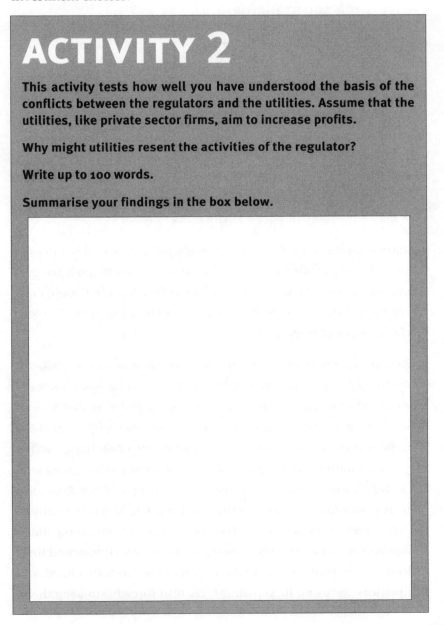

ACTIVITY 2

This activity tests how well you have understood the basis of the conflicts between the regulators and the utilities. Assume that the utilities, like private sector firms, aim to increase profits.

Why might utilities resent the activities of the regulator?

Write up to 100 words.

Summarise your findings in the box below.

Commentary...

Ask yourself what the major determinants of profits are and how they are affected by the regulator. Profits are calculated by subtracting costs from sales revenue. Any moves by the regulator to increase costs, for example, by splitting up British Gas, are likely to be resisted. Sales revenue is heavily influenced by the prices the utilities can charge and the level of competition. So, the water boards would be unhappy with any attempt by OFWAT to keep down price increases and British Telecom would oppose easier access to its network for Mercury, its main competitor.

COMPETITION AND STRUCTURE

Customers, on the other hand, complain that regulators have been far too slow in exposing the utilities to competition.

Ten years after its privatisation in 1984 and despite competition from its only rival Mercury, British Telecom's market share had fallen by just 10 percentage points to 90 per cent. Competition, however, will increase with the government's decision to allow the entry of cable companies and Energis, the National Grid subsidiary; and the decision by the EU to end state monopolies on telephone networks by 1998 may have some impact on British Telecom.

British Gas, sold off in 1986, still controlled 91 per cent of the market in 1993. However, British Gas is beginning to relinquish its grip somewhat on the industrial market after acrimonious battles with its regulator, and the government has decided that its monopoly in other markets will be abolished before the end of the decade.

In electricity (where ministers at least tried to address the issue of competition by establishing an eight-year timetable for liberalising the market) a powerful duopoly, comprising National Power and PowerGen, was left in place in power generation. By 1994, with Nuclear Power (still state-owned) counted in, the generators held the 94 per cent market share they inherited at privatisation with new entrants holding the remaining 6 per cent. The regulator did make an attempt, albeit small, to reduce the generators' monopoly. In return for not being sent to the MMC for dismemberment, PowerGen and National Power, the UK's two major generators, were ordered by the regulator in 1994 to sell off to competitors some of their oldest coal and oil-fired plant within two years, and to cap certain prices. The stock market saw this as no serious threat to the generators and marked up National Power's share price. As with gas, all electricity customers will, by 1998, have the freedom to shop around. Like telecommunications, both the gas and electricity industries will be subject to EU attempts to introduce more competition into the energy market.

The natural monopoly held by the water boards remains, and is likely to remain, simply because of the difficulties of introducing competition.

CONSUMERS VERSUS SHAREHOLDERS – PRICES, PROFITS AND DIVIDENDS

Shareholders Utility shareholders have fared well from privatisation, in terms of rising share prices. They have also received hefty dividend payouts. Consumers have not been so lucky.

This is partly explicable by the mechanisms set in place to protect the customers. It could be assumed that protection of consumers was the job of the regulators. But while each of these watchdogs has a general duty towards customers, they must also ensure financial viability of the utility – i.e. maintaining the ability of the company to raise finance from shareholders, financial institutions, as well as from profits. Regulators therefore must bear in mind that shareholders look favourably on companies with rising profits, increasing share prices and dividend pay-outs. The government appeared to recognise the contradictory position of the regulators, but put in place a bewildering, and therefore not very effective, variety of consumer bodies in the four industries. OFTEL, has four advisory bodies (England, Wales, Scotland and Northern Ireland) to communicate with the director-general. The regulator in addition then appointed an advisory committee for small business, and another for elderly and disabled customers. OFTEL has also organised a Telecommunications Forum for large users. Then there are the 160 or so local advisory committees. Electricity has a quite different set of consumer arrangements. The director-general of OFFER, in consultation with the Secretary of State, appoints 14 consumers' committees, one each for the regional supply companies. These bodies are usually not truly representative of the general body of consumers.

Consumers The consumers' experience of electricity regarding prices has changed over time. Prices rose sharply prior to privatisation. After flotation, the x factors in the initial price formula permitted the regional electricity companies (RECs) to raise their charges by up to 2.5 per cent a year above the rate of inflation. This regime, while increasing prices to customers, was good for shareholders in terms of increases in the value of shares and dividends. (See figure 3.1 on electricity share price relative to FTSE.)

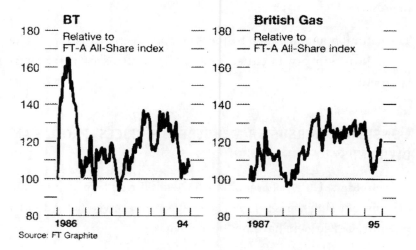

Source: FT Graphite

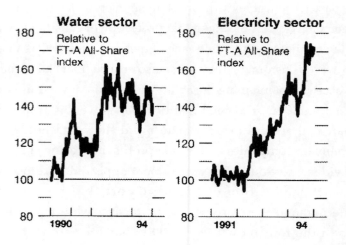

FIGURE 3.1: *Share prices of British Telecom, British Gas, water sector, electricity sector.*

By 1994, East Midlands Electricity had built up so much cash that it gave a special payment of £186 million to its shareholders – even though it had six months previously, written off £130 million spent on diversification projects – this from a company that had more than doubled the dividend pay-out to shareholders over the three years it had been in the private sector. Other RECs have been in a similar cash-rich position. When Professor Littlechild, the regulator, announced the latest formula for the RECs of RPI–2 per cent it was generally considered very lenient and the share prices in the companies soared. New information available to the regulator meant that this judgement was subject to review in 1995.

For most large customers, average electricity prices fell in real terms in the five years after privatisation. However, the very largest customers have experienced substantial price increases due largely to the removal of subsidies they enjoyed before the flotation. It is therefore no surprise that electricity prices have frequently incurred the wrath of big energy users. In 1994, The Energy Intensive Users Group declared that they were being overcharged by £545 million a year for electricity distribution and demanded that the electricity regulatory watchdog, OFFER, clamp down on the prices of the regional electricity companies. The chemical industry maintained that their ability to compete with French and German rivals was being undermined by the high costs of electricity in the UK and called for an 18 per cent reduction in prices. In the autumn of 1994, ICI claimed that electricity prices had doubled since privatisation.

British Gas declares that gas prices for its 18 million domestic consumers by the mid-1990s had, since privatisation, fallen 20 per cent in real terms making them the cheapest in Europe. George Yarrow, of the Regulatory Policy Centre, attributes the fall almost entirely to the lower cost of North Sea Gas than to the efforts of British Gas (see figure 3.2).

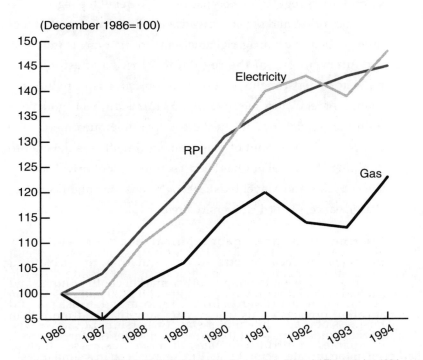

Source: Corzine, R., Gas industry tiptoes into free market, *Financial Times*, 8 Jan 1994.

FIGURE 3.2: *Prices since gas privatisation.*

OFTEL says that overall British Telecom prices have fallen in real terms by at least 25 per cent since privatisation. In 1994, British Telecom said that it was returning £1.4 billion to consumers because of lower prices resulting from the price formula. Most of the benefit, however, has gone to business users where competition from Mercury has been fiercest. While prices for domestic consumers have come down, but not to the same extent, the reductions have been partially offset by significantly higher line rental charges.

Water prices rose by 50 per cent in real terms after privatisation, with the average household water bill going up by about 37 per cent more than the retail price index. The number of water disconnections trebled to 21,000 between 1990 and 1992. Profits of the companies, on the other hand, more than doubled and their share prices have easily outperformed the market.

How the utilities have responded to regulation

The utilities have reacted to regulation in three main ways:

1. **Outwitting the regulator** Managers are continually trying to second-guess regulators. Because of the power of the regulator to influence prices and profits, privatised utilities have spent a lot of time, particularly managerial time, and money trying to minimise the interventions of the regulator. Most have established regulatory departments whose main objective is to reduce the chances of regulatory interference, and to ensure that negotiations with the regulator result in the best possible outcome for the company. 'The amount of management time that is devoted to "fighting" the regulator has been a serious cost of privatisation.' (Bishop, Kay and Mayer (eds), 1994, Privatisation and Economic Performance, Oxford University Press, p12).

2. **Moving into new geographical markets and new products/services** Frustrated by regulation, the privatised utilities have been looking to other markets both at home and abroad for higher rewards. British Telecom and British Gas did business abroad while under state ownership. But now, even companies in intrinsically stay-at-home businesses such as water supply, electricity generation and distribution, have made big moves into foreign markets. The water industry bought into overseas water-treatment plants, environmental consultancies, human resource consultancies, a mineral-water business and a chain of hotels.

Among the water companies, North West and Severn Trent have been among the most active. North West runs water and waste services in Mexico City; it has also won contracts to build and run plants in Melbourne, Sydney and Macau. Severn Trent has bought several American water-and-waste firms, and a firm making computer software for utilities, and has also won a contract in Mexico City.

The regional electricity companies (RECs) embarked on similarly ambitious programmes, expanding from their core business of electricity distribution. All moved into gas supply, most moved into electricity generation of which they knew something, but several went into retailing, and communications.

Since 1989, the electricity and water industries have spent more than £1.6 billion on diversification. But this appears to have been ill-advised given that more than £1 billion of this has had to be written off, mainly as goodwill. And the investments are currently giving the two industries a negative return. The two competing privatised electricity generators have, so far, been more prominent abroad than the 12 regional distribution monopolies. National Power intends by the end of the decade to have invested around £1 billion abroad, with foreign business contributing 10–20 per cent of profits. So far, it has agreed on a £100 million deal in America, and is involved in projects in Pakistan, India and Portugal. PowerGen, the other generator, has won contracts in Portugal and eastern Germany, and is looking for opportunities in East Asia. British Telecom formed a joint venture with MCI, an American telecoms firm, to provide telecoms services for multinationals, and said it would spend $4.3 billion on a 20 per cent stake in its new partner. It had previously bought (and sold) stakes in Mitel, a Canadian firm, and McCaw, an American cellular-phone company. British Gas is involved in deals in Malaysia, Trinidad, Thailand, Indonesia, Bahrain and India. It is active in 45 countries.

All this has prompted fears that domestic customers are financing, through needlessly high prices, foreign investments. The utilities and their regulators deny this. The firms have a legal duty not to cross-subsidise unregulated activities. The regulated parts of their businesses keep separate accounts, which ought (in theory) to bring any such subsidies into the open. Perhaps it is the shareholders who should be concerned.

Privatised firms are looking to alternative markets because they reckon they cannot give shareholders good growth in earnings from their regulated businesses at home. So far, diversification by privatised utilities – both at home and abroad – has been dreadfully unprofitable. British Telecom's stake in Mitel lost the firm $220 million. Plans by electricity distributors to enter generation have mostly borne little fruit; so too have their moves into security alarms. Water companies have suffered from moves into the hotel industry. One explanation for their lack of success may be that they are moving into new geographical or product/service markets with which they are unfamiliar.

3. **Cutting costs in their core businesses** Between 1990 and 1994, British Telecom cut 90,000 jobs, around 36 per cent of its workforce, mostly engineers, operators and clerical staff. In the three years after privatisation, National Power cut back employment from 17,000 to just over 5,000, and PowerGen reduced the number of employees by nearly 60 per cent. British Gas planned to reduce its labour force by 25,000 between 1994 and 1997. Electricity distributors, and water companies have also reduced their labour forces but not to the same extent.

Initially, of course, paying off workers costs the utilities money in terms of redundancy pay but afterwards it helps swell company profits.

Operating Profit (£ million)				
	1990	1991	1992	1993
British Telecom	2,646	3,378	3,253	2,155
National Power	–	427	525	599
PowerGen		223	306	433
British Gas	1,370	1,989*	1,358	−38
East Midlands	–	114	158	162
Severn Trent	164	197	268	298

* British Gas changed its reporting month from March to December.

Source: Extel Microview.

TABLE 3.4: *Profits of privatised utilities*

RECALL:
allow 15 mins

Decribe briefly the three main reactions of the utilities to regulation.

SAT:
allow 25 mins

| Managing tasks and solving problems | ✔ |
| Applying numeracy | ✔ |

ACTIVITY 3

Look at table 3.4 on operating profit. Calculate the percentage change in profits in 1993 compared with 1991 for the utilities.

Give two possible reasons for the decline in British Telecom and British Gas profits.

How high were British Telecom and British Gas profits for last year? (You will find this information in the March issues of the *Financial Times* for British Telecom, and the February issues for British Gas. You could also use Extel cards/CD-ROM for this information. An alternative would be to approach the Public Relations departments of British Telecom and British Gas.)

Now calculate the percentage change in their profits from 1991.

Commentary...

Your table should look like table 3.5.

Operating Profit (£million)

	1990	1991	1992	1993	1993/1991 % change
British Telecom	2,646	3,378	3,253	2,155	-36
National Power	–	427	525	599	40
PowerGen	–	223	306	433	94
British Gas	1,370	1,989	1,358	–38	–102
East Midlands	–	114	158	162	42
Severn Trent	164	197	268	298	51

TABLE 3.5: *Changes in profits of privatised utilities*

The possible reasons for the decline in the profits of British Telecom and British Gas could be connected with the intervention of the regulator, e.g. on prices. Another reason you might have thought of is the regulator's attempts to increase competition for British Telecom and British Gas. Both companies are also having to meet costs of redundancy pay.

UK competition policy

The aim of competition policy is to promote effective competition. The government feels that competition provides the following benefits:

- a wider choice for consumers

- it forces firms to look for ways of cutting costs

- it keeps prices down

- it keeps quality standards high

- it stimulates innovation in the form of new products and new production processes.

Firms, on the other hand, do not always see competition in such a favourable light. They are interested in increasing profits and are likely to see a strong market position as making it easier for them to get higher prices from customers – this could be seen by the competition authorities as abuse of a dominant position. Firms also wish to survive. An operating environment which is often hostile, volatile, and uncertain may be regarded by firms as a threat to survival as well as to profits. To make their environment more stable and predictable, firms may indulge in behaviour judged by competition law as anti-competitive.

Examples of anti-competitive behaviour:

- Limiting competition Firms can charge artificially low prices so that competitors are unfairly forced to leave the market – this is called **predatory pricing.**

- Firms can charge different customers different prices unrelated to any variations in the costs of supplying those customers – this is called **price discrimination**.

- Firms can refuse to supply certain customers, in order, perhaps, to control the marketing and distribution of the product. Kellogg, one of the biggest manufacturer of breakfast cereals, was accused by Shoprite, a discount retailer, of threatening to stop supplies of cereals unless it raised its selling price. Kellogg was not keen on retailers selling its brands at below cost. Sometimes firms can find themselves in trouble with the competition authorities because they have been pressurised by important customers not to supply others. For example, when Aldi, the German food discount retailer, opened for business in the UK in 1990, it complained to the Office for Fair Trading that other large retailers were pressing food manufacturers not to supply it. (If giant supermarket chains like Sainsbury and Tesco use their market power to force manufacturers not to supply other grocery chains, that could be seen as abuse of their dominant position.)

Other examples of anti-competitive behaviour are:

- attempting to prevent rivals taking sales by offering customers such incentives as loyalty discounts that are not related to cost savings

- taking over competitors to reduce the level of competition

- entering into agreements with competitors so as to, for example, avoid price competition or to share out the market. Such agreements are called **cartels**.

RECALL:
allow 20 mins

Name three benefits of competition as seen by the government.

Give three examples of anti-competitive behaviour.

Explain why a firm might pursue anti-competitive policies.

THE LAW AND COMPETITION POLICY

There are a number of statutes or laws relevant to competition policy.

UK Principal Acts

1948 Monopolies and Restrictive Practices Act
(Monopolies Commission created.)

1956 Restrictive Trade Practices Act
(Restrictive Practices Court and Registrar of Restrictive Trading Agreements created. Register of restrictive agreements relating to goods.)

1964 Resale Prices Act
(Cases to be referred to Restrictive Practices Court.)

1965 Monopolies and Mergers Act
(Provision for mergers to be referred to Monopolies Commission.)

1968 Restrictive Trade Practices Act
(Provision made for registration of information agreements.)

1973 Fair Trading Act
(Director General of Fair Trading to replace Registrar of Restrictive Trading Agreements.)

1976 Restrictive Trade Practices Act

(Restrictive agreements relating to services to be
registered.)

1980 Competition Act

(Director General to investigate anti-competitive practices.
Provision for public bodies to be referred to Monopolies
and Mergers Commission.)

European Community

1973 Treaty of Rome

Article 85: Agreements prohibited which affect trade
between member states and prevent, restrict or distort
competition.

Article 86: Abuse of a dominant position within the
common market prohibited.

1990 Merger Control Regulation

Competition policy deals with:

- mergers

- anti-competitive practices carried out by dominant firms

- cartels, where firms come together to agree on common policies

- resale price maintenance, i.e. where producers can tell the
  distributor what price to charge.

In the UK, each of these is dealt with by different procedures
involving a combination of authorities including the Department of
Trade and Industry (DTI).

The Director General of Fair Trading (DGFT) is in charge of the
Office of Fair Trading (OFT). The DGFT is responsible for promoting
and safeguarding producers and consumers through competition,
eliminating anti-competitive practices, and publishing information for
consumers. The DGFT registers cartels operating restrictive practices
through agreements involving price-fixing, market-sharing, bid
rigging, and collusive tendering. The DGFT can refer them to the
Restrictive Practices Court. The DGFT also monitors industry to
identify likely monopoly situations or behaviour by firms which
might adversely affect consumers, and refers monopolies to the
Monopolies and Mergers Commission (MMC) – the Secretary of State
for industry can also refer monopolies to the MMC.

The Competition Act (1980) empowered the DGFT to carry out a preliminary investigation of anti-competitive practices. If firms are behaving in an anti-competitive way then the DGFT can request them to stop or to modify their behaviour. If firms refuse to comply then the DGFT can refer them to the MMC.

The MMC:

- investigates possible abuses by a dominant firm, i.e. a firm or group of firms controlling at least 25 per cent of the market

- reviews the activities of the privatised utilities

- evaluates the likely effects of merger proposals referred to it by the Secretary of State for industry. The test for referral is where the combined asset value of firms exceeds £70 million or where the market share of both firms together exceeds 25 per cent of the market. When vetting mergers, the Commission looks primarily at how it is going to affect competition.

The MMC produces reports with recommendations. It is then for the Secretary of State to decide whether or not to implement the recommendations.

The **Restrictive Practices Court** examines restrictive agreements referred to it by the Director General and decides whether the agreement is contrary to the public interest.

Only resale price maintenance is automatically prohibited (except in relation to books and pharmaceuticals). Everything else is subject to case-by-case examination, and an anti-competitive practice or situation can only be prohibited or modified if, following investigation, it is found to be against the public interest. This is a nebulous concept and sets the UK's competition laws apart from those of most other countries, including those of the EU.

Since 1988, the Monopolies and Mergers Commission has published 112 reports, one-third of the total published since it was set up in 1949. That represents an average of 22 reports a year compared with an average of five a year in the previous 40 years. The average time taken to complete inquiries has come down considerably. Monopoly inquiries which used to take anything up to four years are now dealt with in 9–12 months. Merger inquiries which used to take six months are now completed in three.

Weaknesses of competition policy

Industry complains that the structure of the UK's competition authorities is unnecessarily complex. It argues that there is too much duplication of effort between the Office of Fair Trading and the Monopolies and Mergers Commission. Firms may undergo a preliminary investigation by the OFT and then another investigation by the MMC. They say that this costs them valuable managerial time and money. Firms have mounted a growing number of legal challenges to MMC reports. The Commission has been judicially reviewed nine times. While it has won all nine of its judicial reviews, the cases have drawn attention to ambiguities in the wording of the Fair Trading Act (1973).

Critics claim that the use of the concept 'public interest' to decide whether a merger should be allowed to proceed, or a monopoly allowed to survive intact, is outdated. Some competition lawyers argue that the criteria to be taken into account when judging the public interest, as laid out in the Fair Trading Act (1973), are too vague. This makes it difficult for firms to predict the outcome of an MMC investigation, thereby increasing the uncertainty of their operating environment. A more direct focus on competition issues, so it is argued, would produce a degree of extra certainty for industry in the way monopolies and mergers will be judged.

Defects also exist in the legislation relating to restrictive practices. The law requires parties to any agreement in which two or more of them accept restrictions on their commercial freedom, to provide details of the agreement to the Office of Fair Trading for registration. If they do not, the agreement will be unlawful. But this registration requirement catches a large number of agreements that have no significant effect on competition. The second weakness is that the OFT has inadequate investigatory powers. When it suspects an unregistered agreement is in operation, it can issue a notice requiring details of any registrable agreements. It has virtually no means of proceeding in the face of denials, even where it continues to have strong suspicions. The third defect is that the legislation lacks deterrent effect. There are no financial penalties for failure to comply with the registration requirement. Companies operating anti-competitive agreements do face unlimited fines for contempt of court if they break an order of the Restrictive Practices Court, but in practice fines for contempt in cartel cases have been modest.

Bodies representing consumer interests assert that the Monoplies and Mergers Commission has 'gone soft' in its monopoly-policing role by producing reports favouring big business. Critics say it has paid too much attention to the views of the companies under investigation. Inquiries into photocopiers, instant coffee, soft drinks and compact discs have left monopolies largely intact, compared with the reports that helped to liberalise industrial gas supply and weaken the link between brewers and pubs in the late 1980s. Those who accuse the MMC of going soft believe that the government's rejection of some of the more radical elements of the beer report, and the increased willingness by firms to ask for a judicial review of decisions, caused the MMC to take a more cautious approach. Criticism of monopoly investigations reached a peak with the report on new cars. The Consumers' Association accused the MMC of ignoring an independent report which showed considerable price differentials between cars bought in the UK and on the Continent. Instead, the Association said, the MMC relied too heavily on information given by the manufacturers, which claimed these differentials were not nearly as large in practice as the independent research suggested. The power of companies to lobby the MMC had grown while commercial secrecy and lack of resources prevented consumers having equal clout.

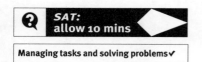

SAT:
allow 10 mins

Managing tasks and solving problems ✔

ACTIVITY 4

Test your understanding of competition policy by assessing whether each of the following statements is true or false.

(a) There are two bodies responsible for competition policy.

(b) The Director General of Fair Trading alone has the power to refer a monopoly to the MMC.

(c) The Secretary of State alone has the power to decide whether a proposed merger should be investigated by the MMC.

(d) Restrictive agreements can involve firms colluding on prices or sharing out the market between them.

(e) Book publishers can specify the price at which books can be sold by the bookseller.

(f) The asset test for the referral of a merger to the MMC is £30 million.

(g) The market share test for the referral of a monopoly is at least 25 per cent.

(h) Cartels are automatically prohibited by competition law.

(i) The concept of public interest is well-defined in competition law.

Commentary...

(c), (d) and (g) are all true statements.

(a) There are three bodies responsible for competition policy: the OFT; the Restrictive Practices Court; the MMC.

(b) In addition to the Director General of Fair Trading, the Secretary of State has the power to refer a monopoly to the MMC.

(e) Arrangements by which firms specify the price at which their customers sell on products may also be restrictive. But book publishers can specify the price at which books must be sold by the bookseller.

(f) The asset test for the referral of a merger to the MMC is £70 million.

(h) Cartels are not automatically prohibited by competition law. Only resale price maintenance is automatically prohibited.

(i) Critics claim that competition law leaves the concept of public interest too vague.

European competition policy

UK business, in addition to UK competition policy has also to comply with EU competition law. Article 85 of the Treaty of Rome prohibits anti-competitive agreements, and Article 86 deals with abuse of market power. They are directly applicable in the UK when trade between member states is affected. Growing levels of international trade and the globalisation of markets mean EU law has an increasing impact in the UK. UK firms can also be affected by EU controls on cross-border mergers.

To enforce its rules, the European Commission has wide powers of investigation and can declare a practice illegal at any time, require changes in agreements, and impose fines on offending firms. Appeals on its decisions can be made to the European Court of Justice. EU competition law takes preference over national law and is directly applicable in member states.

Agreements that may fall foul of Article 85 must be notified in advance to the Commission which can grant an exemption.

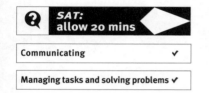

SAT:
allow 20 mins

Communicating ✔

Managing tasks and solving problems ✔

ACTIVITY 5

This activity raises some dangers faced by business regarding EU competition law.

Read the article in Resource 3.

Explain in up to 50 words why a business might unwittingly run up against problems under Article 85 with the EU Commission.

Commentary...

Your answer should include the following points:

Innocent meetings of trade associations intended to promote an industry may be viewed with suspicion by the Commission. It may suspect that the meetings are used as a way of avoiding competition in the industry thus breaching Article 85.

There is a danger that industry meetings where market information is exchanged could end up discussing prices and also result in a breach of Article 85.

If businesses cannot convince the Commission that they have done everything possible to comply with the law then they could face hefty fines of up to 10 per cent of turnover.

EXEMPTIONS

To gain an exemption firms must show that the harmful effects of an agreement are counterbalanced by benefits such as:

- improvement in production or distribution

- reductions in costs

- increase in productive capacity.

In addition, it must be shown that consumers enjoy a fair share of the benefits in the form of lower prices or increased quality.

A number of block exemptions have been granted for agreements between companies including exclusive distribution and purchasing, motor vehicle distribution, licensing of patents and know-how, R&D cooperation, and franchising.

Market share is the most important criterion as far as Article 86 is concerned. For the article to apply, firms must have a dominant market position – shares above 50 per cent usually lead to a presumption of dominance. A market share below 40 per cent is not regarded as implying dominance. The dominance must occur in the EU or a substantial part of it and the firm must be abusing its dominant position.

ARTICLES 90 AND 92

These articles also have implications for competition policy.

Article 90 forbids the distortion of competition through the granting by governments of special and exclusive rights to public enterprises, e.g. where a government protects the monopoly position of a nationalised industry by not allowing new firms to enter the industry. Article 92 says that financial assistance given to firms by the state are incompatible with the common market where they distort trade between member states or damage competing firms.

Date	Case	Significance
1990	ICI and Solvay fined ECU 47 million for alleged soda ash	At the time, the largest ever cartel fine imposed by the European Commission
1991	European Court upholds Commission's right to use Article 90 of Treaty of Rome without seeking prior approval of EC member states to liberalise the telecommunications equipment market	Confirmed Brussels' ability to challenge national monopolies
1991	Tetra Pak fined ECU 75 millions for alleged abuse of its dominant position in the market for cartons and liquid packaging machinery	Currently the largest fine ever levied by the Commission
1991	Commission vetoes Aérospatiale and Alenia's attempt to take over de Havilland, Canadian aircraft maker	The first and only case yet blocked under the merger regulation
1992	Nestlé bid for Perrier cleared on condition that brands are given up to a 'third force' on the French mineral water market	Established for the for the first time that the EC merger task will take into account the impact of duopolies and oligopolies on the market

Source: Financial Times, 23 February 1993.

TABLE 3.6: *European community competition rulings*

MERGER CONTROL

The policy on control of mergers came into force in 1990. Member states recognised that the aim of the single European market to promote competition might be frustrated by firms taking over their competitors in other member states – i.e. cross-border mergers.

The 1989 Regulation gave the Commission important new powers. Previously, it had been able to deal with mergers only after they had taken place and usually because there was abuse of a dominant position. The Regulation requires authorisation for big mergers or joint ventures with a Community dimension. This is held to exist where:

- total world turnover of the firms concerned exceeds 5 billion ECU (£3.8 billion)

- and at least two of the enterprises have turnover above 250 million ECU (£193 million) within the EU

- if more than two thirds of the combined EU turnover is in one member state then it will not be affected by the regulation.

Mergers not meeting these criteria remain under the discretion of national authorities.

The new Regulation aimed to ensure 'one-stop shopping', i.e. that mergers would not be looked at more than once within the EU. The intention was that firms would find the procedure simpler, speedier, predictable, and consistent.

Three exceptions are allowed which erode the 'one-stop shopping' principle.

1. Member states can block a merger on grounds of national security, preserving a spread of ownership of the media, and prudential rules for financial institutions.

2. Member states lacking well-developed national competition policies can invite the Commission to investigate a merger where the combined world-wide turnover is less than 5 billion ECU but greater than 2 billion ECU.

3. Member states can investigate big mergers where competition in local markets is threatened.

In 1993, the Commission reviewed the thresholds and stated an intention to bring them down in order to vet more cross-border takeovers. Although having the support of EU industry, this was frustrated by strong governmental opposition from Britain, Germany and France. Cutting the thresholds would have increased the number of cases automatically examined each year to over 100. It would have allowed the Commission to examine potentially significant cases such as the Reed-Elsevier publishing merger, or the ICI-BASF swap of polypropylene and acrylic glass activities, both of which fell below the existing thresholds.

The main motive for the regulation is to maintain competition. Consequently, the Commission must judge mergers on the basis of the threat to competition. It must be sure that a dominant position is being created or strengthened before it can claim that competition is being impeded. Mergers can be blocked only where they create a market leader, or where the post-merger firm dominates its rivals by exceeding the market share of its biggest rival by a significant margin. There is a presumption in the regulation that a merger will not threaten competition where the combined market shares of the merging firms do not exceed 25 per cent of the common market or a substantial part of it.

PROCEDURES

The EU set up a merger task force to enforce merger policy. Firms intending to merge are obliged to notify the Commission within one week of the deal being announced. The deal will automatically be suspended for three weeks so that the authorities can carry out a preliminary investigation. Companies disregarding the suspension and going ahead with the merger can be fined up to 10 per cent of their combined turnover. Within one month of notification the Commission will decide, on the basis of the potential threat to competition, whether to launch a full investigation. Four months later, the Commission will deliver its verdict. The competition authorities can approve a merger, block it or reverse it if it has already taken place, demand that the plans must be modified before it can proceed, or impose certain conditions on the companies for the merger to go through.

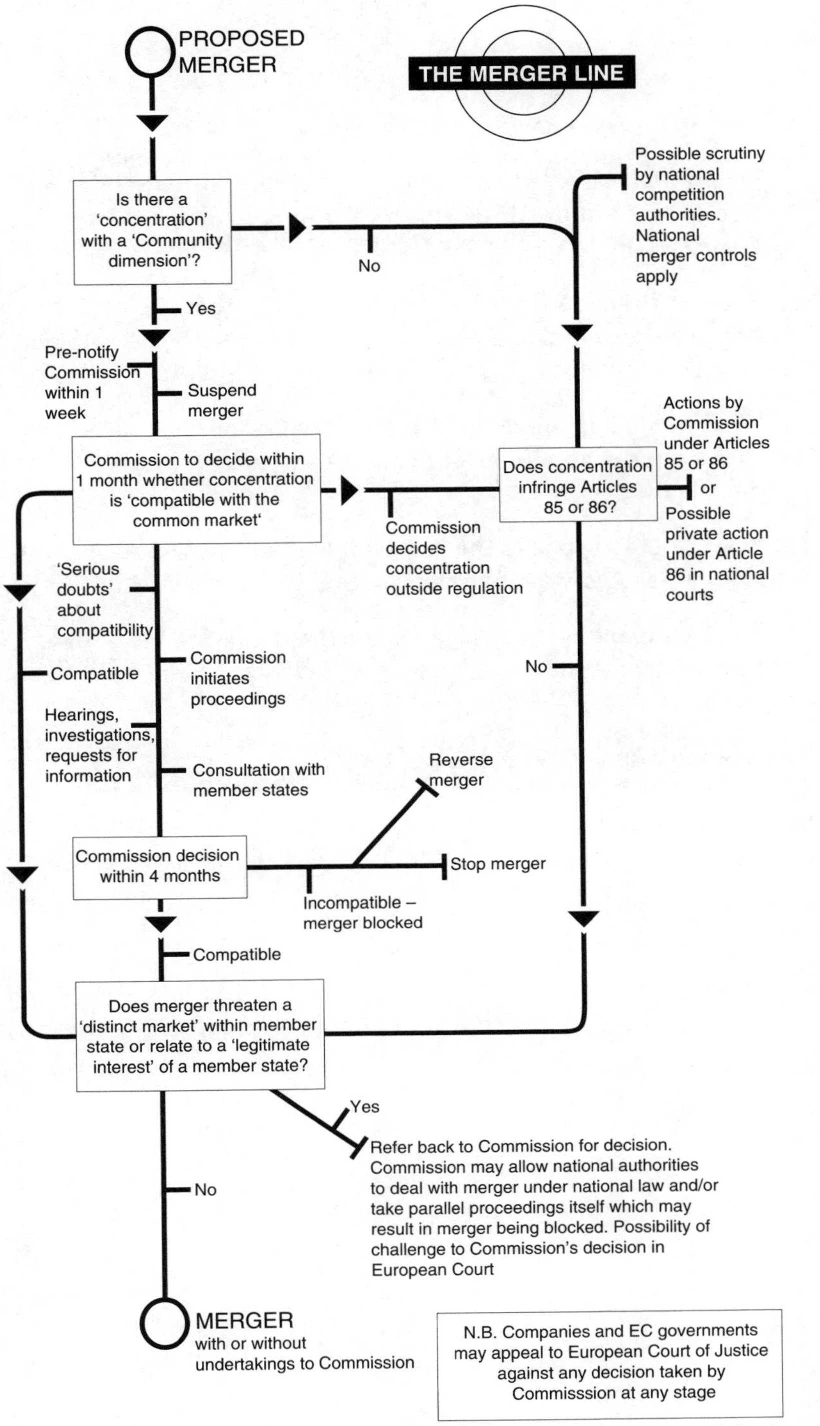
PROPOSED MERGER
THE MERGER LINE
Is there a 'concentration' with a 'Community dimension'?
No
Possible scrutiny by national competition authorities. National merger controls apply
Yes
Pre-notify Commission within 1 week
Suspend merger
Commission to decide within 1 month whether concentration is 'compatible with the common market'
Commission decides concentration outside regulation
Does concentration infringe Articles 85 or 86?
Actions by Commission under Articles 85 or 86
or
Possible private action under Article 86 in national courts
'Serious doubts' about compatibility
Compatible
Commission initiates proceedings
No
Hearings, investigations, requests for information
Consultation with member states
Reverse merger
Commission decision within 4 months
Stop merger
Incompatible – merger blocked
Compatible
Does merger threaten a 'distinct market' within member state or relate to a 'legitimate interest' of a member state?
Yes
Refer back to Commission for decision. Commission may allow national authorities to deal with merger under national law and/or take parallel proceedings itself which may result in merger being blocked. Possibility of challenge to Commission's decision in European Court
No
MERGER with or without undertakings to Commission
N.B. Companies and EC governments may appeal to European Court of Justice against any decision taken by Commisssion at any stage

Source: Rice, R. and de Jonquieres, G., Uncharted obstacle course towards one-stop control systems, *Financial Times*, 21 Sept 1990.

FIGURE 3.3: *The merger line.*

Communicating ✓

Managing tasks and solving problems ✓

ACTIVITY 6

Look at figure 3.3 and answer the following questions:

1. Would firms be able to proceed with a proposed merger if it was declared 'compatible with the common market' by the Commission?

2. What is the time limit for the Commission to make an initial declaration that the merger is compatible with the common market?

3. What would happen to the merger if the Commission found that there would not be a 'concentration' with a 'community dimension'?

4. What would happen to the merger if the Commission found that the merger was incompatible with the common market?

5. What happens if the merger is declared compatible with the common market but threatens a distinct market within a member state?

Summarise your answer in the box below.

Commentary...

Firms would be able to proceed with a proposed merger which was compatible with the common market so long as the merger did not threaten a 'distinct market' within a member state or relate to a 'distinct interest' of a member state.

One month only is allowed for the Commision to make an intial declaration that the merger is compatible and the merger would be examined to see if it infringed Articles 85 or 86. Furthermore the Commission would have to decide within four months whether or not to block it.

If the merger is declared 'compatible' but threatens a distinct market within a member state, it has to be referred back to the Commission.

APPLICATION OF THE REGULATION

So far the EU Merger Regulation appears to have had very little 'bite'. Only one merger has been blocked: the joint takeover of the Canadian aircraft manufacturer De Havilland by Aérospatiale of France and Alenia of Italy. The acquisition would have given the merging companies 67 per cent of the EU market for 20–70-seater commuter aircraft and half of the world market. In other cases, the Nestlé takeover of Perrier for example, and the asset swap between DuPont and ICI, approval has been conditional upon undertakings to sell off part of the acquired business.

The Commission looked at 137 deals between September 1990, when the new rules took effect, and March 1993.

Not subject to EU regulation	15
Approved within one month	113
Approved after full investigation	2
Approved after full investigation with conditions	6
Blocked	1
Total	137

Source: Neven, D., Nuttall, R. and Seabright, P., 1993, *Merger in Daylight*, CEPR, June.

TABLE 3.7 *Mergers referred to the European Commission, Sept 1990 – March 1993*

CRITICISMS OF EU MERGER POLICY

EU merger policy has been criticised on several grounds.

- The treatment of mergers has not always been consistent. An economic argument might be deemed central in one case, then ignored in the next. To satisfy Germany and Britain, which both have tougher merger controls, other members had agreed to make effects on competition the main ground for judging proposed mergers. Yet this clear standard has not been applied.

Instead, the Commission has regularly traded-off the anti-competitive effects of a merger against the gains in efficiency promised by would-be partners.

- Once a merger is approved, the Commission does not have enough staff to monitor undertakings given by the merging firms. The Commission looks for assurances from companies that they will not exploit their market power and that some of the benefits of the merger are passed on to customers. Critics argue that even if the Commission had sufficient resources, it still has little power to enforce the undertakings.

- The Commission has also used economic analysis to justify decisions pressed on it by governments of member states. In other words, some decisions have been made for political rather than economic reasons.

- Would-be mergers have been treated too gently. A handful of borderline cases have been rejigged in secret talks with the Commission to make them acceptable.

- The Commission is influenced too much by big firms and their political lobbyists.

As a result, it does seem that firms in countries with relatively strict merger controls, such as Germany, like having Brussels judge their proposed tie-ups. German firms involved in deals vetted by the Commission rated the new procedures highly.

This points to the need not only for closer co-operation between competition authorities, but also to the need for convergence in national laws and enforcement policies.

ACTIVITY 7

This activity tests your understanding of the application of the EU Merger Regulation.

You are working in the Corporate Intelligence Department of a large UK electronics company wishing to merge with a German competitor.

Your boss asks you to find out whether the merger would need authorisation by the Commission.

1. Use the following information to decide whether the merger needs EU authorisation.

CURRENT TURNOVER (£ billion)	Total	UK	Germany	Other countries
Your company	3	1.8	0.5	0.7
The German company	1.5	0.3	0.8	0.4

2. If you find that the answer is yes, then you must advise your boss on how the company might handle its dealings with the Commission to gain approval. Write a memo to him of up to 100 words with your advice.

Use a separate sheet of paper to record your answer. Summarise your findings in the box below.

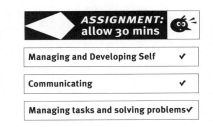

ASSIGNMENT:
allow 30 mins

Managing and Developing Self	✔
Communicating	✔
Managing tasks and solving problems	✔

summary

▶ Utilities after privatisation retained monopoly powers.

▶ Regulatory bodies have been set up to prevent the abuse of these monopoly powers and to promote competition.

▶ There can be conflict between regulators and utilities.

▶ Regulators are criticised by the utilities for impairing their business efficiency and by consumer groups for not introducing enough competition.

▶ Utilities have reacted to regulation in three main ways: by trying to outwit the regulator, by moving into new markets and by cutting costs.

▶ The aim of competition policy is to promote effective competition, providing a wider choice for consumers, lower prices and higher quality standards.

▶ Competition policy is supported by a number of UK statutes, for example, the Fair Trading Act (1973).

▶ Policy is also reinforced by EU regulations and by the Treaty of Rome.

▶ Competition policy has a number of weaknesses and critics: businesses complain that the system is unnecessarily complex and often arbitrary, consumer groups claim that the system sometimes lacks teeth.

Resources

Resources

Samsung plans £450m UK Plant

The *Financial Times*
October 18, 1994

North-east factory will create 3,000 jobs – European HQ to move to London

By John Burton in Seoul, Christine Tighe in Cleveland and Alan Cane in London

Samsung of South Korea, the world's 14th largest industrial group, is to invest £450m to build a manufacturing plant at Wynyard, Cleveland, in the north-east of England.

The factory, which will produce consumer goods ranging from microwave ovens to computer monitors for the European market, will eventually create 3,000 jobs and provide a considerable psychological boost for a region where high unemployment seems endemic.

The Korean company also plans to move its European headquarters from Frankfurt to London as part of the deal. The investment was unveiled yesterday by Mr Michael Heseltine, trade and industry secretary, during a visit to Seoul. He said Samsung was attracted to the UK because of "competitive wage rates without the social charter".

Mr John Bridge, chief executive of the Northern Development Company, the inward investment and economic regeneration agency for north-east England and Cumbria, said he believed Samsung's presence would stimulate investment from other companies in related activities such as plastic injection moulding, metal casing manufacture and wiring systems production.

Samsung's plan is the latest in a series of large investments in the UK by foreign companies. Last month NEC, the Japanese electronics giant, said it intended to spend £530m to build a semiconductor manufacturing plant at Livingston, near Edinburgh.

The UK government offered Samsung £58m in regional grants and loans to secure the project. Together with indirect aid, the support is equivalent to 20 per cent of Samsung's investment.

Samsung's decision follows stiff competition from other European countries, including Spain, Portugal, France and Germany. The Cleveland investment dwarfs other Korean investments in the European Union.

Mr Chan Bea, managing director of Samsung's UK operations, said the decision had been influenced by the proximity of Cleveland to Scotland's "Silicon Glen" where a large number of computer manufacturers, potential customers for Samsung's electronics products, are located.

He said the move was part of Samsung's globalisation strategy and a measure against possible anti-dumping measures by the EU.

Samsung intends initially to manufacture 1.3m microwave ovens and 1m computer monitors annually at the Cleveland site. It will add production facilities for personal computers, facsimile machines, colour display tubes and semiconductors. The plant should be completed by 1999 when it should be generating $2bn (£1.25bn) in turnover, about half the group's total European sales.

Samsung manufactures a broad range of products from semiconductors and personal computers to ships, petrochemicals and medical equipment.

Samsung Electronics was established in the UK in 1969. It makes 700,000 televisions a year in Teeside, and earlier this year, supported by the Department of Trade and Industry, agreed to invest £11m over three years in the plant.

The UK accounts for 47 per cent of all Korean manufacturing in the EU, with 10 Korean firms operating in the country.

RESOURCE 2:

The *Financial Times*
February 2, 1995

Fresh ferment for the brewers

Government intervention continues to weigh heavily on the UK industry, writes Roderick Oram

In a former life, the Old Punch Bowl pub at Crawley in Sussex was a bank branch. It is within earshot of Gatwick airport but most nights it is noisier inside than out. The place is packed with young customers knocking back expensive British cask ales and premium foreign lagers.

Greene King, the brewer which spent £1m to convert it, regrets not a penny. Mr Tim Bridge, chief executive, says takings are far above plan even during the traditional post-Christmas decline in sales. The key to its success is that it appeals to local "circuit drinkers".

The euphemism for "pub crawlers" speaks volumes about the migration up-market of British brewing and pub retailing. The future looks expansive and prosperous for brewers such as Greene King and Whitbread which have best responded to the trend. But the future looks less inviting for others such as Bass and Courage, which are burdened by excess brewing capacity, a product mix of declining keg beers and standard lagers, and too many unimproved pubs.

To a great extent, the winners and losers in the industry can both cite government intervention as the cause of their present state. What worries the industry most is that the government seems unwilling to leave it alone to work through the changes into a modern consumer-oriented industry. Only this week, the Office of Fair Trading said it would investigate the price brewers sell beer to their captive pubs.

"It is the 33rd time since 1966 the industry has been flung into apparent disarray by government intervention," says Sir Paul Nicholson, chairman of the Brewers and Licensed Retailers Association and chairman of Vaux Group.

His message to the government is: "You got it wrong last time and did some damage but that was controllable. Don't get it wrong again and do even more damage which might not be controllable."

The heaviest hand the government has taken to the industry in recent times were the 1989 Beer Orders, made after an inquiry by the Monopolies and Mergers Commission found brewers' ownership of pubs limited competition.

The main aim of the orders was to weaken the hold brewers had on retailing by forcing them to sell some of the pubs they owned. The industry fiercely opposed the orders, arguing the relationship helped guarantee them sales outlets, pub landlords financial support and thus consumers a choice of pubs and beers.

Sir Paul and other brewers fear the latest OFT enquiry is a further assault on the relationship. Some of the pubs they were forced to sell went to small regional brewers but most to independent pub companies that have no links with brewers. The number of pubs not tied to brewers doubled to about 25,000 out of the UK's 65,000 pubs, sparking a battle between Bass and Courage to sell their beers through them.

This triggered a price war in 1992, competition that continues to undermine margins today. The OFT is interested why brewers are selling beer more cheaply to free houses than tied houses.

Consumers have benefited from increased competition from the new independent pub companies and from a proliferation of beer varieties from brewers such as Whitbread which are trying to build new upmarket brands.

But costs include the closure of thousands of pubs unable to justify the investment needed to modernise them. Moreover, beer prices have risen almost 50 per cent faster than inflation over the past six years, partly because of investment in new ownership or refurbishing.

The industry's ability to adjust has been hindered by an ownership logjam, with large parcels of brewing and pub assets owned by companies wanting to leave the UK industry. An example is Foster's Brewing of Australia which owns Courage, Britain's second largest brewer, and half the Inntrepreneur Estates Ltd, a pub-owing joint venture.

The need for the industry to complete its change is ever more pressing. Beer consumption is declining, worsening the problem of excess capacity. There are also still about 10,000 pubs in the UK that cannot justify their economic existence.

One factor is the trend to home drinking. A decade ago 12 per cent of beer was drunk away from pubs. The share is 25 per cent and could hit 30 per cent by the late 1990s.

Another problem is the growing incursion of cross-channel imports and the government's unwillingness to lower excise duties to counter them. Also, the EU must decide in 1997 whether to renew the exemption from competition laws it granted brewers' tied estates.

Of the remedies to the industry's ills, the most pressing is to take out excess brewing capacity estimated at about 25 per cent. The trouble is much of the unwanted capacity is in large, relatively modern plants for key ales owned by big national brewers. These are the mass produced beers that have lost popularity compared with rising consumption of specialist cask ales.

All the easier cuts in capacity have already been taken out: the big brewers by closing some smaller plants; a handful of medium-sized regional brewers such as Boddington and Greenalls have given up brewing to concentrate on retailing through pubs and other outlets.

The industry's ideal solution to the problem of over capacity would be for Courage to be sold to one or more national brewers who would be willing to shoulder the cost of shutting some plants. But if there was a Courage deal in the making, as some in the City suspected, it will almost certainly have been delayed by the latest OFT enquiry. If Courage remains intact, a long period of trench warfare lies ahead for the industry.

The elimination of excess pubs will be a gradual process. If they cannot get the investment they need, they will be sold off. But this does not always remove them from the market: typically pubs sold by large brewers drop down through the ownership chain to a smaller brewer or an independent company. Only when there is no future for it as a pub does it leave the industry, normally to become a home.

A typical candidate for such a demise is an inner-city "back-street boozer" in an industrial town which had once lived on selling vast volumes of beer and not much food or entertainment. A pub estate manager recalls six changes in ownership of one such pub over 12 years before it was finally de-licensed and sold as a house.

For those who fear the current economics of pub owning will mean the end of their local there is some hope. A few villages, for example, are trying co-operative ownership or doubling up the premises with other businesses, such as a hair-dresser or post office. Even if the pub might be open only at the weekends, it is still there.

For the industry, however, the

future lies in upgrading pubs to draw back customers. All brewers have learnt how to brand their pubs in varying formats to appeal to different customers. Scottish & Newcastle is experimenting with a chain called the Rat and Parrot, with big clear windows to encourage women customers reluctant to enter pubs they cannot see into.

Mr Peter Jarvis, chief executive of Whitbread, is not the least embarassed to say that one of his big new pubs "is more like Disneyworld than a boozer" or to talk of a pub visit as a "leisure occasion".

But it is often the new independent companies, such as J. D. Wetherspoon or brewers turned retailers such as Greenalls, which are most successful in running attractive pubs and increasing turnover. Wetherspoon, for example, adds to its estate only by converting large high street premises into pubs. It reckons big beer volumes of, say, 1,500 barrels a year per pub allow it to undercut prices in Whitbread pubs, for example, by 5 to 10 per cent.

As willing as the large brewers are to embrace such strategies, this week's OFT announcement has brought new uncertainty into the industry that is likely to delay the restructuring essential to its future.

RESOURCE 3:

The *Financial Times*
August 17, 1994

The price police —
The sleuthing skills of the EU's competition division

It was more than 200 years ago that Adam Smith, the classical economist, penned his famous dictum that 'people of the same trade seldom meet together, even for merriment and diversion, but the conversation ends in a conspiracy against the public, or in some contrivance to raise prices'.

Several examples during the past decade suggest that his comment is as valid now as then. Last month, a group of carton-board producers were fined record sums after forming what the EC described as Europe's 'most pernicious' price-fixing cartel.

The meetings of the 'massive' 19-strong cartel were disguised as social events of an ostensibly legitimate association known as the Product Group Paper board. These meetings usually took place in Swiss hotels, and occasionally in Nice or Barcelona, to lend credence to the idea of a social gathering.

In 1987, a group of North Sea supply boat operators were accused of running a price-fixing cartel, known as the Coffee Club because its alleged meetings took place in the guise of coffee mornings.

At about the same time, a group of Manchester glass merchants were meeting in private rooms in airport hotels to agree prices. A few years earlier, a pub in Newbury, Berkshire was the meeting point for managers employed by some of Britain's biggest concrete companies who used to discuss how to carve up markets in neighbouring Oxfordshire.

As well as proving Smith's point, these cases illustrate a central problem facing the competition authorities. Although there may be ample grounds for suspicion, how can they prove that companies have agreed to rig the market? If people from the same industry discuss illicit agreements at, say, a trade association meeting or an industry conference, what proof is there that the law has been infringed?

Interviewing staff or examining documents seized after unannounced inspections of companies may yield incriminating evidence. In some instances, carelessness may play into the officials' hands – e.g. documents about a PVC cartel were left on an office window sill by an employee of ICI, the UK chemicals group.

Frequently, however, it requires the skills of a sleuth to prove that illegal price-fixing has actually taken place. Many cartels cover their tracks effectively. The carton-board producers, for example, concealed their activities by drawing up bogus minutes of meetings.

'It is extremely difficult to get evidence of any collusion,' says one observer. He likens the problems faced by the European Commission's competition division to those of the US agents who managed to bring down Al Capone, the Chicago gangster, on tax evasion.

Not surprisingly, trade associations can be a focus of suspicion for competition authorities. In many cases, the origins of trade associations lie in the enforcement of price-setting agreements, in the years when they were legal. To a suspicious eye, the associations still provide a convenient cover to discuss pricing.

'It is clear that the Commission has a jaundiced view of trade associations,' says one association official. 'They believe that an organisation which exists to promote that industry has the capacity to orchestrate the things that go on.'

He adds, however, that in many ways trade associations are unlikely media for cartels. 'The last thing that companies want is a trade association official being there. If they were going to do anything they would do it on the telephone.'

The subject of pricing is particularly likely to crop up in commodity-type industries. Ian Blakey of the British Iron & Steel Producers Association says it is sometimes necessary to stop conversation drifting towards the subject of price.

'You have to be strict with the members. You can talk about market conditions but discussion of prices is not on. People know the rules.'

Frequently, however, it is not flagrant discussion of prices that causes the problems. Trade associations can run into difficulties by exchanging statistics, selling products overseas collectively and establishing industry standards.

The exchange of statistics has proved a thorny issue for the Agricultural Engineers Association. In 1989, the European Commission took exception to its system of collating and supplying information on UK tractor registrations. An appeal concerning the Commission's decision is due to be concluded next month.

The Commission said that the system revealed too much detailed competitive information. However, some tractor makers believe that the Commission's real concern about associations' statistical systems is that they are a way for an industry to police the workings of a cartel. If the Commission wins the appeal case, it is thought possible that it will take action against the statistical systems run by some 22 other trade associations.

The wide scope of the competition authorities' interests demonstrated by this example shows that it may be possible to get unwittingly into difficulties. That raises problems for associations and companies alike.

There are pitfalls for the unwary. Senior executives may be unaware of what their subordinates are doing. 'It can be middle management who unbeknownst to the board get the firm into difficulty,' says Sue Hankey of lawyers Cameron Markby & Hewitt.

The excuse is sometimes ignorance. Not everyone realises, for example, that the exchange of information between competitors is illegal. 'A problem with sales people is they don't always realise they are infringing any legislation,' says Richard Spiller of lawyers D.J. Freeman.

But the competition authorities are not impressed by pleadings of innocence. Companies need to show they have done everything possible to comply with competition law. Smiths Concrete, accused of taking part in a concrete cartel, appealed successfully against a fine on the grounds that it had taken all reasonable steps to prevent staff from taking part in unlawful agreements.

The heavy fines imposed by the Commission, which has the power to fine offenders up to 10 per cent of their worldwide annual turnover, has concentrated the minds of senior management on these issues. Organisations increasingly feel the need to be seen to comply with both the letter and the spirit of competition law.